THE FIRST ONE HUNDRED YEARS

THE FIRST ONE HUNDRED YEARS

A Centennial Anthology Celebrating
Antiochian Orthodoxy
in North America

With a Foreword by
The Most Reverend Metropolitan PHILIP

Editors:
George S. Corey
Peter E. Gillquist
Anne Glynn Mackoul
Jean Sam
Paul Schneirla

ANTAKYA PRESS
ENGLEWOOD, NEW JERSEY

© 1995 by The Antiochian Orthodox Christian Archdiocese of North America, 358 Mountain Road, Englewood, New Jersey 07631 U.S.A.

All Rights Reserved. Published June 1995. First Edition.

Written permission must be secured from the copyright holder to use or reproduce any part of this book, except for brief quotations in critical reviews or articles.

Rights to "Schism and Parallel Hierarchies: Antioch During the First Crusade" reserved by the author, John Lawrence Boojamra.

Portions of "The Martyrdom of Early Arab Christians: Sixth Century Najrān," appeared in *The Martyrs of Najrān*, by Irfan Shahîd. Copyright 1971 by the Société de Bollandistes.

Library of Congress Cataloging-in-Publication Data

The first one hundred years : a centennial anthology celebrating Antiochian Orthodoxy in North America / with a foreword by The Most Reverend Metropolitan Philip ; editors George S. Corey ... [et al.]. — 1st ed.
    p. cm.
Includes bibliographical references.
ISBN 0-9624190-2-8
    1. Antiochian Orthodox Christian Archdiocese of North America—History. 2. Orthodox Eastern Church—North America—History.
I. Corey, George S.
BX738.A753F57   1995
281.9'7—dc20   95-14094
                                                             CIP

Committee for the Centennial Anthology

The Most Reverend Metropolitan PHILIP

The Right Reverend Bishop ANTOUN

The Right Reverend Bishop BASIL

The Committee for the Centennial Anthology wishes to acknowledge the work of the authors of articles included in this volume as well as the work of the editors.

FOREWORD

Emma Lazarus (1849-1887) wrote the following words inscribed on the Statue of Liberty which stands, majestically, in the harbor of New York City like a beacon of hope:

> Give me your tired, your poor,
> Your huddled masses yearning to breathe free,
> The wretched refuse of your teeming shore,
> Send these, the homeless, tempest-tossed, to me:
> I lift my lamp beside the golden door.

Around the turn of this century, thousands of tired and poor sailed from the sunny shores of the eastern Mediterranean, seeking economic opportunities, social justice and freedom in the United States of America and Canada. They were told that "the streets of America were paved with gold." Thus, they left the simplicity of their villages in Lebanon, Syria and Palestine pursuing their dreams across the sea. Some of them were left to die from starvation in the seaports of North Africa. Some were left in Marseille, France, thinking they were already in New York City. Some of them landed in South America, not by design, but rather by accident. Many, however, were fortunate enough to reach these blessed shores of the United States of America and Canada. Perhaps very few of them were able to read these immortal words inscribed on the Statue of Liberty. "Give me your tired, your poor . . . ."

They were tired, poor and mostly illiterate. They had neither relatives nor friends to welcome them at Ellis Island. But despite the foreign environment and the monumental difficulties they faced, they were determined to challenge the unknown and leave their heroic marks on the plains and prairies of America. It is evident, therefore, that the early immigrants did not bring with them any material wealth; they brought something more precious than gold or silver. They brought their social and spiritual values which left lasting marks on the soul of America.

It did not take them long to discover the streets of America were not paved with gold. And nothing was going to save them except their faith in God, hard work, honesty and decency. They peddled their merchandise from city to city and from town to town to the point of exhaustion. When they could no longer walk they stopped and founded a worshipping community, very often without the help of priests and bishops. Their two most cherished institutions were the Church and the family.

In 1895, the Antiochian Orthodox Christians in North America were fortunate to have Archimandrite Raphael Hawaweeny in charge of their spiritual life. This saintly, scholarly and mission-minded priest became their bishop in 1904, and laid the foundation of Antiochian Orthodoxy in this hemisphere. He founded *The Word* magazine, translated many liturgical books, authored many religious articles and served his flock with apostolic zeal until he fell asleep in the Lord in February, 1915. The seeds which Bishop Raphael planted in the North American soil germinated and flourished through the splendid efforts of his successors. Thus, the Antiochian Archdiocese grew from thirty parishes in 1915 to one hundred and ninety-one parishes in 1995. The decade of the sixties was a defining moment in the direction which this Archdiocese was destined to take. The doors were open for North Americans who were seeking refuge, theological meaning and stability in the Orthodox Church; they were welcomed home.

Besides the spiritual legacy which Bishop Raphael Hawaweeny and the early pioneers left, there is a literary legacy which must be celebrated as well. Although most of the first immigrants were illiterate, some of them were men of letters who left their indelible marks on Arabic language and literature. No one can write the history of Arabic literature in the twentieth century without devoting many pages to the Pen Bond (*al-Rabita al Qalamiyya*). The Pen Bond was founded in 1920 by distinguished poets and writers such as Kahlil Gibran, Mikhail Naimy, Iliyya Abu Madi, Nasib 'Arida, Nadra and his brother 'Abd al-Masih Haddad, and others.

The decline of the Arab Empire was paralleled by another tremendous decline: Arabic literature became mere form, void of substance, boring verbosity. The members of the Pen Bond and their companions revolutionized Arabic literature and created a new school of literary expression which will continue to influence Arabic literature and language for many years to come. Their poetry was marked by a strong sense of longing for their villages and the simple lives they left behind. Moreover, it expressed the eternal tension of the immigrant who constantly lives in two spheres: one in his new country and one in the old.

This Centennial Anthology is written to celebrate the memory of all Arab immigrants: the rich and the poor, the clergy and the laity, the literate and the illiterate. In this volume, you will read about the legacy of these immigrants and the rich heritage which they have received from past generations. I am eternally grateful to the distinguished scholars who have contributed to this work. It is my hope you will enjoy reading it — lest we forget.

January 5, 1995　　　　　　　　+Metropolitan PHILIP (Saliba)
Englewood, NJ　　　　　　　　 Antiochian Orthodox Christian
　　　　　　　　　　　　　　　Archdiocese of North America

CONTENTS

Foreword VII

PART ONE:
One Hundred Years of Witness and Service

PAUL D. GARRETT
The Life and Legacy of Bishop Raphael Hawaweeny 3

NAJIB E. SALIBA
Arab Immigration to North America 31

ALIXA NAFF
The Arab Immigrant Experience 51

ISSA J. BOULLATA
The Contributions of Arab Immigrants in North America
    to Arabic Literature 79

PART TWO:
Christian Influence on Arabic Civilization

MICHEL NAJIM
Syriac and Arabic Theological Thought 101

JOHN LAWRENCE BOOJAMRA
Schism and Parallel Hierarchies: Antioch During the First Crusade 115

SUSAN ASHBROOK HARVEY
"There Were Also Many Women There:"
    Women and the Foundation of the Church 141

IRFAN SHAHÎD
The Martyrdom of Early Arab Christians: Sixth Century Najrān 169

GEORGE SALIBA
Antioch and All the East:
    Indian Science and the Early Syrian Fathers 189

GEORGE N. ATIYEH
Contributions of Christians to Arabic Civilization 219

PART THREE:
The Antiochian Orthodox Christian Archdiocese of North America

ANTONY GABRIEL
A Retrospective:
 One Hundred Years of Antiochian Orthodoxy in North America 243

JOHN W. MORRIS
Toward a Middle East Peace:
 A Chronicle of Efforts for Peace and Justice in the Middle East 293

Contributors 315

Selected Bibliography 317

This volume is dedicated to the memories of all those — bishops and priests, men and women — who labored in this vineyard before us.

May their memories be eternal!

PART ONE:

One Hundred Years of Witness and Service

THE LIFE AND LEGACY OF BISHOP RAPHAEL HAWAWEENY
by Paul D. Garrett

Introduction

When he fell asleep for the last time in this world, during the night of February 26/27, 1915, reclining in the armchair to which failing health had increasingly confined him, Bishop Raphael Hawaweeny had just completed, without fanfare, the tenth anniversary of his episcopal consecration. This decade marked the culmination of twenty-nine years in Holy Orders,[1] all but nine in North America. While intensely devoted to the land of his birth and with his talents much-sought by the Antiochian hierarchy later in life, he never celebrated a Divine Liturgy in his Syrian homeland. He was destined to pass his fifty-five years as a wanderer upon the earth, tossed by historical events, forced to adapt to three rapidly-changing cultures.

He completed his course an honored and revered figure, whose passing was mourned as premature. In life he stood shoulder to shoulder with some of the greatest figures of twentieth century Orthodoxy, a lively and spirited era, but because he was spared living through the most searing crises to befall Christendom since the Roman persecutions, he was for decades relegated to footnote-status — the first Orthodox Christian hierarch to be consecrated on the territory of the New World — his greater significance often being overlooked. That at the centenary anniversary of his arrival at the port of New York on November 14, 1895, the memory of Bishop Raphael continues to grow in stature is truly remarkable. And the more closely he is examined within the context of his times, the more brightly his memory shines.[2]

Such an examination is rendered difficult and somewhat frustrating by the nature of the sole major source available. *'Awatif al-abna' nahwa khayr al-ru'asa' wa a'taf al-aba'*, cover-titled, simply, in English *Life of Bishop Raphael*,[3] is a 336-page volume coming from the pen of the future Bishop Emmanuel (Abo Hatab), then still serving in deacon's orders. It can best be characterized as a treasury of memories of a beloved spiritual father by his spiritual son, as is seen from a literal rendering of the title: "The affectionate benevolence of our Father, the munificent pastor and most benevolent of fathers." Its style throughout is unabashedly reverential,[4] readily understandable in an author thirty years his subject's junior, a man recruited in 1908 from Tripoli to serve as the bishop's deacon — whose "job description" in the Orthodox East typically includes traveling companion, administrative assistant, secretary, and confidant. He and the Reverend Basil Kherbawy, ordained St. Nicholas Cathedral Priest in 1907, were the two people closest to Raphael in America, and Kherbawy's writings do not focus on his mentor as did Deacon Emmanuel's.[5] Emmanuel still had access to the late bishop's diaries and files — now most likely lost — and clear memories of the stories told during their long hours of travel together.

The *limitations* of the primary source lie partially in how soon after the fact it was created, for it is clearly aimed at the contemporary Arab American reader. It demonstrates little concern for expanding upon those things which were common knowledge and self-evident to them, but largely lost today. It betrays a strong anti-Greek sentiment which may have been the writer's, the subject's, or both. More importantly, however, *'Awatif al-abna' nahwa* suffers from the common affliction of the biographical genre in Arabic literature, which Daniel J. Boorstin in his monumental tour of history, *The Discoverers*,[6] characterizes through a quotation from a fourteenth-century Muslim historian:

> History is the knowledge of the annals and traditions of prophets, caliphs, sultans, and the great men of religion and of government. Pursuit of the study of history is particular to the great ones of religion and of government who are famous for the excellence of their qualities or who have become famous among mankind for their great deeds. Low fellows, rascals, unfit people of unknown stock and mean natures, of no lineage and low lineage, loiterers and bazaar loafers — all these have no connection with history.[7]

Biography has from time immemorial been the major genre in Arabic historical writing, seen in the majority Muslim population as "a 'conversational science' helpful for political wisdom and social skill, a source for illustrations but not for demonstrations."[8] The Muslim historian/biographer at the height of the Islamic Empire saw himself as a compiler and chronicler, not a critic, and naturally tended towards sycophancy; as a result, their "records of events became as suspect as they were fulsome."[9] Christian writers fell into much the same line, despite the differing views of history in the two faiths. Only after World War I — that is, after Bishop Raphael's death and Deacon Emmanuel's writing — did Arab scholars begin to turn their attention away from the "golden era" and begin to scrutinize more modern times through the eyes of the Western critical methodology.[10] The attempt to examine Raphael's life and times more critically, to fill in the periods when he could be considered still "of unknown stock ... of no lineage and low lineage," and his ministry among those who were almost entirely of such description, is laborious — and nowhere near complete. The present article will attempt only to place Raphael Hawaweeny in the context of his times and indicate the various influences which formed him.

The Young Raphael Hawaweeny

Raphael was a product of the *Tanzimat* reforms which swept nineteenth-century Ottoman Turkey, of which his native Syria was a province. After enduring eleven centuries of discrimination and sometime outright persecution at the hands of their Muslim conquerors and rulers, Ottoman Christians, after the promulgation on November 3, 1839 of Sultan Abdul-Majid's landmark *Hatt-i Sharif* of Gülhame, and more so the *Hatt-i Hümayun* of February 18, 1856, were promised:

> energetic measures to insure to each sect, whatever the number of its adherents, entire freedom in the exercise of its religion. Every distinction or designation tending to make any class whatever of the subjects of my Empire inferior to another class, on account of their religion, language, or race, shall be forever effaced from administrative protocol.[11]

Soon they were tasting the fruits of freedom in their native land. For Christians of Raphael's generation, however, regardless of denominational affiliation — Orthodox, Melkite, or Maronite — these documents, sometimes referred to (somewhat inaccurately) as an "Ottoman Bill of Rights," were less significant than the tragic events which came to be known as the "Black Year" of 1860. People, in fact, reckoned themselves to be so-much-younger or so-much-older than the brutal massacres of their co-religionists that fateful spring and summer at the hands of Druze and Muslim mobs. The massacres were a horrible culmination of two decades of brutal inter-confessional civil war in the region. Raphael was born, probably in November,[12] in Beirut, where his parents fled prior to the riots of July 9-16, 1860, which ravaged the Bab Tuma quarter of Damascus. Nearly desperate to find some means of preventing the reoccurrence of such horrors, the survivors and their children showed great zeal towards the ideals of universal education and inter-confessional harmony, and in many instances turned to publishing as the best means of achieving these goals. We shall find the adult Raphael numbered in their ranks.

On the broader, world-wide level, Orthodox Christians of the generation of Raphael's parents and teachers had seen their church emerging from centuries of isolation and dependence on the West.

They began experiencing a renaissance in theological study. Seminaries and academies flowered, again accompanied by mass publishing.

The Antiochian Patriarchate established a seminary at the Balamand Monastery near Tripoli in 1833, but its "first run" lasted only through 1842. Three years later, however, in 1845, two new schools opened in the Empire, one in Jerusalem run by the Brotherhood of the Holy Sepulcher, and a second on Halki Island, in the Sea of Marmara offshore Constantinople, run by the Ecumenical Patriarchate. The adolescent Raphael yearned for education, but soon learned that for non-Greek Orthodox Christians, the *Tanzimat* freedoms did not exclude discrimination by their Hellenic co-religionists.

Greeks had for centuries occupied most of the episcopal sees in the Balkans and the Levant, and maintained a general policy of limiting the advancement of pious native men beyond the parochial ministry. This had been the *status quo* in the Patriarchate of Antioch for nearly two centuries, since 1721, as the "Ionians"[13] virtually occupied it (as they did the ancient patriarchates of Alexandria and Jerusalem), ostensibly in order to "save" it from falling further into false union with Rome. In doing so, they virtually forced their subjected lower clergy and faithful into the waiting arms of the Russians, who were intent on the simultaneous political and religious penetration of the region.

In Russia, four theological "academies" (what we would term graduate schools) and innumerable "seminaries" had existed since the eighteenth century, and readily opened their doors to foreigners. Those who escaped within their portals the hateful discrimination they experienced at home responded enthusiastically, coincidentally, becoming imbued with a brand of patriotism still anachronistic in their homeland. Moreover, they so cherished the mysteries which they succeeded in learning that they spared no effort to pass them on to the next generation.

Raphael's earliest ecclesiastical career followed the age-old Middle Eastern pattern; his potential was noted by the patriarchal Archdeacon[14] Athanasius Atalla, and he was taken in and raised through adolescence in the patriarchal complex, St. Mary's, in Damascus. Raphael came of age towards the end of the thirty-five year reign of Patriarch Hierotheos, a partisan, no doubt, of the Hellenic cause (he survived the massacre of 1860 because of a summons to Constantinople for deliberations over the "Bulgarian Schism" within the Great Church), yet not entirely closed-minded when it came to filling vacant thrones with Arab prelates. When a very strong proponent of education, Ioakeim III, ascended the Ecumenical Throne in 1858, he offered a scholarship to Halki for one new Antiochian candidate.[15] After some hesitation, Hierotheos blessed Raphael to accept the opportunity, and he enrolled in 1879. In 1886 he was graduated as a "Teacher of Orthodox Theology," having written his thesis on *Holy Tradition and its Authority*.

After briefly serving in the entourage of Hierotheos' successor, Patriarch Gerasimos, by-then Deacon Raphael was blessed to advance his education at the Kiev Theological Academy in 1888. He was allowed to complete only one academic year, however, before being pressed into service by the patriarch as rector of the Antiochian *Metochion*[16] in Moscow, probably because the Russians had come to appreciate his nationalist spirit; they rejected the pro-Greek candidates proposed by Damascus. At Gerasimos' request, Deacon Raphael was ordained to the holy priesthood on June 16, 1889, in Kiev, and elevated to the rank of Archimandrite on July 28th, following his arrival in the ancient Russian capital. He would serve there through 1892, as a cleric of the Church of Antioch, succeeding in reducing by one-fifth the *Metochion*'s 65,000-ruble debt, and arranging for twenty-five Syrians to enroll in Russian schools.

Raphael Hawaweeny in Russia and America

In March of 1891, however, Father Raphael's life began to take the sharp turn which would see him change "jurisdictions" from Antioch to Moscow, and bring him to his life's ministry in the New World. When he learned of the ecclesiastical "coup" in Jerusalem, removing the excessively pro-Russian Patriarch Nikodemos from his throne, and the installation of Gerasimos, patriarch of Antioch, on the Throne of St. James,[17] Raphael's reaction was clear:

> I was made very happy at these glad tidings, a happiness unequaled, because I thought that now there is a chance to battle for the liberation of the See of Antioch from the yoke of spiritual slavery to strangers of Greek tongue and origin. I myself will persevere in fighting and will use all the power given to me through my position to realize this wish.[18]

He wrote home to various metropolitans in Syria and influential lay friends in Damascus and Beirut, and found that a good many Arab Orthodox clergy shared his yearning for such liberation. They had acquiesced to the election of Patriarch Gerasimos in 1885, but were increasingly unwilling to remain silent now that another opportunity had arisen. In the path to realizing their dream stood a great deal of money in Istanbul and Jerusalem, both dedicated to preserving the status quo, and the general malaise of the rank-and-file Orthodox faithful. Reasoning that this could be overcome only by convincing Orthodox Russia of the gravity of the situation in Syria, Raphael submitted a number of articles to various newspapers exposing the arrogant and uncanonical nature of the Greek occupation of the apostolic See of Antioch, and the contempt which their self-defensive neglect of education had inspired among the people. The Russians did not learn the Syrian side alone; a rival "ecclesiastical diplomat" answered him letter for letter, vigorously promoting the Panhellenic side, until the tsar ordered the editors to print no more.

In Damascus, a six month impasse ensued, as the eight Arab bishops[19] who by then constituted a majority of the twelve man Holy Synod of Antioch, put forth three strong candidates from among their ranks, but were loudly opposed by the four Antiochian Greeks backed by a chorus from Constantinople and Jerusalem. They charged the Arabs with "*phyletism*," that exaltation of nationality over faith in the Church which the Greek Patriarchs had somewhat cynically condemned as heretical in the context of the "Bulgarian Schism."

Two Greek candidates were added to the slate, including the eventual victor, Bishop Spyridon of Tabor (Jerusalem Patriarchate).[20]

"Reliable sources" in Damascus assured Father Raphael in Moscow that victory had come only after the Ionians promised the electors of Damascus ten thousand Turkish lira, badly needed for maintaining their schools, churches, and other institutions, in exchange for their convincing two Arab metropolitans to change their votes. Raphael's patriotism and concern for canonical order in his distant church were strained beyond endurance by this news, and as he had dared do while still a student at Halki in 1885, Raphael again spoke out against blatant simony. Patriarch Spyridon placed Raphael fourth on his list of enemies to be silenced and eliminated.

A high-placed acquaintance in the Russian ecclesiastical administration, Vladimir Karlovich Sabler,[21] arranged a reconciliation between the suspended Father Raphael and the patriarch. Allowed to save face, Sypridon forgave Raphael and permitted him to stay in Russia, but nowhere prominent like Moscow or St. Petersburg. Finding himself abandoned by his spiritual birth-mother, Damascus, Raphael asked for a parish assignment somewhere within his newly-adopted family. Sabler, however, sought to assuage Raphael's sorrows by arranging an assignment teaching Arabic. Accordingly, Raphael moved south to Kazan' and accepted a teaching position at the famed Anti-Muslim Missionary School. He would doubtless have been assigned to teach and to take part in the massive task of translation needed to advance the cause of the Gospels across the largely Muslim southern steppes of the Russian Empire, had he not received a letter from some Syrian Orthodox immigrants in Brooklyn, New York, and been approached about service in North America by the head of the American Mission, Bishop Nikolai.

Since the 1880s, periodic economic dislocation across the Balkans and the Levant, coupled with industrial expansion in the New World, where wages five-to six-times greater than those available at home were transformed by imagination into tales of "streets paved with gold," created the necessary impetus for mass emigration. Orthodox Christians (and their Uniate relatives) inhabited many of the bleakest regions of Russia, and in the years of Raphael's coming of age, began making the dreadful — but always hopeful — transatlantic crossing and the painful transition to American or Canadian life. Their writings show that their greatest sorrow was finding none of the familiar comforts of their faith in a foreign land, and having to choose between assimilating to a Western creed, waiting patiently for an itinerant pastor to wander briefly into town, or simply drifting away from the faith. Communities and parishes sprung up by popular initiative, and permanent clergy came naturally to be viewed as hired personnel by the community "bosses."

Orthodoxy in America: the Background

Only one Orthodox ethnic group had followed the more traditional path of organized mission. The Holy Synod of the Church of Russia in 1794 dispatched a team of monks to Kodiak Island, south of the Alaskan mainland, to minister to the spiritual needs of Russian fur trappers assigned to exploit the archipelago, and more importantly, to Christianize the native population. Three years later the Russian Synod consecrated a bishop to head this seemingly successful mission, a man destined to perish at sea en route to his primitive episcopal see. A successor was appointed only in 1840, but Innocent (Veniaminov)[22] was such an extraordinary man that he placed an indelible mark on the American Church.

Following the sale of Alaska to the United States in 1869, the Russian mission declined drastically in numbers and faced formidable trials. By Raphael's early adult years, the see was for all intents and purposes *in partibus* (since virtually all the emigrés from Imperial Russia were persecuted dissenters — Jews or nihilistic revolutionaries — neither disposed to joining the bishop's flock) and the Russian Holy Synod neared the point of dissolving it.

Beginning in 1890, however, masses of Rusyn Uniates, led by the pioneer Uniate priests John Volyansky, Alexander Dzubay, and, preeminently, Alexis G. Toth, sought refuge from Latin domination under the Russian bishop's jurisdiction, and the mission received a last minute reprieve. An energetic forty-year-old Rusyn, Nikolai

(Ziorov) was consecrated to the episcopacy and charged with advancing the project. In 1895, after several years in Alaska, Nikolai travelled to St. Petersburg on a mission to recruit a brotherhood of clergymen to care for the diverse and ever-growing flock.

In Kazan', meanwhile, Raphael had received an invitation from the New York Syrian emigrés to come and pastor them. They had briefly been served by two itinerate priests, but this did not suffice to advance their spiritual and communal progress. Raphael paid a visit to Bishop Nikolai in St. Petersburg, was assigned by the Russian Holy Synod to service in North America on June 17/29, 1895, and made his way across Europe and the Atlantic in Nikolai's retinue. The patriarch of Antioch offered no objections to Russia's inclusion of the so-called "Syro-Arabs" into its North American diocese, or to Raphael Hawaweeny's pastorate.

Bishop Nikolai (1851-1916) as a seminarian in Moscow had observed the dwindling days of Metropolitan Innocent's earthly life and ministry, and never forgot the impression. In America he found the great hierarch's memory vividly alive across Alaska, where he had served the years of his parochial ministry and early episcopacy, breaking all the standards of nineteenth-century clergy and hierarchs by sparing himself no hardship in visiting the most geographically remote of his spiritual children. The ceremonialism and aloofness so characteristic of Russo-Byzantine episcopal practice was utterly foreign to St. Innocent's nature, and it became traditional among his successors to forego the "usual amenities." Both bishops' extensive writings abound with vivid descriptions of the horrors of travel around the rim of the Northern Pacific basin.

In 1893, 1896, and 1897, Bishop Nikolai established a new pattern for the hierarchy by traveling the rails coast to coast, talking with clergy and parishioners, offering directions and exhortations, and primarily the example of his own courage, energy, enthusiasm, and love for work. He praised the people's zeal and growth when this was in order, and admonished those who were in error. The clergy more than occasionally felt his temper and strong will, and were touched when he made amends. Writing about Bishop Nikolai, the

Jesuit priest Emerikh Bodichka, describes the spirit of turn of the century North American Orthodoxy into which Raphael Hawaweeny fully entered:

> Although he signs himself "Humble," he [Nikolai] does not sit home in his chambers, but as a forty-five year-old energetic person, he makes great travels, hundreds of kilometers to *far off Canada*, where, as soon as he hears of Russians or Slovaks, visits their communities, preaching to them with wild fanaticism that no other faith can save Slavs than Orthodoxy.[23]

Father Raphael embraced this philosophy whole-heartedly. Nikolai proposed stationing him in Chicago, near the geographical center of the American mission. This would have made particular sense for one pastoring the immigrant population which more than any other spread out to every nook and crany of the continent. Raphael, however, saw the importance of close contact with the primary colony which was in New York, out of which the peddlers' vast, thin web of relatives and former fellow-villagers, were stretching coast to coast.

Immediately he established a chapel on the second floor of a decrepit building at 77 Washington Street in Manhattan, at the center of the original "Little Syria." He established his residence at 120 Pacific Street in Brooklyn, nearer to where the community's center was gradually shifting. This completed, he took to the rails in mid-1896, visiting some thirty colonies between New York and San Francisco, touching the lives of some seven thousand Arabic-speaking immigrants.

Over the course of five months on the road, he never stayed in one place for more than four days; often his ministrations took under twenty-four hours before he hastened back to the station. His spirit was troubled by the restrictions on his straying north or south of the straight-line path, so in 1898-99 he made multiple sorties out of the "Mother of the Churches" and back again, then completed a great meandering loop through the untouched northern tier of states: Michigan, Indiana, Illinois, Wisconsin, Minnesota, Nebraska, and Iowa; and a more linear penetration of Dixie — into Georgia, Alabama, Louisiana, and Texas — en route to California.

The detailed journal of his northern travels[24] show that while his primary mission was to Orthodox Arabs, he denied his ministrations to no one. Melkite and Maronite Christians, Muslims and Druzes all attended his services, often as in Savannah, Georgia, outnumbering the Orthodox by two-to-one. He took great pains to prevent the importation to the New World of the confessional divisiveness of their homeland. He commiserated in particular with the Maronites' dissatisfaction with their spiritual plight in immigration.

When home in Brooklyn, Raphael devoted much of his time to writing. In 1898 he compiled a nearly nine hundred page compendium of liturgical services in Arabic.[25] He began writing to friends in the Middle East, recruiting clergymen and potential ordinands. He also worked closely with the dean of the east coast Russian clergy, Reverend Alexander Hotovitzky. With the peripatetic bishop residing still in San Francisco, Father Alexander was charged with helping newly-arrived clergy to acclimatize to America, and with editing the newly-founded, mostly Russian, *Russian-American Orthodox Messenger*. Raphael served nine years as censor for the journal. Clear in its pages is the certitude among the top echelons of the Orthodox mission that the ancient faith had to adapt to its new environment in order to bear witness to the truth which it alone preserves to those who hunger for it. While at the grass roots level reclamation of the Uniate masses to Orthodoxy continued to be the overarching concern of the mission at large, it is clear that a wider consciousness of pan-Orthodoxy was alive.

This came to be more heavily emphasized under Bishop Nikolai's successor, Bishop Tikhon (Bellavin, 1865-1924). Appointed in 1898, the future "All-Russian Patriarch" (and later "Confessor-Saint") proved no less energetic in his pursuit of the Innocentian legacy — despite having never laid earthly eyes upon him. Because he shared a common background with the Rusyn portion of his new flock and several years' episcopal experience in missionizing Uniates, there was apprehension among non-Rusyns that he might not understand the ethnic diversity of the North American flock. Raphael voiced this caution when, after pledging the complete loyalty of "the whole twenty-thousand Orthodox Syro-Arab colony, both in New York and the whole United States," whom he represented, he asked that in return Tikhon "continue to show all of us Orthodox Syro-Arabs who live within your divinely-protected Diocese, the same maternal love, paternal care, and archpastoral attention that your Most Reverend predecessor [Nikolai] showed us." Responding in equally concrete terms, the bishop vowed he would be

> equally well-disposed to all Orthodox of whatever nationality, for Orthodoxy is catholic; if in Russia we do not experience that catholicity, so to speak, it is because all Orthodox there are Russians. But here, outside of Russia, where under the roof of an Orthodox Church the Russian, the Greek, the Arab, etc., are all straining equally — the concept of catholicity is fully clear for us.[26]

The clergy found themselves trusted as advisors by their bishop, and the people encouraged to make full use of their gifts as members of the Body of Christ. The immediate impression which Tikhon left was the happy, if disarming, one of a completely atypical Russian prelate, most unpompous and completely unpretentious. In his office, he spoke simply and with humor and tact. He reproved lovingly and with a disarming air of jocularity. He was utterly simple and genuinely friendly. People responded to him with undisguised love. He was accessible and responsive to the people's needs, meticulous about details, yet able to grasp "the big picture." Anything that could be blessed he blessed — and as expeditiously as possible.[27]

During his first year, Tikhon proved as good as his initial word to Father Raphael. As he crisscrossed the continent, he took pains to celebrate with the Syro-Arabs, who responded, in the florid words of a Galveston, Texas folk poet, with "profound love for the Archpastor of all Orthodox" in North America. In the autumn of 1902, when the long-awaited time came for the consecration of two St. Nicholas churches in greater New York, Bishop Tikhon first blessed the renovated building[28] at 301-303 Pacific Street in Brooklyn, on Sunday, October 27, 1902. Then, on November 10, 1902, he went downtown for obsequies at the Russian Cathedral. To Father Raphael's flock he proclaimed:[29]

> We rejoice because we are your brothers in faith. We have with you one Lord, one faith, one system of sacraments, and, here in America, one hierarchical principle. We rejoice also because, just as in your homeland of Syria, the Russian people cooperate with you in preserving your faith and nationality, so too, here, we have helped in building your church. Here is a donation from our most pious Emperor, and a mite from the spiritual authorities and local Russian people. Therefore your church is near and dear to us as well. Let today's celebration of consecration bring us even closer together and bind us with the unbreakable bonds of faith and love for Christ Jesus, to the greater glory of the Orthodox Church and to our common good.

Bishop of Brooklyn

Realization of the "one hierarchical principle in America" meant, in Bishop Tikhon's mind, consecration of bishops to head the various national churches. While serving eight months on the Russian Holy Synod in 1902-03, Tikhon received authorization to initiate his plan. On December 14, 1903, he served as chief celebrant in the consecration of Archimandrite Innocent (Pustynsky) as vicar of Alaska, and returned to New York with permission to consecrate Archimandrite Raphael to the episcopacy as vicar of Brooklyn and the Syro-Arab Mission.[30] The historic event took place on February 29, 1904.

The vagaries of history would eventually dictate that the Syro-Arabs would be the only non-Russian people to receive a bishop of their own nationality prior to the break-up of ecclesiastical unity in the wake of World War I and the Bolshevik revolution in Russia. The plan was otherwise, however. On March 25, 1905, "Greek Independence Day," Bishop Tikhon ordained a Greek, Michael Andreades to the holy priesthood, and happily would have helped the quarter of a million Greeks solve their mounting "episcopal question," had any more than a handful of them been willing to recognize his canonical authority.[31] In September, 1905, Archbishop Tikhon[32] elevated Reverend Sebastian Dabovich, the first American-born Orthodox priest, to the rank of archimandrite, and named him official Head of the Serbian Mission, destined (it was vainly hoped) to follow Bishop Raphael into the episcopacy.[33]

Shortly before his transfer home to Russia and the immense burdens which would befall him after 1917, the beloved archbishop presided over a clergy conference in Cleveland's St. Theodosius Church — an event that would become a paradigm for all Orthodox jurisdictions in America[34]— and purchased a beautiful and tranquil farm property near Mayfield, Pennsylvania, on which to build America's first Orthodox cloister. Bishop Raphael concelebrated with him the consecration of St. Tikhon's Monastery on May 17/30, 1906,[35] and built a summer home for himself there, which would be open to other clergymen when vacant. His hierarchical schedule dictated that they had almost unlimited access.

Realizing he could not be physically present everywhere, and that the peddler's life most typical of his flock would not make it feasible to incorporate all of them into parishes, Bishop Raphael expanded the literary ministry which he had always exercised by founding a diocesan magazine, *al-Kalimat* (The Word). As a close collaborator with Reverend Hotovitzky on the Russian *Messenger*, he knew first-hand the plight of American Orthodox editors/publishers: they do not simply peruse and pass on the plethora of articles which cross their desks from willing contributors; they write nearly every word of every article of every issue.

And so it was over most of the course of *al-Kalimat*.[36] The pages are filled with probing historical and theological articles and minutely-detailed chronicles of Raphael's never-flagging travels in the Innocentian tradition. These included the joyful founding and consecration of churches, and the less enviable archpastoral task of disciplining priests and preventing schisms among immigrants from different regions and villages of the Middle East.

Maronite opposition to his ministry stiffened with his ascendancy to the episcopacy, fanned by the writings of Na'um Mukarzal in the pages of the weekly newspaper *al-Hoda* [*The Guidance*]. Rhetoric — matched by the Orthodox Najib Diyab in *Mir'at al-Gharb* [*Mirror of the West*] — turned to street violence in Brooklyn a mere eight months after Raphael's consecration, resulting in charges that he had placed a bounty on his opponents' [Najib Maloof and Mukarzal] heads and, within the sacred precincts of his cathedral, blessed the weapons to be used in annihilating the Maronites. Raphael, guarded from assault by a cordon of Brooklyn detectives, surrendered, was booked, pleaded "not guilty," and was eventually exonerated at a cost of thousands of dollars in legal fees.[37]

Despite all the problems of his high office, which never really yielded their poisonous fruit until after his death and the divisiveness of the Russy-Antacky era,[38] Bishop Raphael endeavored to be the "salt of the earth" and the "light of the world" (Mt. 5.13-14). At his own expense he distributed copies of *al-Kalimat* to the Middle East and to emigrés on every continent, leaving himself penniless at the end of his life. Day and night he labored over fresh and in some cases premiere translations into Arabic of the liturgical books of the Orthodox Church.[39]

Following the restoration of the Antiochian Patriarchate to Arab hands in 1898, Damascus tried innumerable times to lure him home. The Archdiocese of Latakia asked unanimously that Metropolitan Meletios nominate Raphael as his successor on the day he departed to ascend the patriarchal throne. The aging metropolitan of Beirut sought Raphael as his auxiliary the same year. Zahleh (in 1901), the patriarchal vicarate in Damascus (in 1904), Tripoli (in 1908)[40] and Marsine (as late as 1914) were all offered to him with considerable insistence. But he repeatedly declined, citing the even greater need of caring for the flock in emigration. Nevertheless, he maintained the most intimate of communications with his Mother Church.

Patriarch Meletios made clear the degree of rapprochement achieved and Antioch's orientation now to the Church in the New World:

> The heart of the holy Church of Antioch is glad today, and the souls of her archpastors and children rejoice, seeing that blessed plant — our beloved son-in-the-Lord, the archimandrite Raphael, who has been cared for so much by our late predecessors *[sic.]*, and who became for us the object of a great hope as he grew in stature and success under the care of the sister Church ... of Russia, ... has now reached the high order of the episcopate by the will of God. ... The metropolitans of the holy See of Antioch do still consider him as a member of our body, since he comes from our midst, and we number him as one of us in faith and in virtue of his responsibilities over our Syrian children, dispersed in North America.... [41]

In the pages of *al-Kalimat*, the bishop reveals time and again how he was consulted before virtually every important decision in the patriarchate and informed of the outcome directly thereafter. He publicized these matters in his journal for the faithful's edification, along with his voluminous correspondence with Old World hierarchs. Often the subject was the importation of clergy to serve the needs of the parishes which had grown to thirty in 1913, or their return home when life in North America weighed too heavily upon them or their families. The tension which all bishops felt between training these priests to deal with the North American situation realistically and in advancing American and Canadian born men to the priesthood — most often without specific training — weighed on Raphael's very cautious soul.

The bishop never broke the formal canonical bonds with Russia. Indeed, he became ever-more deeply involved in the life of the Russian-American Diocese, administering it when the archbishop was summoned to attend synod meetings or was replaced at the helm of the diocese. He accommodated the liturgical needs of the Russian "cathedral folk" across town in Manhattan on the eve of great feasts, when a "normal" liturgy would be unthinkable, and he maintained his connections with St. Tikhon's Monastery and St. Platon's Seminary in Tenafly, NJ.[42] Bishop Raphael saw no conflict in serving as the veritable envoy of Antioch in North America, and regularly confessed this to be his understanding and practice.[43]

North America also teemed with refugees from the patriarchates of Constantinople, Alexandria, and Jerusalem, and Raphael kept up a conscientious and voluminous correspondence with these ancient centers of Christendom. Deacon Abo Hatab maintains that "these other churches considered him an ecclesiastical leader who possessed the true faith and correct teaching — a good chief and leader...."[44] The Russian hierarchy seems not to have objected to this arrangement; it certainly mirrored its own orientation of keeping one foot planted firmly in each world. The Russian Consistory's only complaint about Bishop Raphael was that he was *too busy* to visit frequently enough and to contribute articles to its journal.

More so than any bishop of the time (with the possible exception of St. Tikhon), Raphael accepted the realities of life in North America, and refused to rail against and fight with the flock. Superficially, photographs show him slowly evolving from a stern sphinx-like archimandrite bearded *à la Russe* on his arrival to a carefully groomed and kindly-visaged gentleman-priest in clerical collar and tailored business suit. More profoundly, when he saw his young people drifting away from the church because they did not understand the Arabic of their elders, he did not insist on Saturday classes in the forgotten tongue. Rather he instituted English language Sunday school instruction and services in the new vernacular. He found time in his schedule to collaborate with such pioneers of the anglicizing of Orthodoxy as Isabel F. Hapgood and Reverend Nathanael Irvine.

In Bishop Raphael one can see incarnate St. Innocent's 1867 call for an English-speaking hierarchy and clergy, and the inevitable adoption of English for liturgical and educational purposes.[45] The bishop could afford this attitude, of course, since he had become absolutely fluent in English (as well as Arabic, Greek, and Russian; he was comfortable in Turkish and French, and able to pursue theological studies in Latin) and was a powerful, much sought-after speaker in the non-orthodox churches of New York.

A very significant part of Raphael's coming to grips with American society lay in the area of ecumenism. In the "native lands" of Orthodox Christianity, the Orthodox faith was either an established and virtually uncontested state religion, or an underdog to another state religion — persecuted or badly-disadvantaged, or one party in a more-or-less constant "holy war" among multiple sects. Catholicism was generally viewed as a "known threat" seeking to absorb the Orthodox; Protestantism was seen as a deformed sect of Catholicism, fortunately isolated in lands that few Orthodox ever had any cause to visit. Nowhere was the reality of having to live in "peaceful coexistence" with other faiths as equals encountered. North America was such a land, and Raphael quickly became highly-esteemed for his gentility.

The most natural and friendly relations between the Orthodox and western Christians occurred with the Episcopalians, since they were not outwardly proselytistic and were openly helpful, morally and financially, to the plight of the immigrants. Contacts between Canterbury and Moscow dated back to Metropolitan Philaret's tenure as metropolitan[46] and by the turn of the twentieth century had grown particularly fruitful, with individual hierarchs of the Russian Church privately expressing hopes for a corporate reunion of the two confessions and the recognition of the validity of Anglican Orders.[47] Among them were the progressive archbishops of North America: Tikhon, Platon, and Evdokim. Orthodox hierarchs and clergymen were regularly invited to address the annual general conventions of the Episcopal Church, including Raphael in 1910 when he declared,

> I hope the day is not far off when we will no longer say, "our church, your church," "our bishops, your bishops," but will say, "our church, our bishops," just as we now say, "the Head of the Church is our Lord Jesus Christ."[48]

Prompted and supported by Archbishop Platon, Raphael took two concrete steps towards that end. First, he accepted on October 13, 1908, a vice presidency in the newly-formed Anglican and Eastern Orthodox Church Union.[49] More significantly, in June of 1910, he authorized Episcopalian ministrations to Orthodox Christians in a number of carefully-delineated situations where they could not avail themselves of the services of an Orthodox priest.[50] Within fifteen months, however, he withdrew the edict and reluctantly severed all connections with the Union. Factors had included complaints about a number of individual Episcopal clergymen over-stepping the boundaries of the decree and reports of a significant number of Orthodox lay people misunderstanding its intent and taking it to mean a state of *de facto* union — something no individual bishop was empowered to conclude.

Close contact with representatives of the Anglican side left both Raphael and Platon with a two-fold outlook: a "personal regard and love" for them individually, but as strong a certitude that authentic, theologically-based union was not yet possible. In judging Bishop Raphael's actions on these matters — and the two *cannot* be separated — one must bear in mind the atmosphere of hope which pervaded his day and was never fully vanished until our own times. Indeed, in Europe and the Middle East the dark days of World War I and the almost as desperate inter-war period forced all Christian believers closer together. Often in desperation, both sides administered the sacraments to believers of the other confession along the lines proposed and authorized by Bishop Raphael.

Meanwhile, signs of theological *rapprochement* continued to grow at least through World War II, most notably in the work of Meletios (Metaxakes) of Constantinople/Alexandria, supporting and vindicating the attitudes of the earlier decades. Bishop Raphael's actions should be viewed as wholly understandable historically — and equally courageous.

Like St. Innocent, Raphael was not able to be diverted by his many side interests and pursuits — primarily in the areas of language and literature, the natural sciences, and theology — from the main focus of his calling: ministering to the flock. As early as 1909 his travels caused him to grow gray and triggered a painful case of rheumatism which kept him bed-ridden for an extended period. Heart disease progressed, and in 1914 he was incapacitated for an even longer period. He recovered and undertook a major visitation of his parishes.

In January of 1915, he sought medical help. On February 22, the Russian Bishop Alexander (Nemolovsky) paid a visit, and found him confined to an armchair. From it he had worked feverishly to complete his Arabic translation of the *Euchologion,* then said his "Lord, now lettest Thou Thy servant depart in peace." He entrusted to Alexander the archpastoral staff which he had received nearly eleven years earlier, begging him to see that it be passed on to a worthy successor. Throughout the Arab and Russian parishes prayers went up for his recovery. But this was not the will of God. Bishop Raphael had completed the way he should go, and departed this life shortly after midnight on February 27, 1915.

Vested by Bishop Alexander and the area Arab and Russian clergy, he lay in state for a full week as special permission was obtained from the city of New York to inter his remains beneath the altar of St. Nicholas Cathedral, and twenty-three of the clergymen whom he had left orphaned across the continent gathered to bid farewell to their father. Alexander was joined in presiding at the services by Metropolitan Germanos (Shehadi) of Seleucia/Zahleh, who had been allowed by Bishop Raphael to come to America to collect money for an agricultural school in his diocese.

The funeral proper was celebrated by twenty-three Arab priests, eighteen Russians, three Greeks, and four deacons. As the masses wept and wailed and would not be comforted, clergymen and poets vied with one another to praise the departed's qualities in the most exalted terms. But none surpassed the tribute paid him three years before in the pages of a Brooklyn daily by the Episcopalian cleric T. J. Lacy: a "rare man," reminiscent of the apostle Paul himself, sitting in the lowly quarters of Rome, receiving all visitors in patience, sympathy, and hospitality. He wrote,

> I consider Bishop Raphael as one of the most outstanding men in our city, a worthy prelate, an outstanding scholar, a selfless Christian, a friend of the poor and a social worker among his compatriots — a man of whom our Brooklyn can be proud.[51]

No better words were spoken to summarize the life of Raphael Hawaweeny, however, than those uttered by Archbishop Platon (Rozhdestvenskii) on March 11, 1911, when the North American diocese feted the Syro-Arab bishop's fifteenth anniversary in its midst.

> I am thankful to God, the Father of our Lord Jesus Christ, who has let me reach this glorious day to embrace with a holy kiss our beloved brother and loyal friend Raphael. ... *May his anniversary be immortal and eternal.* Yes, our holy brother. Why can it not be immortal? Have you not worked in the Lord's field so that your seeds have brought forth fruits and yielded ten-fold? Have you not made Orthodoxy and piety to grow, and preached the faith and the Gospel of salvation? Were not you, when you arrived, the only shepherd of the small flock, and are now the master of their pastors? Have you not ... visited the United States, Canada, and Mexico, preaching, counseling, teaching, and performing services? Have you not given of your time, health, and money for your magazine in order to protect your blessed Church? Have you not become ill from serving? Have you not suffered grief,

persecution, hunger, nakedness, even arrest, for Christ's sake? And in all this you stood firm. Yes, may your anniversary be immortal with the righteous and upright church fathers whom you are imitating....[52]

NOTES

[1] He was ordained deacon on Dec. 20, 1885, in the chapel of the Theological School at Halki; and priest on June 16, 1889, in the chapel of the Theological Academy in Kiev, Russia.

[2] Bishop Raphael's veneration has reached the stage that the Holy Synod of Antioch has taken up the question of his canonization. Brief accounts of Bishop Raphael's life have been published several times in periodical literature. See: William Essey (Bishop Basil), "Lest we forget — Raphael, Bishop of Brooklyn," *The Word* 20.5 (May 1976), 12-14; "Bishop Raphael of Brooklyn," *Orthodox Life* 43.6 (Nov./Dec. 1993), 22-32; Paul D. Garrett, "Pascha, 1901," *The Word* 28.4 (April 1984), 15-16; Michael Laffoon, "The 75th Anniversary of the Falling Asleep of Bishop Raphael," *The Word* 34.3 (March 1990), 4-7 (which unfortunately introduces certain factual errors, e.g., that Raphael was born in Damascus, was destined by his parents for the priesthood, etc., which have been incorporated in other presentations, e.g., "Bishop Raphael (Hawaweeny)," in George A. Gray and Jan V. Bear, eds., *Portraits of American Saints* (Los Angeles, CA: Diocesan Council and Dept. of Missions, Diocese of the West, Orthodox Church in America, 1994), 55-58; Paul D. Garrett, "Envoy from Antioch: the Life and Ministry of Bishop Raphael Hawaweeny," *Again* 16.4 (Dec. 1993), 6-9. Discussions of his ministry and leadership in texts on the Arab immigration are sparse; neither Philip K. Hitti's *The Syrians in America* (New York: Doran, 1924) nor Alixa Naff's *Becoming American: The Early Arab Immigrant Experience* (Carbondale, Ill.: Southern Illinois University Press, 1985) includes a comprehensive picture of Bishop Raphael, despite the fact that both devote considerable space to questions of religion and ethnic (largely clerical) leadership.

[3] Emmanuel Abo Hatab, *'Awatif al-abna' nahwa khayr al-ru'asa wa a 'taf al-aba* [Life of Bishop Raphael] (New York: Mir'at al-Gharb, 1915). The text is substantially translated into English with some additions from other sources, by André G. Issa in his unpublished M.Th. thesis for St. Vladimir's Seminary, *The Life of Raphael Hawaweeny, Bishop of Brooklyn, 1860-1915* (1991).

[4] Over one-third of the volume is given over to a collection of flowery posthumous paeans to Raphael; Issa omitted these from his translation.

[5] Kherbawy's *Tarikh al-Wilayat al-Mutahhidah wa al-muhajarah al-suriyyah* [History of the United States; History of the Syrian emigration illustrated] (New York: 1913) provides virtually no biographical information on Raphael.

[6] Daniel J. Boorstin, *The Discoverers* (New York: Random House, 1983), 559.

[7] Quoted by Samir Khalaf in his article "Communal conflict in Nineteenth-century Lebanon," in *Christians and Jews in the Ottoman Empire: The Functioning of a Plural Society. Vol. 2: The Arabic-Speaking Lands* (New York: 1982), 123-24.

[8] Boorstin, 559.

[9] Khalaf, 560.

[10] Raphael Patai, *The Arab Mind* (New York: Charles Scribner's Sons, 1973), 247-51. Joseph Hajjar states that Arab ecclesiastical historians in the modern sense emerged only in the 1950s and 1960s, each focusing closely — almost exclusively, except for polemical purposes — to "their own Churches, their own 'confessional nations,' their own Patriarchates." (See his "Church History and Consciousness in the Eastern Churches of the Arabic World," in *History —Self-understanding of the Church [Concilium, 67]*, tr. Paul Burns (New York: Herder & Herder, 1971), 133-38. The major treatment of the Orthodox Patriarchate of Antioch is Assad Rustum's three-volume *Kanīsat Madīnat Allāh Antākia al-'Uzmā* [The Church of God's City, the Great Antioch], (Beirut, 1952-58). That the "traditional" biographical form has not died out entirely, see the 1964 treatment of Bishop Raphael's schoolmate at Halki, *Jirasimus Masarah fi difa`ihi `an al-`aqidah al-Urthudhuksiyyah*, by Ghifra`l Salibi (n.p., 1964).

[11] Quoted by Samir Khalaf in his article "Communal Conflict in Nineteenth-Century Lebanon," in *Christians and Jews in the Ottoman Empire: the Functioning of a Plural Society. Vol. 2: The Arabic-Speaking Lands* (New York: 1982), 123-24.

[12] Birthdays were not yet celebrated in the Middle East. In official documents in America, Raphael cited Nov. 8, 1860 as his birthday.

[13] Greeks living in still-"irredenta" Asia Minor.

[14] Later Metropolitan of Homs.

[15] Gerasimos Massara was sent to Halki in 1875, by the future Antiochian Patriarch, Meletios al-Dumani. He became the first Arab graduate of the institution, and went on to serve as metropolitan of Beirut. He shared with Raphael a life-long interest in liturgical translation, and in 1920 headed the delegation to America which brought Metropolitan Antony Bashir to our shores.

[16] *Metochion* (deriving from the Greek *metochê*, participation) began as the "satellite office" of one monastery to another, charged with maintaining brotherly unity between institutions; later it evolved into the present sense, as the virtual embassy of one autocephalous Orthodox Church maintained at the primatial see (and usually political capital) of another, charged with looking after the distant church's interests — economic and otherwise.

17 Theofanis George Stavrou, *Russian Interests in Palestine, 1882-1914* (Thessaloniki: Institute for Balkan Studies, 1963), 159.

18 Abo Hatab, 19, quoted in Issa's English translation, 8.

19 Four times during his brief reign Patriarch Gerasimos had advanced four Arabs to the episcopacy, not by choice, but for lack of available Ionian candidates. His predecessor was responsible for the other four.

20 Gavriel Karapatakes, *To Antiochion Zetema* (Constantinople: 1909), 24-26.

21 Vladimir Karlovich Sabler, *Polnyi pravoslavnyi bogoslovskii entsiklopedicheskii slovar'*, reprint, (Moscow: 1992), vol. 2, cols. 1978-79.

22 See Paul D. Garrett, *St. Innocent, Apostle to America* (Crestwood, NY: St. Vladimir's Seminary Press, 1979).

23 *Budapesti Hirlap*, n. 94 (Apr. 4, 1897); emphasis in the original.

24 "Iz missionerskogo dnevnika Arkhimandrita Rafaila [From the missionary diary of Archimandrite Raphael]," *Russian-American Orthodox Messenger* (hereafter cited: ROAM) 3.15, 422ff.

25 al-Ta'ziyah al-haqiqiyyah fi al-salawat al-ilahiyyah [True Consolation in the Divine Prayers].

26 *ROAM 3.1*, 14-15.

27 *ROAM* 3.2, 50, 52-53, 58; 5.11, 227; Tikhon, archbishop of New York, *Zavety i nastavleniia* (New York: lzd-skii komitet pri sv.-nikolaevskom kafed ral "nom sobore," 1924-26), 7-8; Rojdestvensky, "Patriarch," 34.

28 Despite Raphael's best efforts, the Arab American communities could not raise the $19,000 needed to erect a new church; instead, they purchased and remodeled a Swedish Lutheran church for $7,000.

29 Tikhon, *Zavety i nastavleniia*, 98-99.

30 Tikhon, *Zavety i nastavleniia*, 125-28 (sermon to the flock delivered Jan. 18, 1904).

31 For the Greeks' negative attitude towards Russian primacy, see Demetrios Constantelos' contribution in Miltiades Efthimiou and George A. Christopoulos, eds., *History of the Greek Orthodox Church in America* (New York: Greek Orthodox Archdiocese of North and South America, 1984), 13-18.

32 Elevated to this dignity by the Holy Synod in August for "his extraordinary zealous service and special labors." See *ROAM* 9.10, 200-201; and 9.11, 203.

[33] Tikhon, *Zavety i nastavleniia*, 157-58; and *ROAM* 9.19, 376.

[34] *ROAM* 9.12, 245-46.

[35] *ROAM* 10.11, 207ff.

[36] Archdeacon Emmanuel Abo Hatab assumed a good deal of the burden following Raphael's grave illness in 1914, and continued its publication for one year after the bishop's death.

[37] Afforded melodramatic headline coverage in the *New York Times* and *Herald*. See description and analysis in Naff, *Becoming American*, 223-27.

[38] Raphael deftly weathered a first attempt at schism in Montreal in 1910, which proved a mild precursor of events after his death; see Issa, 76.

[39] Including the *Great Euchologion*.

[40] On this occasion, Raphael's name was dropped from consideration by the Antiochian Holy Synod, since he was already bishop of Brooklyn, and Apostolic Canon 14, 1 Nicea 15, Chalcedon 5 all forbade transfers "city-to-city." See below.

[41] Letter to Bishop Tikhon dated March 11, 1904; English translation by the V. Rev. John Meyendorff in "Notes and comments: the Patriarch of Antioch and North America in 1904," *St. Vladimir's Theological Quarterly* 33.1 (1989), 83-86.

[42] The V. Rev. Joseph Allen reports having held a now-lost photograph of Bishop Raphael stepping out of a Model-T Ford at the seminary entrance. Anyone having copies of this — or any other documents pertaining to Raphael — is asked to contact the Antiochian Village Heritage and Learning Center, P.O. Box 638, Ligonier, PA 15658-0638.

[43] Most clearly following the death of Patriarch Meletios in 1906, when he stated that he shared the late primate's view that Brooklyn was a diocese of the Antiochian See, "though in name it belongs to the Russian Holy Synod." See *al-Kalimat* 2.5 (1906), 93-96; quoted in English in Issa, 62.

[44] This despite the fact that the official organ of the Ecumenical Patriarchate, *Ekklesiastike aletheia,* ignored the fact of his consecration in its reports from America.

[45] Garrett, *St. Innocent,* 276-77.

[46] St. Innocent's predecessor yielded an absolutely enormous influence on Russian Church policy and practice; his encouragement of good relations between the Orthodox and Anglicans in 1832 would have sufficed alone to create the atmosphere we are discussing. Reinforcement was provided, however, in 1896 when

Pope Leo XIII declared Anglican Orders invalid. Orthodox resentment of the papal presumptions threw them naturally to the opposite position.

[47] In 1903 the Holy Synod of Russia declared to the Ecumenical Patriarchate that it viewed the Anglicans as preservers of the apostolic faith rather than Rome, and in 1905 established a committee for joint dialogue.

[48] *ROAM* 14.22, 342.

[49] *ROAM* 12.20, 395.

[50] *ROAM* 16.17, 330 and 16.18, 344-345. Raphael's conditions dealt with affinity and attestation of civil divorce in marriage; insistence on triple immersion in baptism with encouragement to seek chrismation as soon as possible; and limited the administering of confession and communion only to Orthodox Christians on the point of death — and allowed their subsequent burial. It specified that these ceremonies be administered by the Episcopalian clergy according to the Eastern Rite as found in English in Miss Hapgood's *Service Book*. The periodical literature of the era is replete with stories of Jesuit and other proselytizers drawing isolated Orthodox away, of atheism taking hold among others, and of Episcopalian clergy providing the only help to the Orthodox in combating the situation: informing the Consistory so it could dispatch a roving missionary; bucking up the ancestral faith of individuals so put upon, etc.

[51] Quoted in Russian translation in *ROAM* 16.19, 358-60; my rendition back into English.

[52] *al-Kalimat* 7.7 (1911), 125; quoted from Issa , 81-82.

ARAB IMMIGRATION TO NORTH AMERICA
by Najib E. Saliba

Arab immigration to North America starting in the closing decades of the nineteenth century was essentially from Greater Syria[1] and constituted part of Syrian emigration to many parts of the world.

This article[2] discusses the background and causes of Syrian emigration in the period approximately between 1880 and 1920, with special focus on North America. This period witnessed the first wave of Syrian emigration worldwide which was effectively interrupted by World War I and, as far as entry into the United States was concerned, by more stringent immigration laws.[3]

An Historical Background

During the last forty years of Ottoman rule, Syria was administratively divided into three provinces (vilayets) and three autonomous districts called *mutasarrifiyyas* (usually subdivisions of vilayets).[4] The province of Aleppo included northern Syria and parts of southern Turkey; the province of Syria included central Syria (mainly the cities of Ḥamā, Ḥimṣ, and Damascus) and Transjordan; the province of Beirut, which was created in 1888, included the coastal districts of Latakia, Tripoli, Beirut, southern Lebanon, and northern Palestine (the districts of 'Akkā and Nāblus). The autonomous districts included the district of Jerusalem, that of Dayr al-Zawr in eastern Syria, and the district of Mount Lebanon.

Of all these administrative divisions, that of Mount Lebanon played a pioneering role in emigration. The district of Mount Lebanon was established as a consequence of a tragedy and was abolished in the midst of another tragedy, World War I. It was established in the wake of European, mostly French, intervention in a sectarian civil war in Syria in 1860, during which several thousand Christians perished.

The Ottoman sultan, acquiescing to European pressure on behalf of the Christians, issued a decree setting up Mount Lebanon, an area of about two thousand square miles, as an autonomous district with a governor responsible directly to the Sublime Porte in Istanbul. The governor, an Ottoman Catholic Christian but not from Mount Lebanon, was appointed by the sultan and approved by the six European powers which guaranteed Mount Lebanon's autonomy.[5] Assisting the governor was an administrative council composed of four Maronite Christians, two Greek Orthodox, one Greek Catholic, three Druzes, one Sunnite Muslim and one Shi'ite Muslim.

From its inception in 1861 to its fall in mid-1915, Mount Lebanon was better governed, administered, policed and its people better educated than the rest of Syria. Many observers noted that its people enjoyed unprecedented tranquility, security and prosperity.[6] They also enjoyed exemption from military conscription and high taxation, two notorious facets of late Ottoman rule. Because of these favorable conditions the residents of Mount Lebanon were envied by their less fortunate neighbors. As the saying went, "Happy was he who had a goat's resting place in Lebanon."

Economically, however, the situation was not totally satisfactory. Mount Lebanon was cut off from the fertile hinterland, the Biqā' plain, as well as the plains of Sidon and Tyre. Its territory was largely mountainous and little suitable for agriculture. With a high birth rate, little farming and virtually no industry, emigration served as a safety valve to what might otherwise have been an explosive situation.

The relative peace and tranquility which prevailed in Mount Lebanon for over half a century totally disappeared with the onset of World War I. As soon as the Ottoman Empire entered the war on the side of Germany, the Allied fleets blockaded Syria's coasts and prohibited the entry of all imported food supplies. Local production was not enough to feed the population.

In addition, Ottoman military authorities confiscated wheat and other grains in order to assure adequate food supplies for the army.

Famine spread all over Syria and was particularly acute in the area of Mount Lebanon.[7] Survivors of that calamity still relate horror stories of the war years, stories of people who starved to death in the streets while others frantically went through garbage looking for something to eat. People of moderate means sold or mortgaged their land, homes and other belongings for small quantities of food. This was how some of the modern feudal families in Lebanon acquired their large land holdings. Ironically, food supplies, according to some accounts, were not always absent from the market. Monopoly and high prices, however, made commodities beyond the reach of the common man.

An absence of private and public relief agencies contributed to the severity of the situation. Although Ottoman authorities undertook some relief measures, those measures were totally inadequate. Some Ottoman officials, in collaboration with wealthy local opportunists, benefited at the expense of the poor. As thousands starved to death during the four years of war,[8] suspected leaders and politically conscious notables suffered from imprisonment, house arrest, exile into central Anatolia and hanging.[9] Jamal Pasha, the Turkish military governor of Syria, drew no distinction between Muslim and Christian.

If Mount Lebanon enjoyed satisfactory living conditions before the war, the same was not true for the rest of Syria. Although conditions varied slightly from one province to another, public security on the whole was wanting. The people were subjected to the arbitrariness of government officials, the police and tax collectors. There was barely any security for life and property.[10] Villages at the edge of the desert were constantly exposed to bedouin raids and pillage; urban areas, likewise, suffered from sectarian unrest and other sources of tension.

One could ask, "Where was the government at this time?" The government was weak and its intervention could not be depended upon. High public officials were sometimes unwilling or unable to preserve public order. Insufficiency of or inaccessibility to security forces tied the governor's hands. In order to keep the balance of power in the sultan's favor in a given province, the commander of army troops did not take orders from the governor, the highest public official in the province, and did not always work harmoniously with him.

Furthermore, peaceful relations between the empire on the one hand and its dissatisfied minorities and the imperial powers on the other were a rarity from 1850 onward. Conditions of war invariably led to withdrawal of almost all security forces from the provinces to the scenes of hostility, leaving the Syrian provinces under-policed and exposed to lawlessness and domestic strife. At such times, public security was obviously at its worst.

The general economic situation was also unsatisfactory. Ottoman authorities followed a laissez faire economic policy. Economic development was not deemed within the purview of governmental duties. Without official concern and encouragement, agriculture — the mainstay of the economy — and industry were in a state of decline.[11]

Agriculture, for example, had long suffered from neglect, from peasant ignorance, from pests, from inadequate rainfall, from bedouin marauders, from foreign competition and from dependence on centuries-old methods of farming, threshing and winnowing. Whole villages at the edge of the desert were deserted by the peasants for lack of security and the fields were turned into desert. The annual yield of wheat, barley and maize had progressively fallen. Particularly affected was the cultivation of cotton. Left unprotected from the competition of Egyptian and American cotton, Syrian production of that commodity had practically ceased by World War I.[12]

The situation in industry was hardly better. For years, observers of the Syrian economy had noted the decline of the previously vigorous textile industry. Although estimates of the number of workers and looms left in operation varied, there was general agreement that the trend was downward. The problems which hurt the cotton and silk industry the most included high domestic taxation and lack of protective tariffs in the face of heavy competition by cheap machine-made goods imported from abroad.[13]

In addition, a shift in native tastes to European-made clothing led to a shrinking domestic market. The opening of the Suez Canal in

1869 not only hurt Syria's transit trade with Iraq and Iran, it also dealt a serious blow to its silk industry in the international market for it greatly facilitated the transportation of Chinese and, particularly, Japanese silk to European markets at competitive prices. Syrian silk could not hold its ground. Subsequent attempts to open the American market to compensate for the loss of the French one proved fruitless. In 1889, Syrian production of silk was reported to have been twenty-five percent below that of previous years. Silkworm disease and the felling of mulberry trees during World War I for fuel accelerated the decline. In the early 1920's, Syria's production of raw silk (cocoons) was little more than one-sixth of what it had been in 1910[14] (down from 6,100,000 kilograms to 1,300,000).

The problems of the textile industry, however, were not unique. The same situation was generally true in other industries such as the production of olive oil and alcoholic beverages, tanning, dyeing, wood engraving and jewelry making.

An already bad economic situation was made worse by the empire's entry into the war and the establishment of the draft. Males between eighteen and forty-five years old were drafted. In a land not accustomed to military service, conscription was very unpopular. Of the 240,000 conscripts about 40,000 were killed and approximately 150,000 deserted.[15] Many others fled their homes and lands to escape the draft. Undoubtedly, this reflected negatively on the security situation and the economy, particularly agriculture.

Emigration

Evidence indicates the number of emigrants from Syria was small, discontinuous, and largely to Egypt prior to 1878.[16] Emigration picked up steadily in the 1880's and the 1890's and increased sharply in the first fourteen years of this century, peaking in 1913 and 1914.

There is virtual consensus among the sources that the Christians of Mount Lebanon set the pace in emigration. Although conflicting estimates make it impossible to state with certainty the number of Lebanese who emigrated before 1900, it is estimated that probably over 5,000 emigrants had settled in the United States by 1899 and over 1,000 in Canada by 1901.[17] Others went to Australia and the countries of South America. Of a population estimated at 442,000 in 1913, Mount Lebanon lost more than 100,000 to emigration by 1914,[18] more than one-fourth of its population.

It did not take other Syrians long to catch up with the Lebanese. Very soon emigrants were leaving from Damascus, Jerusalem, Ramallah and the many other towns and villages.[19] By the 1920's, the Syrian community in Egypt numbered over 50,000 of whom more than 15,000 were Orthodox Christians.[20] Probably about 4,000 Syrian emigrants had settled in Australia by 1903,[21] over 3,000 in Canada by 1921,[22] and some 80,000 to 100,000 in Brazil by 1922.[23] Others settled in Argentina and Mexico, among other locations.

A large number of Syrian emigrants went to the United States before 1920. It is impossible to accurately determine their number and place of origin in Syria. Part of the difficulty stems from the fact that early Syrian emigrants were entered in United States immigration records as Arabs, Turks, Asiatic Turks, and sometimes as Greeks and Armenians.[24] It was only after 1899 that the Immigration Service began to classify such immigrants as Syrians. Even then, the 1910 United States census listed no immigrants of Syrian origin in the United States.[25] Following an inquiry, however, another official report put the number of Syrian emigrants who entered the United States between 1899 and 1910 at 56,909.[26]

Table I shows the number of Syrians who entered the United States annually from 1899 to June 30, 1919, a total of 89,971. The sharp decline in the number of immigrants beginning in 1915, and continuing through 1919, reflects the conditions of war years as well as United States literacy restrictions.[27] The figures, however, need some explanation.

The total number included only those who had declared their intention to stay in the United States permanently. It did not include those who might have subsequently returned or those who might have decided to stay following their entry. Moreover, it ignored the deceased and did not include those who had entered the United States before 1899. Taking these factors into consideration, a conservative estimate of Syrian born immigrants in the United States in 1920 might well have exceeded 100,000.[28]

Table I
Syrian Emigration to the United States, 1899-1919

Year	Emigrants
1899	3708
1900	2920
1901	4064
1902	4982
1903	5551
1904	3653
1905	4822
1906	5824
1907	5880
1908	5520
1909	3668
1910	6317
1911	5444
1912	5525
1913	9210
1914	9023
1915	1767
1916	0676
1917	0976
1918	0210
1919	0231
Total	89,971

Source: Annual Report Commissioner General Immigration, 1919, 168 (cited by Ḥitti, *The Syrians in America* [New York: George H. Doran Company, 1924], 62-65).

An overwhelming majority of Syrian immigrants entered the United States at New York City's Ellis Island. A few entered through Boston, Providence, Philadelphia, New Orleans, Mexico or Canada. The journey between the shores of Syria and Ellis Island took over a month. Ports of call usually included Alexandria, Athens, Naples, Marseilles and Liverpool.

On the way, transfers from one ship to another were not uncommon. Immigrant accounts are replete with stories of swindling by ticket agents at the ports of Beirut and Tripoli, overcrowded ships, horrible food and sea sickness. Sometimes tickets were bought presumably for passenger ships but good only for cargo ships. After about a month between the sea and the sky, the exhausted immigrants finally arrived at Ellis Island where they were given a physical examination. Those found physically fit were allowed to disembark. The sick, especially those with communicable diseases like trachoma, were forced to return aboard the same ships to their points of origin.

Before disembarking, however, those immigrants who did not speak English and who were not met by a friend or relative were "tagged." The tag included the name and destination of the immigrant and the name and address of his sponsor. With these formalities completed, the immigrants finally got their first glimpse of New York City.

Since Ellis Island was the major port of entry, New York City saw the rise of the most important Syrian colony in the United States at the turn of the nineteenth century.[29] It saw the establishment of the first Syrian businesses in the mid-1880's, the first church (Maronite) and newspaper in 1891 and 1892 respectively,[30] and the first Syrian organizations. Numerically, the size of New York City's Syrian colony ranged from 10,000[31] in 1895 to 15,000 or 20,000 around 1913.[32]

The Syrian quarter on Washington Street was within a "stone's throw" from Wall Street, observed Mikhail Naimy[33] (Mikhā'īl Nu'ayma) in 1911. "Here, the dialects of the Lebanese villages intermixed with those of Beirut, Damascus, Ḥims, Ḥamā, Jerusalem, and Aleppo," he added. "One feels at home" in the Syrian quarter, noted Archpriest Basil Kherbawy at about the same time.

Not all Syrian immigrants, however, made New York City their home. Those who did not seek their fortunes in that city for one reason or another, fanned out to the many cities and towns in the interior of the country. Although the northeastern region of the United States attracted the most, not a single state in mainland United States was without Syrian immigrants. A few even went to Hawaii, Alaska and Puerto Rico.

Table II reflects cities in the United States with the largest concentrations of Syrian immigrants in the early 1920's.

Table II

City	Immigrants	City	Immigrants
New York	7,760	Paterson (NJ)	1,252
Detroit	3,858	St. Louis	987
Boston	3,150	Fall River (MA)	971
Chicago	1,672	Philadelphia	914
Worcester (MA)	1,448	Akron	883
Cleveland	1,440	San Francisco	773
Pittsburgh	1,406	Springfield (MA)	696

Source: Hitti, *The Syrians*, 67 (based on the 1920 U.S. Census).

Causes of Emigration

Although we do not know exactly how many people emigrated from Syria, we are much better informed as to why they left. Considerable literature, including numerous accounts written by Syrian-born immigrants as well as those taken from personal interviews, leaves no doubt that the vast majority emigrated primarily because of economic factors. Whether they emigrated to Egypt, Australia, North or South America, the main motive for emigration was economic betterment.[34] "We heard that the streets of America were paved with gold," said one respondent. Many immigrants believed that it would only take them a short time to get rich and to return home to enjoy the fruits of their labor.

American Christian missionaries who were well established in Syria helped the Syrians discover America in the last quarter of the nineteenth century.[35] They helped spread the idea of a better life overseas. Missionaries, however, lamented the flight of the educated to America. They wished that their graduates would stay to help educate their compatriots. To keep their teachers, Russian Orthodox missionaries increased faculty salaries to discourage emigration.[36]

In the case of Mount Lebanon (unlike the rest of Syria) overpopulation was also an important factor in immigration. As already stated, the Lebanese had no access to the fertile plains of the Biqā', Sidon, and Tyre. The rest of Syria was unattractive to them because of its economic backwardness and its lack of political and economic security. Thus they turned to emigration.[37]

The opening of the Chicago and St. Louis fairs in 1893 and 1906 respectively were instrumental in attracting and distributing Syrian immigrants across the country.[38] Among the Syrian goods displayed at these fairs were tapestries, icons, strings of beads and crosses, items for which Palestine was noted. There is hardly any doubt that the general economic backwardness of Syria, the lack of economic enterprise, economic insecurity, ruinous taxation and, most importantly, the awareness of a better life elsewhere, drove the Syrians to emigrate.

Political insecurity and an almost total absence of freedom of expression drove many intellectuals to emigrate. Because of the native and foreign schools which were established in Syria, the country experienced an intellectual awakening in the second half of the nineteenth century.[39]

The city of Beirut was the hub of this intellectual activity. Besides its native schools, there was the Syrian Protestant Mission (later known as the American University of Beirut) and Saint Joseph's University. In addition, Beirut included several printing presses, newspapers and magazines. In 1881, the American printing press alone issued 57,500 books, more than two-thirds of which were sold that same year.

As a result, a renaissance occurred in the Arabic language. The reading public increased and writers began to discuss serious topics such as better government, social equality, due process of law, improved economy and improved communications. Stimulating this intellectual movement was the relative freedom of thought and expression which existed in Syria until 1880. However, with the expulsion of the liberal and reformist governor, Midhat Pasha, from the province, censorship was applied to the press and all other forms of intellectual expression. Sultan 'Abd al-Ḥamīd and his over-zealous agents gradually squeezed all life out of the press and subjected writers and journalists to imprisonment, fines, and expulsion. Thousands of books were burned or buried underground to keep inspectors away.

Faced with tightening Ḥamīdian censorship and economic emaciation at home, Christian and Muslim intellectuals alike fled Syria and took refuge in Egypt, Europe and the Americas.[40] Perhaps the largest community of these intellectuals settled in Egypt after 1882. Under British control, the Egyptian press was relatively free to publish, especially on topics unrelated to British-Egyptian relations. Consequently, authors, editors and journalists flocked to Cairo and Alexandria, twenty-eight and nineteen respectively. This colony of Syrian political refugees left its mark on the Egyptian press. Well-known and long-lasting Egyptian papers and magazines were established by Syrians.[41]

Religious persecution in Syria, particularly the 1860 massacres, has often been cited as a major factor in emigration. The literature dealing with this topic is controversial, emotional, and not entirely consistent. Popular belief and some accounts tend to overemphasize its importance.

Sa'īd B. Ḥimadeh, for example, stated that emigration developed gradually from 1860 to 1900 at an average of three thousand emigrants annually.[42] The American missionary, Henry H. Jessup, told of a "thousand refugees," presumably Christians, who emigrated to Alexandria aboard a Russian steamer in the wake of the Damascus massacre of 1860.[43] Muḥammad Kurd 'Alī, on the other hand, referred to "some" who emigrated to Egypt, Istanbul and elsewhere in the Mediterranean area.[44]

An examination of much of the literature dealing with emigration, including numerous accounts written by emigrants as well as personal interviews, indicates that on the whole religious discontent was a supplementary rather than a primary factor in emigration. While available evidence supports growing emigration from Syria after 1880, there is no convincing proof of a significant and sustained outflow of emigrants in the previous two decades. Hence, the oft-repeated assertion that religious persecution drove Christians to emigrate is untenable and needs considerable modification.

Extant accounts written by emigrants themselves do not substantiate the persecution thesis. Seldom did an emigrant indicate that he had left his homeland because of religious persecution; seldom did he indicate that he had left permanently. On the contrary, many expressed a desire to return, having "become rich."[45] A. Ruppin, a German scholar, reported that one-third to one-half of the emigrants returned and invested their savings in land and in new homes.[46] It is highly unlikely that so many would have returned if religious persecution had been their primary reason for leaving.

The fact that sustained and progressive emigration came after 1880, two decades after the 1860 massacres, coupled with the fact that the early emigrants came largely from the autonomous district of Mount Lebanon, which had a Christian majority and enjoyed political stability, indicates that religious persecution played a minor role in emigration. Surely, some emigrants complained of religious fanaticism, bigotry and personal quarrels with Muslims or Druzes. These complaints, however, were placed after others, such as Ottoman misrule, political oppression, lack of freedom, inequality and lack of economic opportunity.[47] Moreover, some respondents mentioned that they had gotten along well with Muslims and had many Muslim friends.

In only one account, that of the Orthodox Christian 'Arbīli (Arbeely) family, the first known Syrian family to emigrate to America,[48] is religious persecution named as a primary reason for leaving. The 'Arbīlis, an upper-class family of nine individuals, witnessed and miraculously survived the sectarian massacres of

Damascus in 1860. Having moved to Beirut, a relatively safer place, Yūsuf 'Arbīli decided, eighteen years after the massacres, to leave the Ottoman Empire altogether "for the progress of my children." Having been discouraged from emigrating to Russia by the Russian consul in Beirut, he decided to come to the United States. The 'Arbīlis settled in New York City and Washington, D.C.

Religion, if not a primary cause of emigration, was important in determining the destination of the emigrants. Most emigrants to Egypt were Muslims and almost all the early ones to the West were Christians.[49] Despite the fact that the Christian emigrant was usually a Maronite, Orthodox, or Melkite, denominations not very common in the Western world, he could still live as Christian, subscribe to Christian beliefs and worship and pray to the Christian God without constraints.

The Muslim, by contrast, while he could feel at home in Egypt, faced psychological, religious and cultural obstacles in the West. What would become of him, his children and his religion in the land of the "infidel?" It was reported that a certain Muslim bought his ticket and set off for America in 1885. Having learned that America was "*bilād kufr*" (land of unbelief) and had no mosques, he changed his mind and got off the boat. Largely for religious reasons the Syrian Muslim initially shunned emigration to the West, leaving that option almost totally to the Christian.

Other factors also influenced Syrian emigration. Stories of economic success abroad created a mental disposition favorable to emigration.[50] The early emigrants themselves, either through correspondence or after an occasional return home, encouraged their relatives and former neighbors to emigrate.[51] Emigration became popular. Some even borrowed the money or mortgaged property[52] to purchase their tickets, which cost approximately 230 to 250 francs for a one-way fare to South America and 190 francs to New York City.[53]

Transportation was regular, monthly and sometimes weekly, and emigrants were not encumbered in those days by lengthy immigration forms, visa applications, passports or medical examinations. They only needed to go to the port where they would buy their tickets. Ticket agents often determined their destinations for them.

Emigrants to the United States took their physical examination before debarking at New York harbor or Boston. The sick were not permitted to disembark. In one case, a Lebanese mother and her two children came to join the father in Worcester, Massachusetts. The children were not allowed to land because of illness. In another case, a Lebanese was denied entry in 1908 because of trachoma; he returned home and came back to the United States in 1913.

As Ottoman international problems multiplied precipitating war, conscription and a ban on emigration, candidates for the draft "paid off" smugglers or high Ottoman officials to look the other way while they slipped aboard ships bound for foreign lands.[54]

Present data indicate that some 68 percent of the immigrants were men and the majority of the men (probably 60 percent) were young, on the average in their mid-twenties and unmarried.[55] A small minority were married and perhaps 12 percent of these brought their families with them. The ratio of women to men increased after 1900, as wives and children joined husbands and fathers in the *mahjar* (place of emigration).[56] The emigration of the young, the unattached, was most serious. Many villages lost their young blood and became like shelters for senior citizens. A village in Mount Lebanon called "Bayt Shabab," or the home of youth, was nicknamed "Bayt al-'Ajazah," or the home of the aged.

With the possible exception of the educated minority and the intellectuals, the early emigrants were predominately poor peasants. Few had some education while the majority were illiterate.[57] Less than one-fourth were professionals or skilled. As immigrants they were so absorbed in economic matters that they neglected the world of the mind and failed to avail themselves of the educational opportunities in their adopted country.[58]

The impact of emigration was both negative and positive. Although the immigrants benefited materially and a few educationally, a large number of them remained attached to the "old country" and never adjusted fully to life in the *mahjar*. On the national level, emigration depleted Syria's manpower, causing shortages of labor, reinforcing economic stagnation.[59]

Since most emigrants were young, emigration deprived Syria of hundreds of thousands of productive people. This hemorrhage of young blood had deleterious effects on agriculture and the silk and weaving industries of Mount Lebanon. The terraces, which the Lebanese peasant had laboriously constructed over the years to preserve his soil and maintain its productivity, lay untended.

Emigration also had a major impact on the religious balance in Syria. It depleted the Christian population and increased the numerical imbalance between Christians and Muslims.[60] In the long run, emigration was responsible, to no small degree, for the economic, political, and social retardation of Syria.

On the positive side, Syria's economic losses were partially compensated for by an increase in Syrian exports[61] and by remittances from abroad. In the case of Mount Lebanon, those remittances constituted on the eve of World War I, some 41 percent of its budget.[62] Many of those red-roofed houses, so characteristic of the present-day Lebanese landscape, were paid for with money earned overseas.[63] In addition, the emigrants contributed to famine relief efforts in Syria during World War I.[64]

In the interwar period and during World War II, the emigrants lobbied extensively for the independence of Syria and Lebanon from France. As that independence was achieved and foreign armies withdrew, both governments initiated programs to tie the emigrants closely to their native land. Plans to encourage the emigrants not only to pay annual visits to the "old country," but to invest part of their savings in it as well, were quickly undertaken. Moreover, in its effort to consolidate emigrant Lebanon with resident Lebanon, the Lebanese government made Lebanese citizenship readily available to the emigrants (who actually never lost it in the first place) and their offspring, enabling them to hold property, public office, and vote in elections should they choose to do so.

NOTES

[1] The term Greater Syria includes present-day Syria, the Republic of Lebanon, Palestine, and the Kingdom of Jordan.

[2] This article is adapted from my book *Emigration from Syria and The Syrian-Lebanese Community of Worcester, Massachusetts* (Ligonier, PA: Antakya Press, 1992).

[3] In 1917 the U.S. Congress introduced literacy restrictions, thus closing the U.S. to illiterate immigrants. Moreover, the more stringent immigration laws introduced in 1924 almost totally closed the U.S. to Asiatic immigrants.

[4] For a brief account of Ottoman administration in Syria see the author's doctoral dissertation, *Wilāyat Sūriyyā* (the Province of Syria) (Ann Arbor: University of Michigan, 1971); see also Yūsuf al-Ḥakīm, *Sūriyyah wa-al-'Ahd al-'Uthmāni* (Beirut, 1966), 5.

[5] K.S. Salibi, *The Modern History of Lebanon* (London: Weidenfeld and Nicolson, 1965), 110.

[6] *Ibid.*, 142; Yūsuf al-Ḥakīm, *Beirut wa-Lubnān fī 'Ahd Āl 'Uthmān* (Beirut, 1964), 14.

[7] There are many moving accounts about the famine which afflicted Mount Lebanon during World War I. See al-Ḥakīm, *Beirut wa-Lubnān*, 245-51; Laḥd Khāṭir, *'Ahd al-Mutasarrifīn fī Lubnān: 1861-1918* (Beirut, 1967), 200-207; Ibrahim al-Aswad, *Tanwīr al-Adhhān fī Tārīkh Lubnān* (Beirut, 1930), 3:57; Nasīb 'Arīḍah, ed., *al-Funūn*, part 5 (New York, Oct. 1916), 459-62. This issue of *al-Funūn* was dedicated to the victims of the famine in Syria.

[8] Estimates vary. L. Khāṭir (200) put the number of Lebanese victims at 100,000; Muhammad Kurd 'Ali put the number of victims in all Syria at 120,000; see his *Khiṭaṭ al-Shām* (Damascus, 1925), 3:135.

[9] About 40 people were hanged in Beirut and Damascus in 1916 because of political activities. See al-Ḥakīm, *Beirut wa-Lubnān*, 234-38; Kurd 'Ali, 141-45.

[10] See chapter six of the author's dissertation, *The Province of Syria*, on government and public security in Syria; Basil Kherbawy, *History of the United States* (Brooklyn, N.Y., 1913), 748. This book is in Arabic and contains a section on Syrian emigration, 725-911.

[11] Author's dissertation, 307-309.

[12] Saʿīd B. Ḥimadeh, *Economic Organization of Syria* (Beirut, 1936), 79; Charles Issawi, "British Trade and the Rise of Beirut," *International Journal of Middle East Studies* (IJMES), 8:1, (1977), 91-101; Charles Issawi, *The Economic History of the Middle East, 1800-1914* (Chicago: University of Chicago Press, 1966), 208.

[13] Issawi, *IJMES*, 8:1 (1977), 99; *Economic History*, 208, 221 and 281-82; Ḥimadeh, 80.

[14] Author's dissertation, 313; Philip K. Ḥitti, "al-Sūriyyūn fi al-Wilāyāt al-Muttaḥidah," *al-Muqtaṭaf*, 60 (1922), 120; Edmond Bishārah, "al-Ṣināʿāt fi Sūriyyah wa-Lubnān," *al-Muqtaṭaf*, 60 (1922), 355, 358; Ḥimadeh, 123, 137; August Adib, *Lubnān baʿd al-Ḥarb* (Egypt, 1919), 104.

[15] Kurd ʿAli, 145; al-Ḥakīm, *Beirut wa-Lubnān*, 223.

[16] Kurd ʿAli, 93; Elie Ṣafā, *L'Émigration Libanaise* (Beyrouth, 1960), 10, 120.

[17] Yūsuf al-ʿĪd, *Jawlāt fi al-ʿĀlam al-Jadīd*, (Buenos Aires, 1959), 529, 613; Elaine Hagopian and Ann Paden, *The Arab-Americans* (Cypress, Calif.: Medina University Press, 1969), 21.

[18] Pierre Rondot, *Les Institutions Politiques du Liban* (Paris, 1947), 28-29 (cited by Michael W. Suleiman in *Political Parties in Lebanon* [New York: Cornell University Press, 1967], 18); Philip Ḥitti, *A Short History of Lebanon* (St. Martin's Press, 1965), 207; A. Ruppin, in Issawi's *Economic History*, 270, table 2. Other estimates put the number of Lebanese emigrants by 1914 at 300,000 or close to it. See Adib, 104; Kamal Karpat, "The Ottoman Emigration to America, 1860-1914," *IJMES* (17:2, 1985), 175-209.

[19] al-Ḥakīm, *Beirut wa-Lubnān*, 42-43; Ḥitti, "al-Sūriyyūn," 22-23, 121; Issawi, *Economic History*, 272.

[20] Issawi, *Economic History*, 269; *al-Kalimat* (Brooklyn, 1914), 108-111. Donald Reid in his *Odyssey of Faraḥ Anṭūn* (Chicago: Bibliotheca Islamica, 1975) put the number of Syrian Christians in Egypt in 1907 at 34,000 according to the Egyptian census of that year (27). Later on (51) he put their total number at 30,000 in 1920. This may well be an underestimate since the great bulk of Syrian emigrants came to Egypt following the British occupation of 1882 (Kurd ʿAli, *Khiṭaṭ* [Damascus, 1926], 4:153-54).

[21] Yūsuf ʿAbbūd al-Khūri, "al-Sūriyyūn fi Ustrālyā," *al-Maḥabbah* (Beirut, 1903), 600-602.

[22] Kherbawy, 892-93; Hagopian-Paden, 21, n.7.

²³ Tawfīq Ḍaʿūn, "al-Sūriyyūn fi al-Barāzīl," *al-Muqtaṭaf*, 61 (1922), 228-31; Elie Ṣafā (p. 190) put the number of emigrants who entered Brazil between 1904 and 1913 under the designation of "Turks" or "Syrian" but mostly of "Lebanese" origin at 46,003.

²⁴ Hitti, "al-Sūriyyūn," 16-17.

²⁵ *Ibid.*, 16-18 (Hitti cited the U.S. Thirteenth Census Reports, 1:1006, 1015).

²⁶ *Ibid.*, 22.

²⁷ In 1917 the U. S. Congress introduced literacy restrictions thus closing the United States to illiterate immigrants. Yet more restrictions would follow in the racially colored laws of 1924 which virtually closed the United States to Asiatic immigrants.

²⁸ Other estimates put the number considerably higher. See Karpat, 185, 208, n. 47; Kherbawy, 789-90; Amin al-Ghurayyib, *Akhbār wa-Afkār* (Beirut, 1912), 101-102; Yūsuf N. Maʿlūf, *Khizānat al-Ayyām fi Tarājim al-ʿIẓām* (New York, 1899), 268; Philip and Joseph M. Kayal, *The Syrian-Lebanese in America* (Boston: Twayne Publishers, 1975), 69; Ayad al-Qazzaz, *Transnational Links* (Sacramento: Cal Central Press, 1979), 17.

²⁹ *al-Kalimat* (1905), 27-28.

³⁰ Maʿlūf, 263, 266, 298-306; Kherbawy, 780, 791, 824.

³¹ Karpat, 208, n. 47 (quoting the *New York Times*).

³² Kherbawy, 825; Hitti puts the number of Syrians in New York City in 1920 at 7,760 according to the 1920 census (see Hitti, *The Syrians*, 67). This figure may well be an underestimate.

³³ Mikhail Naimy, *Sabʿūn*, 2 (Beirut, 1964), 9.

³⁴ *al-Manār* (Beirut, 1899), 490; *al-Maḥabbah* (Beirut, 1902), 599; *ibid.* (1903), 382; *al-Kalimat* (1909), 348-50; *al-Jāmiʿah* (New York, 1906), 54-56; Kherbawy, 764, 770, 786; Maʿlūf, 259-65; Nasīb ʿArīḍah, *The Syrian-American Directory* (New York, 1930), 148; *al-Sameer* (New York, April 1st, 1931), 1092-94; Salom Rizk, *Syrian Yankee* (New York: Doubleday, 1946), 16; Abraham M. Rihbany, *A Far Journey: An Autobiography* (Boston: Houghton Mifflin, 1914), 277; *The Syrian World*, 11:2 (Aug. 1927), 50-51.

³⁵ Kherbawy, 768; Aridah, 159-60; Eldridge Mix, "Pilgrims of Today: Our Syrian Colony," *The Worcester Magazine* VI:2 (1903), 56-59; John A. DeNovo, *American Interests and Policies in the Middle East, 1900-1939* (Minneapolis: University of Minnesota Press, 1963), 7-8; Joseph L. Grabill, *Protestant Diplomacy and the Near East* (Minneapolis: University of Minnesota Press, 1971), 31;

Vincent N. Parrillo, *Strangers to These Shores: Race and Ethnic Relations in the U.S.* (Boston: Houghton Mifflin, 1980), 320; Rihbany, 120, 121, 144.

36 *al-Kalimat* (1911), 291.

37 Hitti, *Short History*, 206; al-Ḥakīm, *Beirut wa-Lubnān*, 43; al-Ḥakīm, *Sūriyyah*, 240.

38 Hitti, "al-Sūriyyūn," 22-24; Nicholas A. Naḥḥās, *The Mirror of Antioch in North America* (n.p., ca. 1923) 16; *al-Kalimat* (1905), 27-28; Lucius H. Miller, *Our Syrian Population* (reprint, San Francisco, 1969), 5.

39 Tawfīq Ali Birrū, *al-'Arab wa-al-Turk fi al-'Ahd al-Dustūri al-'Uthmāni, 1908-1914* (Cairo, 1960), 14-17; al-Ḥakīm, *Sūriyyah*, 98-101, 191; Salibi, 139-40; author's dissertation, 317-32.

40 al-Ḥakīm, *Sūriyyah*, 60; al-Ḥakīm, *Beirut wa-Lubnān*, 33; Hitti, "al-Sūriyyūn," 121; Sulaiman al-Bustāni, *al-Dawlah al-'Uthmāniyyah qabl al-Dustūr wa-Ba'dah* (Cairo, 1908), 27-28, 42-45; Rihbany, 156-57.

41 Salibi, 147-48; author's dissertation 332-42; Himadeh, 16; Issawi, *Economic*, 272; Reid, 22, 35-36, 47; see also D.J. Cioeta, "Ottoman Censorship in Lebanon and Syria, 1876-1908," *IJMES* 10:2 (1979), 167-86.

42 Himadeh, 16; see also Issawi, *Economic*, 269; Reid, 20.

43 Henry H. Jessup, *Fifty-three Years in Syria* (New York: Fleming H. Revell Company, 1910), 204.

44 Kurd 'Ali, *Khiṭaṭ*, 3, 93.

45 Ma'lūf, 265; Kherbawy, 772.

46 In Issawi, *Economic*, 271-72. During the U.S. economic depression of the 1930's more Syrian immigrants entertained the idea of return; see *al-Sameer*, April 15, 1931, 9-11.

47 Naḥḥās, 12-14; Murād Abū Mādi, *al-Sanābil* (1952), 9; Ibraham 'Arbīlī, "Fi Tārīkh al-'Ā'ilah al-'Arbīniyyah wa-Muhājaratihā ilā al-Wilāyāt al-Muttaḥidah," *al-Kalimat* (1913), 152-53.

48 *al-Kalimat* (1905), 27-28; "Fi Muhājarat al-Duktūr Yūsuf 'Arbīlī, *al-Kalimat* (1913), 488-97, 490, 495.

49 Hitti estimated the number of Maronite Christians in the U.S. around 1922 at about 100,000; Orthodox, 90,000; Muslims, 8,000; Druzes, 1,000; see "al-Sūriyyūn," *al-Muqtaṭaf*, 61 (1922), 16; Hagopian-Paden, 4; A. Ruppin in Issawi,

Economic, 272; Abdo A. Elkholy, *The Arab Moslems in the United States* (College and University Press, 1966), 17, 22. Karpat believes that Muslim emigrants numbered more than previously thought.

50 Ḥitti, "al-Sūriyyūn," 122; al-Ḥakīm, *Sūriyyah*, 240; *al Jāmi'ah* (1906), 55; 'Arīḍah, 149, 159; Tawfīq F. Ḍa'ūn, *Dhikrah al-Hijrah* (Brazil, 1946), 56.

51 Wadī' Abū Rizq, "al-Sūri fi Ustrālyā," *al-Maḥabbah* (1903), 381-85, 382; al-Ḥakīm, *Beirut wa Lubnān*, 42-43; Ḥitti, "al-Sūriyyūn," 122; Da'un, "al-Sūriyyūn," 228-29; Kherbawy, 772.

52 *al-Muqtaṭaf*, 60 (1922), 122; *ibid.*, 61 (1922), 228; Kherbawy, 772; Naimy, *Sab'ūn*, 1 (Beirut, 1962), 96-97.

53 Issawi, *Economic*, 271-72.

54 al-Ḥakīm, *Sūriyyah*, 241; Ḥitti, "al-Sūriyyūn," 121; al-Bustāni, 115-16; Ḥimadeh, 14; Rizq, 41; *al-Kalimat* (1909), 409.

55 Ḥitti, "al-Sūriyyūn," 125 (citing Reports of Imigration Commission, 1:97); Hagopian-Paden, 8; Sa'īd Abū Jamrah, "Ni'mah Yāfith," *al-Muqtaṭaf*, 65 (1924), 161-71, 166.

56 Karpat, 180.

57 Kherbawy, 772; Naimy, 96-97; Hagopian-Paden, 5; Abū-Jamrah, 165; Issawi, *Economic*, 271; Ḥimadeh, 16-17. This is to be contrasted with the emigrants of the 1950's and the following years. See Hossein Askari and J. Cummings, "The Middle East and the United States: A Problem of Brain Drain," *IJMES*, 8:1 (1977), 65-90.

58 Ḥitti, "al-Sūriyyūn," 436-38; Abū Rizq, 382.

59 Adib, 106; *al-Sameer*, April 1st, 1931, 1094-95; *ibid.*, April 15, 1931, 9-11; Albert H. Hourani, *Syria and Lebanon* (Oxford University Press, 1946), 35; Aḥmad W. Zakariyyā, *al-Rīf al-Sūri* (Damascus, 1955), 81-82.

60 Kherbawy, 823; Karpat, 192.

61 Ma'lūf, 262.

62 A. Ruppin in Issawi, *Economic*, 271; Jonathan C. Randal, *Going all the Way* (New York: Viking Press, 1983), 46.

63 Kherbawy, 820; al-Ghurayyib, 101-102; Adib, 106.

64 *al-Kalimat* (1915), 37-38, 106-107.

THE ARAB IMMIGRANT EXPERIENCE
by Alixa Naff

When Father Raphael Hawaweeny arrived to serve as pastor to the Arab Orthodox community in New York City in 1895, the migration of Syrian-Lebanese from the eastern shores of the Mediterranean to the eastern shores of the United States was gaining momentum. Both spiritual leaders and immigrants left to their successors a record of achievement on which to build.

The Arabic-speaking migrants to the United States came in two major waves. The first wave arrived between 1880 and 1940.[1] The second wave came after World War II. The first wave is distinguished from the second in a number of significant ways. Its members were overwhelmingly unsophisticated village farmer-artisans. The second wave had and continues to have a very large component of educated, bilingual, politicized, and nationalistic individuals. While the first wave was generally Christian, the second is mainly Muslim. Because the first wave came from what was the Ottoman province of Syria which included the administrative district of Mount Lebanon, they called themselves Syrian. The second wave came from a variety of independent Arab nations collectively known, since World War II, as the Arab world. They call themselves Arabs.

The first wave came to an America that was in the process of urbanizing and industrializing, accelerated by a multitude of advance technological innovations such as railroads, steel mills, telegraph and telephone communications, electricity, and automobiles. The second wave came to a country which had filled its borders, experienced two world wars, and had become the world's leading industrial scientific technological and military power.

Until the 1924 Immigration Quota Act which virtually halted immigration from non-western Europe, America welcomed the "poor ... huddled masses" of Europe and western Asia with few immigration restrictions. By 1965, with the passing of the Immigration and Nationality Act, it favored skilled and professional foreigners.

Currently, Americans of Arab descent number perhaps over two million of which half or more are descendants of the first wave.

From the Homeland to the New Land

In the last quarter of the nineteenth century, the spreading revolution in communications and transportation accelerated industrialization and urbanization, primarily in the populous regions east of the Mississippi. On the other hand, railroad networks, expanding westward, opened vast areas of the United States for cultivation and the exploitation of resources while sparsely populated states and territories sought inhabitants. These developments required the recruitment of industrial and agricultural labor. Agents of industry and steamship lines began then to recruit labor from abroad. As a result, millions of poor and illiterate laborers and peasants — predominantly European — flooded to America triggering a virulent anti-foreign sentiment before and especially after World War I. In response, Congress passed a series of restrictive immigration laws culminating in the Quota Act. Syrian immigration under this system was restricted to 100 annually.

The vanguard of Syrian immigrants were merchants and artisans from Syrian trade centers. Urged by the tyrannical but trade-minded Ottoman Sultan Abdel Hamid II, they traveled to the Philadelphia Centennial Exposition in 1876 to show their wares. If these trailblazers were not the first from their homeland to discover American economic opportunities, they at least had the foresight to see the larger potential.

The Syrians were not driven to America on a mass scale from either economic desperation, religious persecution or political oppression. Although these conditions were more evident in Syria proper than in Mount Lebanon, far fewer emigrants, even Christians, left Syrian villages and towns.

Historians, including such pre-eminent Middle East scholars as Albert Hourani and Philip Hitti, agree that in the late nineteenth century, Mount Lebanon was not a place to flee from. Hitti wrote that the people of Mount Lebanon "enjoyed a period of cultural flourish and economic prosperity and achieved a state of security and stability unattained by any Ottoman province, European or Asian...."[2] By their own testimony, the immigrants came to improve their economic condition and to return home in a year or two wealthier and prouder than when they left.

Later, others would join the pioneers for a variety of reasons such as evading personal problems or joining relatives. Muslims, Druzes and some Christians escaped Turkish military conscription after 1908 and many who had suffered through the famine of World War I also emigrated. It was while they were pursuing their get-rich-quick goals that they discovered the ideals of freedom, democracy, and opportunity and they embraced them fervently.

It may have been the tales of undreamed-of wealth and the impression of streets paved with gold that launched a chain migration which ultimately would draw thousands of kinsmen and countrymen to the North American continent and into the mainstream of society. News of their success spread by word of mouth like wildfire throughout the region. A few stalwarts gambled on the rumors and sailed for America. Soon their glowing reports and money orders triggered an exodus. More effective were the dazzling testimonies of returned villagers who sported serge suits, gold watch fobs, and shined leather shoes.

Faris N. visited returning cousins in 1895. "I asked them about work there," he wrote in his memoirs. "They said it was in trading and one could make three English pounds....I said 'Three English pounds!' Then I returned home and said 'Mama,...I want to go to America and I will be away from you for two years.'" Within a few weeks Faris left with 32 others from his village. That same year,

Mike H. emigrated with 72 others. "All of my village of 'Ayn 'Arab rushed to America. It was like a gold rush."

Most of the uncertainties of travel were alleviated in numerous ways, further encouraging emigration. For example, letters from America containing detailed travel instructions, warnings against pitfalls, and providing assurance of work on arrival at a specific destination lowered the level of anxiety. Moreover, in response to the emigrant traffic, a network of entrepreneurial services evolved to facilitate travel even as it exploited the travelers. Syrian agents circumvented Ottoman restrictions against emigration, booked steamship passage to Europe, and smuggled emigrants to the ships anchored at sea. "We hid in the woods for over eight hours before we could leave at night in dinghies," said Elizabeth B. In European ports, too, agents were helpful in many ways including changing money, writing letters, and booking passage for New York. However, it was not uncommon for the naive villagers to find themselves deposited in Canadian, Mexican, Caribbean, South American, even Australian ports, victims of the free-wheeling culture of the network where each opportunistic, often unscrupulous, entrepreneur had his price.

By World War I, immigration records show that about 100,000 Syrians had been admitted into the United States and by 1930, according to census and immigration records, the immigrants and their descendants numbered about 206,000. Official figures tend to be unreliable for several reasons — among them faulty recordkeeping — especially before World War I. Before 1899, immigrants from the eastern Mediterranean were registered as from "Turkey in Asia." However, in 1899, the Bureau of Immigration, convinced that most of these were from Ottoman Syria, added a "Syrian" classification to its register. This not only improved the accuracy of the records, but gave the Syrians a way of identifying themselves in a land teeming with immigrants from various national origins. Also, while most arrived through the port of New York, a substantial number entered at other United States ports of entry or smuggled themselves across Canadian and Mexican borders. In addition, the itinerant immigration occupation of the Syrians, their relatively rapid assimilation, their historic fear of questioning officials, and their relatively high rate of outmarriage which diluted their ethnic identity made counting them even more difficult.

On average, the number of Syrian immigrants, insignificant compared to the flood of migrants passing through Ellis Island, doubled annually.

More than 90 percent of the early arrivals were Christians from Mount Lebanon who, as a result of western and American schools and churches, were more receptive to undertaking the adventure when American opportunity beckoned. They were overwhelmingly of the Eastern rite faiths, mainly Orthodox Christian, Melkite, and Maronite. Because they feared that they could not maintain their Islamic way of life in a Christian country, perhaps as few as 5 or 10 percent were Muslim and even fewer were Druze.

Most of the pioneers were young and adventurous single men, although married men did not hesitate to travel. Over one-third were women and about 17 percent were children under fourteen years of age. The men were generally farmers who also engaged in a craft or trade to supplement the family income. They were poor, but not destitute and most were underschooled or uneducated. It was not uncommon for a family to borrow money or mortgage land at usurious rates to send a member or two to fulfill its dream of greater wealth and status. Few were intellectuals and professionals.

Although in the United States before World War II they called themselves Syrians, rarely would they have had to do so in the homeland. Even more rarely would they have had to refer to themselves as Arabs although they clung proudly to their Arabness. The Syrian and Arab references were cultural rather than nationalistic since there was neither an independent Syrian or Lebanese political entity to which nationalism could be tied.

Among themselves, the Syrians identified by family name, religion and place of origin. These were the most meaningful and reflexive identity factors for them. While this grouping served the purposes of the Ottoman government in the homeland, it was a source of disunity in the new land.

Once past the United States customs, the immigrants, bursting with anticipation, dispersed. Many, perhaps most, made their way to their respective destinations — generally a supplier's peddling settlement — assisted by relatives, friends, immigration officials, or on their own. Others were attracted to the New York colony by its reputation in the homeland. A small neighborhood in lower Manhattan, it was the Syrian's mother colony and the wellspring of enterprise. As one observer wrote, "It was the dumping ground for new arrivals."[3]

Its narrow, crowded streets bustled with peddlers and would-be peddlers who sought bargains from a bazaar of manufacturers, wholesalers, and retailers. There were Syrian-owned hotels and restaurants and residents who seemed to conduct much of their lives outdoors. Ethnic churches and newspapers gave the colony the impression of long, deep roots.

The Peddling Life

Syrians, on the whole, came to peddle dry goods from farmhouse to farmhouse in the countryside and house to house in the towns and cities of America. That trade was the magnet that drew the pioneers — men, women, and children — away from their families and they pursued it assiduously. If they happened to land in Canada or South America, they pursued it there also. Other ethnic groups peddled, but none except German Jews so completely identified with the trade.

Syrians were attracted to peddling because it required no capital, no advanced training or knowledge of English. Moreover, it suited their individualistic nature and it yielded wealth more quickly than they had hoped for.

Peddling was the most fundamental factor in the assimilation of the Syrians in America, and the major source of their success. It enabled them, for example, to see America and experience its way of life first hand while it forced them to learn English rapidly. It took them into American homes and raised their aspirations. In pre-World War I America, it spared them the uncertainty of finding factory work and facing layoffs. Finally, because they were itinerant most of the time, it spared them a ghetto mentality.

By 1900, Syrians had covered the nation in a network of peddling routes that radiated from peddling settlements making opportunities for thousands of newcomers. By 1910, they were reporting destinations in all states and territories, which explains the broad distribution of Syrians in North America.

Despite its hardships, they preferred peddling to the drudgery of the factory and the isolation of farm life. Only a relatively few found it too difficult or too demeaning. They joined the labor force or gambled on some other entrepreneurial endeavor such as a fruit stand.

Habib I. Katibah aptly described this pioneer, or peddling, period as "the most romantic and colorful period, the period of discovery, adventure, and colonization."[4] It was the period in which their impressions of America were shaped — not by what they understood, but by what they saw. Busy and lighted streets, tall buildings ("I used to count the stories of every one I saw," mused Frank A.), electrically-lit rooms, police who were not to be feared, and an abundance of consumer goods filled them with wonder.

A variety of unsorted fragments of American life perplexed them: Fourth of July and Thanksgiving celebrations, raucous political parades, workers' strikes, and hooded men burning crosses. When they sought explanations, they turned to veteran immigrants and the supplier in the peddling settlement who tended to interpret American life through their own skewed comprehension of it. Their reminiscences are like snapshots of pre-World War I America — its landscapes and its people — taken through the lens of peasants originating in a world as alien to Americans as America was to them.

Peddling settlements were the home bases from which peddlers plied their trade. They were formed around a supplier — a veteran peddler who decided to settle down in a well-chosen location. He would then recruit peddlers from his or from nearby villages. Elizabeth B. recalled how fifty or sixty men and women arrived in Ft. Wayne, Indiana. The women, wearing long colored dresses, carried bundles on their shoulders. In the settlements, the immigrants instinctively grouped themselves by kin, faith, and place of origin.

In his role as businessman, leader, and often founder of a settlement, a supplier served many functions critical to peddlers' success. He provided merchandise, frequently on credit, suggested routes, and banked their savings. Supplier and peddler formed an interdependent relationship firmly based on tradition that validated the supplier's leadership and limited his excesses. It was also based on economic self-interest. Since peddlers joined the settlement voluntarily, they could also leave when their personal and material objectives were better served elsewhere.

In the settlement, newcomers, with the help of veteran peddlers or relatives, outfitted themselves with suitcases and a *kashshi,* the notions case that was the peddlers' constant companion. They were also taught a few tricks of the trade, the value of American currency, and how to make the maximum profit.

On the road, peddlers were mobile department stores. They greeted the customer who answered their knock with "Buy sumthin', Maam?" and then presented a bazaar of merchandise — almost anything that a housebound urban housewife or isolated farmwife would need or desire. There were notions, ribbons, icons, jewelry, gingham, calico, work and children's clothes, and much more in the heavy packs. Peddlers' women produced for sale a variety of such attractive items as laces, doilies, crocheted tablecloths, embroidered bedspreads, and decorative handsewn items. Out of a deeply engrained dedication to the family welfare, women and children also peddled.

From New York to California and from Maine to Texas, the Syrians covered the nation with peddling routes. No region was too remote or forbidding to them. Some stalwarts trudged for months over half a continent of dirt roads before returning to the settlement. Others returned in days or weeks.

Rigs and later automobiles allowed them to carry more merchandise and to cover more territory. When some graduated to selling prestigious imported rugs and linens purchased from wholesalers in the New York colony, they began to refer to themselves as salesmen, dressed smartly, and developed a wealthy clientele.

Generally speaking, peddlers were welcomed by their customers because they brought more than merchandise to their doors. News and stories as well as "wisdom of the East" and products "from the Holyland" excited their imaginations. The Syrian peddler became so much a part of America before World War I that they entered American popular literature.[5]

Peddling was a more hazardous occupation than Syrians anticipated. They preserved their experiences in a body of witty anecdotes that glorify cunning and ingenuity. Bewilderment, loneliness, fatigue and fear are lightly concealed beneath the contrived humor. Many dealt with the hardships of climate, lack of language skills, and finding lodging.

For example, Anisee Z.'s husband, desperate to find lodging on a wintry night in rural Nebraska, pushed past the gentle rebuffs of a farmer and his wife. He repeated "thank you" as he moved to the warm fireplace and then to the prepared dining table. The farmers acquiesced. The next morning, he thanked them, in passable English, for the warm bed and welcomed meal. They parted friends. Alaya H. told of a novice who returned from peddling in a small town in South Dakota and railed at his brother for sending him out with "this small box" indicating his notions case. "Everyone told me to 'go away, small box.'" He had stumbled into a small pox epidemic. The Arabic language has no "p" sound.

The anecdotes also tell of rebuffs and insults, relentless heat, parched throats, frozen extremities, hunger, and nights spend in cold barns or schoolhouses. They recount incidents of rigs mired in mud; of companions robbed, beaten, killed, or lost; of farmers' guns and barking dogs. "How do you tell a dog to go away if he/she/it doesn't understand Arabic?" asked Selma M. On the other hand, Matt I. reflected the general attitude of Syrian peddlers when he said "We endured a lot but enjoyed this country because we were free to make money."

For their stringent habits of perseverance, hard work, frugality and self-denial, Syrian peddlers reaped tangible rewards. Their accumulated savings allowed them to pay debts, send promised remittance home, and pay the fares of family members to America.

In the pioneer years before World War I, a peddler could average one thousand dollars or more annually while American laborers averaged about six hundred and fifty dollars. As a result, they discovered that while their success in the United States enhanced their personal self esteem and status, their remittances enhanced their families' honor and status at home. Moreover, the deep satisfaction with their success raised their aspirations and convinced them to settle in America and to enjoy the family life they yearned for.

On the other hand, they made a valuable contribution to American commerce. By distributing the products of small American industries throughout the country, they helped these industries grow, thereby fostering the economic health of the nation.

By hastening Americanization, peddling contributed to its own obsolescence. Shortly before World War I, Syrians had begun to outgrow it as an immigrant occupation and its services to the American consumer was replaced by department stores and the increased use of mail order houses. Few Syrians mourned its end. What they came gradually to mourn was the end of the adventure and camaraderie that made the hardships more tolerable.

The End of an Era

Peddlers gave up their suitcases and their nomadic life and opened family businesses in the cities and towns throughout the country where peddling had distributed them. Dry goods and grocery stores were most common, but according to a 1908 Syrian business directory, businesses ran the gamut — everything from banking, wholesaling, and manufacturing to poolrooms, restaurants, and movie houses — all with no experience. They were compulsive about being in business for themselves. Failure was common but not daunting.

The average business began as a small family concern with very little capital. It required long hours, sixteen or more, and the assistance of the whole family. Store and home were commonly a staircase or door apart and there was much shuttling back and forth. In addition to their domestic burdens, women worked in the family stores and often operated them alone when necessary. As with peddling, they developed skills that proved valuable to community building. Store owners' children, when not in school, worked at their parents' side. Most of the major Syrian national manufacturing, wholesaling and retailing establishments evolved from such modest beginnings.

Since Muslims began migrating in greater numbers during the decline of the peddling era, they tended towards family businesses or were attracted to factory work by higher daily wages of five dollars for eight hours of labor initiated by the Ford Motor Company during World War I. Some of the most populous Muslim communities are found in industrial centers such as: Toledo, Ohio; Michigan City, Indiana; and Dearborn, Michigan — which has since become the largest Muslim settlement in America. The Druze, whose migration paralleled that of the Muslims, tended to shun factory work.

Settling Down

In small towns, pioneer peddling settlements were little more than small clusters of peddlers and their families, relatively homogeneous in religious beliefs and village origins. In cities, however, Syrians of different faiths and origins mingled in poorer immigrant neighborhoods. Peddlers and wage earners lived side by side, generally in crowded, poorly furnished quarters suited to their itinerancy, frugality and impermanence.

After weeks or months of frustration and loneliness on the road, peddlers gravitated to their respective settlements to refresh their spirits and revel in a sense of belonging among friends and relatives. They relished their ethnic food, music, and dance, caught up on news from home and shared peddling anecdotes.

Settlements were, in fact, way stations — havens of continuity with the past which helped to ease the adjustment to the present. Of formal ethnic authority and institutional life, there was little. The role of the supplier was pivotal. In addition to his economic services, he involved himself in the social and communal welfare of the peddlers and their families. He counseled them, mediated conflicts, frequently godfathered their children and intervened in problems with the community. On one such occasion, a supplier explained to neighbors and the police summoned to arrest them, that the men relaxing on the porch of their boarding house at day's end were not in their "nightgowns." They were in their native garb, usually worn outdoors in the homeland.

Inevitably, settlements, often located in ethnically-mixed immigrant neighborhoods, would mature into stable communities based on traditional groupings. Married men sent for their wives and children; bachelors searched for brides in settlements, often in vain, or sought them in the homeland.

The shortage of marriageable women accounted for the unexpectedly high percentage of ethnic (but rarely religious) outmarriages among Syrian immigrants before 1940. Immigrants became naturalized citizens, bought homes, educated their children, and followed the middle-class course out of old neighborhoods into better ones and ultimately into suburbs. The process was slower among the fewer Syrian industrial laborers than among the entrepreneurs.

Settled in the various regions of the country, the Syrians adopted the respective social attitudes, manners, and regional accents. They became New Englanders, Southerners, or Middle Westerners. In general, their relations with other Americans — on the road and in the communities — were sufficiently smooth that they were only dimly aware of the often virulent xenophobic movements that swept America before and after World War I.

More sectarian than nationalistic, relatively few in number, thinly dispersed, inconspicuous as an immigrant group, and socially unthreatening to Americans, the Syrians were spared much of the hostility expressed towards other immigrant groups. Some Syrians anglicized their names primarily to overcome the difficulties in the spelling and pronunciation of Arabic names. Generally, the Syrians felt comfortable in America.

Wherever Syrians lived, village life and customs were maintained. More populous and congested communities were often noisy especially as celebrations and quarrels spilled into the streets.

Coffee-houses, stores, and restaurants supplied from New York provided traditional fare.

The Family and its Values

Although the Americanization process seeped into the settlements, families retained much of their native traditions and values. They continued especially to cherish family honor and solidarity. In return for loyalty, the family provided its members with protection and a sense of identity. Syrian values centered on pride in one's family name and ancestry, dedication to its religious beliefs, respect for elders, and loyalty to parents in their old age. They also prized generosity, hospitality and individualism much as they had done in the homeland.

The tendency of defining themselves by family name, religious sect, and place of origin bred among the Syrians factionalism and community fragmentation. On the other hand, the obligation to defend and enhance family honor and status produced a competitive spirit that in turn bred an ethic of hard work, thrift, perseverance, shrewdness and conservatism quite compatible with the cherished American values of the time.

In addition, the fear of bringing shame and dishonor to the family name seemed to discourage most Syrians from committing crimes or accepting charity, even during the Great Depression of the 1930s. Given the economic opportunities and similarity in the two systems of values, the Syrians readily became as success oriented free enterprisers as their American hosts.

Hardly a Syrian immigrant family was unaffected by the Americanization process, most notably in the breakdown of the patriarchal extended family into nuclear units and the alteration in parent roles. Sons, impelled by American education and economic opportunities, began to establish their own households when they married. The authority and disciplinary role of the father, not unexpectedly, was eroded by his long absences from home as he peddled or nursed a small business. Still, conscious of family honor, fathers rarely relinquished their authority or the appearance of it.

Patriarchal discipline was not so much abandoned as shifted to mothers who, in such cases, bore the greatest share of child rearing. But if fathers lost ground as disciplinarians, they retained the respect, if not always the love, due them as head of the family and prime symbols of authority. The mothers' role was as deputy and enforcer of the absent fathers' will. Constant parental supervision, from the family's point of view, was essential in order to prevent a breakdown in the moral behavior of the children and the consequent appearance of parental weakness and loss of face.

Children were expected to participate fully in the family's economic welfare. Whereas a minority of sons and daughters peddled at an early age, many, perhaps the majority, of store owners' children were prepared for life behind a counter. School-age children, when not in school, were at their parents' elbows, waiting on customers, making change, stocking shelves, and imbibing the shrewdness of operating an independent business on meager resources. They were inculcated with the parents' work and thrift ethics and the lesson that family unity and self-denial were essential to the family's goals.

Proof of this was in the family's financial ability to upgrade its status with the purchase of a modest home and gradually equip it with modern conveniences. It could also purchase an automobile, open a business for a son and perhaps send another to college.

With all of their attraction to America, Syrian parents, however, disapproved of their children growing up "like American children" without the restraints of Syrian values. In pressing Old World values on them, parents failed to comprehend the pressure on their children to conform to American ways and drove them to live in two worlds: Syrian in that of their parent's, and American in what was essentially their own where they strove to gain experience.

In time, change invariably — but cautiously — edged parents toward their children's views. Forces spawned by the Americanization process gradually softened rigid attitudes. The parents' ambivalence toward American culture, contacts with Americans in business, the acquisition of American middle class material symbols and, finally, the infiltration into the home of the English language with its new ideas, tastes, and manners moderated the influence of tradition. Parents could only with difficulty close the door against the tide of change.

Daughters only marginally benefited from their parents' gradual liberalization. About the age of puberty, the behavior of girls was reined in and it continued to be watched carefully by their parents. Girls were allowed, however, to adopt the latest fashions, even those of cutting hair and shortening hems. Unmarried girls remained in the patriarchal home until they married, frequently to a husband of their parents' choice. Convention and religion allowed men greater latitude than women in the choice of spouses. In what they wanted for their children and what they expected from them, parents were resolute.

By building a relatively sound economic base for the family and instilling in them the native values, parents facilitated their children's upward mobility.

Women

Relatively few Syrian families — Christian, Muslim, or Druze — succeeded in America without the help of one or more women. Their economic participation contributed significantly to the general economic satisfaction of Syrian immigrants and to the impetus to settle permanently in America.

The earnings of wives, mothers, daughters, and sisters, their sacrifices and labor, staved off poverty and failure in many cases and in many more enabled the family to improve and accelerate economically and socially. Not only did they peddle, sew, and crochet, they also worked in textile mills and in factories, took in paying boarders, and clerked in stores. They displayed a surprising capacity for economic aggressiveness, pushing and prodding their menfolk forward.

When their men failed or faltered from weakness, poor judgement, or ill health, women took up the breadwinning challenge successfully with courage and often with surprising ingenuity. Because of them, more capital was accumulated, more small businesses started, more money sent to the homeland, and more fares bought to bring relatives to America. Neither illiteracy nor the traditional protective customs toward women seriously hindered their efforts.

The collective earnings of the family helped convey the impression of success enjoyed by Syrians. At the same time, wives and mothers did not shirk the homekeeping role assigned by society and expected by their men. Sisters and daughters, too, proved to be pillars of support in the home and in stores.

Since the family looked to its sons for its future welfare, daughters frequently set aside their dreams in favor of their brothers' goals — even to postponing or foregoing marriage without which a female's status and self-esteem in Syrian society is jeopardized. If marriage was the only realistic aspiration of daughters in the homeland, in America they had other options. Hopes for a high school education, for example, or an independent career were dashed by the demands of the family. The belief that education and independence were unessential to marriage or would hinder a girl's chances for marriage was deep-seated.

Subtle changes in Christian women's status and self-esteem began before World War I in oblique and uncertain ways. Pre-war competition for their hand in marriage and the family's dependence on their economic role as well as interaction with Americans instilled in women a greater sense of self-importance and allowed them to acquire new strengths. With these advantages, they would gradually achieve modest gains in liberalizing the traditional restraints and smoothing the roughest edges of male dominance. They would break the taboo of sexual segregation in churches and social gatherings and would deprecate early or arranged marriages.

Many women adopted the prevailing styles and make-up, marcelled their hair (the youngest and most daring bobbed it), and stopped covering their heads. There began a trend toward fewer children, fewer time-consuming Arabic meals, and pre-arranged social visits. Even the time-honored preference for male children waned.

This was no conscious liberation movement. The majority of the women, caught between the heritage of the past and the demands of immigrant life, had little free time to cultivate new ideas or act on new hopes deliberately. Their progress was made in the shadow of those realities. They moved cautiously lest they overstep the bounds of convention and bring dishonor on the family and the displeasure of their men. Yet, the changes became sufficiently discernible to be discussed in the ethnic press in the twenties between traditionalists and modernists.

With their new confidence, women took on leadership roles aimed primarily at preserving group cohesion and values, particularly among the young. They formed charitable societies, raised funds to build and support churches, and planned programs to promote ingroup marriages.

For many women, clubs and societies represented a welcome change from spending leisure time almost solely visiting neighbors and relatives and a respite from domestic drudgery. Some used them to elevate their status. A handful discovered there a forum for creative expression which convention discouraged. Such creative talents as writing poetry and prose, designing, and decorating were revealed. Social events and religious celebrations were used to present plays and recitals written and directed by women. The opportunity for self-expression further enhanced self-confidence.

Stricter religious and social sanctions made liberalization far more difficult for Muslim and Druze women, and more difficult for the former than the latter.

The first generation passed on its gains to its American-born daughters who chafed under the remaining restrictions. Letters published in the *Syrian World,* an English-language journal aimed at the Americanized second generation, reveal the extent of their discontent and the gap between daughters and their parents. Their arguments for greater freedom in their social life and in the choice of spouses were supported in the press by modernists who pointed out that the parents belonged to a country about which their children knew very little and had never seen.

Institutions

Institutions which presuppose permanence were well advanced in the New York colony, the leading business, cultural, and intellectual community. Since it was the most populous and financially able to build and maintain them, places of worship, newspapers, and associations appeared in it early in the 1890s. Most Syrian communities, however, lacked these essential requirements. Therefore, even such revered institutions as places of worship did not keep pace with Syrian immigration and distribution. Church building was necessarily spotty and mosques were not built before the late 1920s. Leadership in founding them was assumed by the more enterprising and prosperous in both Christian and Muslim centers.

Eastern rite churches whose liturgies would be conducted in Arabic or Syriac and which were central to group cohesion were the first concern of Christian Syrians. The first — one Orthodox Christian, one Melkite, and one Maronite — were built in New York. By 1920, eighty-two, and by 1930, one hundred and twelve Eastern rite churches were scattered around the country, most in the east. Many communities were visited by itinerant priests.

With vast regions unserved by a priest, many families joined the "American" churches they had been attending. Maronites and Melkites attended Roman Catholic churches while the Orthodox found the Episocopal churches more compatible with their beliefs. Community leaders, alarmed by the erosion of adherents, worked to stem the losses.

Dr. Ibrahim Arbeely, president of the Syrian Orthodox Benevolent Society of New York City, invited Archimandrite Raphael Hawaweeny who was teaching Arabic language and literature in Russia in 1893, to "come to America to minister to his fellow countrymen."[6] He arrived in 1895.

After he was named head of the Syrian Orthodox Ecclesiastical Mission of the North American Archdiocese of the Russian Orthodox Church in 1895, Raphael Hawaweeny began assiduously to organize parishes. Before his death in 1915, he consecrated about thirty churches. By the time the Maronites and Melkites — which had come under the jurisdiction of the Roman Catholic Church in America — were permitted to organize dioceses and appoint their own bishops in 1966, the battle to win back the "Latinized" descendants of the immigrant generation had been virtually lost.[7]

Dr. Ameen Haddad, a graduate of the American University of Beirut is credited with bringing the small Syrian Protestant community in Manhattan together in the mid-1890s and helping to found the Syrian Protestant Church in Brooklyn in 1907. As the Americanization process advanced, some Eastern rite churches responded by Americanizing several aspects of their services. In the process, they inadvertently advanced assimilation by diluting the distinction between themselves and the "American" churches.

Only in four Muslim concentrations were mosques known to have been built before World War II. Defending their traditions against the pressures of Americanization was necessarily more difficult for Muslims than for Christians. Although Muslims have no priesthood and can pray in any ritually uncontaminated space and are allowed to make up missed prayers, the mosque and its religious leader (*imam*) are central to Muslim religious heritage and identity, as well as symbols of community unity.

A Muslim, working and living in a non-Muslim society makes essential religious compromises. It is not usually possible to observe the Muslim day of prayer on Friday, pray five times a day, and fast during the sunlight hours of the holy month of Ramadan. Without the availability of a mosque, Muslims came together to conduct prayer and rituals in private homes by the best informed among the group. Infrequently, they might be visited by an itinerant *imam*.

The Druze remain without a place to worship because the faith does not permit religious elders and teachers to migrate, nor can they be trained in foreign lands. The Druze community is tightly knit by an identity that is distinctive from their countrymen — an identity that is based on traditional tribal values and memories of past persecution because of an esoteric religion whose doctrines, its mysteries and symbols, are known only to an elite minority.

The Arabic Press

Perhaps the institution that most contributed to the relatively rapid assimilation of the Syrians was the ethnic press. From its inception, it presented many aspects of American social, economic, and political life to its eager readers as its immigrant editors and publishers understood them. While it educated, it idealized and oversimplified. At the same time, it fostered self-education and good citizenship.

In addition, it published, in 1895, a textbook for learning English and American customs and manners and it made available Arabic books published in the homeland and in America.

Furthermore, its columns and editorials kept the homeland alive in their minds. The works of the renowned emigré writers and poets (among them Kahlil Gibran), who were revolutionizing traditional Arabic literary styles, often appeared first in the press. Never before could these predominantly village-centered Syrians, unschooled or newly self-taught, have had the opportunity to read so much about the society, politics, history, and literature of the homeland and the world.

The impetus for the Arabic press was a handful of intellectual immigrants. So keen was the Syrian penchant for publishing that between 1892 and 1907, twenty-one Arabic publications appeared, seventeen of them in New York. By 1930, the number exceeded fifty. Most were short-lived. Nevertheless, it was remarkable that so many publications could be even temporarily supported by so small a population, for most of whom newspaper reading was a habit acquired in America.

Kawkab Amirika, the first newspaper, was published by Najib and Ibrahim Arbeely, members of an early immigrant family of professionals and intellectuals. Of the others that followed, three lasted into the post-World War II period. The most durable and influential was *al-Hoda*. Published by Na'um Mukarzal in 1898, it spoke for the Maronites. The next year, Najib Diyab launched the Orthodox

Mir'at al-Gharb. The Druze and Muslim *al-Bayan* did not appear until 1911. Established from the start on a sectarian basis, the newspapers deepened community fragmentation.

Ironically, the advance of Americanization between the wars resulted in the decline in the use of Arabic and thereby the ethnic press. English was the first language of the American-born Syrians. English, or a corrupted form of it, was more commonly used than Arabic by their parents in business and increasingly at home.

In addition, restrictive immigration laws limited the entry of new immigrants who would have kept the language alive. Not only were the publishers disturbed by this development, but parents and church leaders became alarmed that the young were losing their cultural roots. Attempts by community leaders to teach Arabic to the youth who were ardent consumers of such innovations as moving pictures and radio programs were defeated by the pace of assimilation.

It was partly in recognition of these developments that Sallum Mukarzal published the *Syrian World.* Its editorials and articles, written by him and leading writers in the Syrian community, tried to balance the urgent need to generate an interest in Syrian history and culture with the irrepressible Americanization process. Because of its short life and small elitist readership, it failed to achieve its publisher's goal and hardly left a mark. However, its quality and purpose has been unmatched in the Syrian American and Arab American communities. In fact, the pre-World War II Arabic press in general achieved a national status that remains unequalled.

The innovative emigré literati influenced by European and American free verse, had little influence on the Syrians in America, notwithstanding the revolutionary effect they had on literature in the Arab world, whose content was alien to their experience. Hardly a name from this group is known to them except that of Gibran. The works of American authors of Syrian descent such as William Blatty of *Exorcist* fame, Vance Bourjaily, and poet Samuel Hazo reflect little or no influence of the emigré writers on their style or subject matter.

Voluntary Associations

When the Syrians learned to organize democratically around a common purpose or cause, they practiced it with a vengeance. Often the number of clubs and societies in existence was out of all proportion to their own numbers in America. Like the newspapers and journals, most were short-lived.

Clubs evolved from the need to help the needy and bury the dead in early peddling communities. Later, they organized for a variety of purposes. In addition to charitable societies, there were clubs to encourage the study of English and good citizenship; others encouraged naturalization and promote better understanding between Syrians and other Americans. There were even societies based on place of origin whose purposes were to modernize their respective villages with schools, orphanages and new churches.

Whatever the stated aim, the most common organizing purpose was group solidarity and continuity, mainly through ingroup marriage. Increasingly, as the Americanization process advanced, groups feared the growing drift of the youth. Like sectarian clubs, family and place of origin clubs created a social life centered on group identity. Annually they brought together families to festivities where patriarchs and matriarchs reigned and youths were encouraged to find spouses. Syrian organizations tended to be exclusivist, perpetuating factionalism.

Homeland politics were not generally reflected in Syrian-American organizations before World War I, but they were not immune to the political vicissitudes in the old country. One notable exception, however, was the Lebanon League of Progress founded in 1911 by the publisher of *al-Hoda* to promote a French-supported Maronite-dominated Lebanon.

In 1924, two events in the former Ottoman province of Syria signalled attempts to separate Maronite-Lebanese nationalism from a developing Syrian Arab nationalism: the creation of Greater Lebanon out of Syrian territory by the French mandate government and the adoption of a secularist identity by the Maronites with the Phoenicians of the region's distant past.

In America, many non-Maronite immigrants from the incorporated Syrian areas rejected the Lebanese identity, fuelling a heated controversy over whether clubs should be called Syrian-American or Lebanese-American or Syrian-Lebanese American. The controversy subsided only when Syria and Lebanon achieved full independence after World War II. Multiple social divisions in the community tended to inhibit the ability of Syrian-Lebanese anonymously to support causes or participate in organizations or institutions involving non-primary groups.

The persistence of traditional restraints in the associational life of Syrians after more than a generation of Americanization began to disturb increasing numbers of the Americanized second generation. They complained of the factional tendencies of the Old World views and practices, not the least of which was gender segregation and sectarian-based clubs.[8] New clubs which seemed to appear everywhere in the country in the 1920s found a medium for their grievances in the *Syrian World* and a mentor in its publisher.

Sallum Mukarzal was a champion of Americanization and a critic of excessive traditionalism. Yet, he was an advocate of upholding the ethnic heritage. There were appeals in letters published in the journal to break the cultural isolation which some sensed, appeals which eventually developed into calls for a national federation. The dialogue ended abruptly when the *Syrian World* closed in 1932 but not before the idea of federation had taken roots in spite of traditional obstacles and failed attempts.

That same year, a regional federation of clubs "of any persuasion or purpose" was formed in Boston. Although hampered by the depression and internal conflicts, the Eastern Federation of Syrian-Lebanese American Clubs was successful enough to inspire three other regional federations. Two survive to this day.

All sponsored social activities, provided scholarships, and worked to enhance relations between Syrian-Lebanese and the American community. Aside from food, music and dance, little of Syrian, Lebanese, or Arab heritage were evident in their gatherings.

Well-assimilated, the Syrian-Lebanese Americans nevertheless retained the values that are rooted in an ethnic culture they understood in its irreducible elements: family unity and honor, hospitality, and generosity. The degree to which Americanization had overtaken their institutions explains, in part, why they were so slow to comprehend the significance of political events unfolding in the homeland. When they finally did, it was primarily as Americans and secondarily as Syrian-Lebanese. The formation of a single national secular organization would not appear until after 1976 in reaction to the anti-Arab sentiment that swept America.

Politics

For decades before World War II, the Syrians felt no need to gain influence as a group in American life. Emphasis on individual achievements, whether in business or later in prestigious professions required neither political parties nor other lobbies. Syrians, however, voted at least as faithfully as the rest of the population.

The majority of Syrians voted Republican because in the twenties when they became politically aware, that party was ascendant. Those who voted Democrat, followed the party's regional platform: conservative in the South and more liberal in the North. They could not, however, be relied on to vote as an ethnic bloc. If national political machines thought them too few and too fragmented to court, small town ward bosses did not.

Before World War II, one or two Syrians aspired to national public office although more ran for or were appointed to public office at the local level. After the war, they won and continue to win elections at every level of state and local government and were appointed to a wide range of public offices.

In 1958, the first descendant of a Syrian immigrant won a seat in Congress. Twenty years later, then Representative James Abourezk of South Dakota became the first Syrian in the United States Senate. That year, five Syrian-Lebanese Americans were in the House of Representatives. One was a woman: Mary Rose Oakar was elected to Congress from Cleveland, Ohio, in 1976 and remained until 1992 underscoring her distinguished record. Currently, Nick Joe Rahall of West Virginia and Spencer Abraham of Michigan are serving in the House of Representatives. George Mitchell of Maine served as Senate majority leader from 1988 until his resignation in 1994. At the other end of Pennsylvania Avenue, John Sununu, former governor of New Hampshire, served former President George Bush as chief of staff.

One of the most distinguished Syrian public servants was the late Philip Habib, son of a Brooklyn grocer. Toward the end of a long career with the State Department, Dr. Habib became the key negotiator in the peace talks that ended the Vietnam War. When he retired in 1980, he was summoned to arrange a cease-fire across the Lebanese-Israeli border. In 1992, newly-elected President Bill Clinton appointed Donna Shalala, chancellor of the University of Wisconsin in Madison to his cabinet as secretary of Health and Human Services.

Other descendants of the first wave of immigrants (now identifying as Arab Americans) are among America's leaders and contributors in all fields of endeavor. Perhaps the most famous is consumer advocate Ralph Nader. A number stand out in the field of entertainment: the late comedian and actor Danny Thomas (also founder of St. Jude's Children's Hospital in Memphis, Tennessee, reknown for the research and treatment of catastrophic children's diseases); television and stage actor, Jamie Farr; Oscar winner, F. Murray Abraham; and composer and singer Paul Anka. Dr. Michael DeBakey made medical history in heart surgery. In journalism, Helen Thomas has been covering the presidential beat since the administration of John F. Kennedy. The first woman to attain the presidency of the White House Correspondents Association, she holds eight honorary degrees and is recognized informally as the dean of the White House press corps. Arab Americans are also well represented in local governments and bureaucracies and in the academic, business, financial, scientific, art, music and sports communities.

More American than Syrian or Lebanese

In its eagerness to succeed, the immigrant generation neglected to preserve its cultural heritage. Much of it, in any case, centered on village life and its mythology. About the great Arab-Islamic contributions to world civilization, immigrants knew little and what they did know was selective and biased by religious affiliation. The village view of Syrian-Lebanese culture left the children poorly informed about their ethnicity. Consequently, of the kind of significant national and political events that in other nations produced national heroes and kindled national pride, the descendants knew little. The void, therefore, was filled from the well of American myth and history. They adopted such heroes and role models as American founding fathers, politicians, film stars and athletes.

Thus, the Americanized children of the first immigrant wave showed scant interest in or knowledge of their ethnic origins. Their parents' homeland bore little relation to the American reality. Later attempts by the group leaders to arouse an interest in the ethnic heritage were, on the whole, unsuccessful except occasionally for ethnic food, dance, and some music. They were, at this point, more American than Syrian or Lebanese.

By the post-World War II period, they selectively retained elements of their Syrian upbringing that accorded with their American perspectives. However, respect for family and the success ethic were indelibly stamped on their character. They raised their children according to their generation's practices; they relished ethnic food but usually on special occasions; and, those who did not attend church regularly, at least observed religious holidays. While they maintained family bonds, they also carried on a life detached from family.

Members of the third and fourth generations are more remote still from the culture of the first. The 1960s ethnicity movement in the United States sent some to their parents in search of cultural pegs on which to hang their identity, but parental knowledge is often superficial based only on being Syrian or Lebanese or of one religious affiliation. Grandparents add little more than nostalgic reminiscences of a distant past. If political, social and economic events had not reactivated immigration from the Arab world and an interest in their ethnic roots, Syrian-Lebanese Americans might have assimilated themselves out of existence.

NOTES

[1] This article is based on data in over 100 taped oral history interviews with immigrants who arrived from the late 1880s to about 1940 conducted in numerous Arab American communities in the United States and Canada. In addition, it draws on a large body of family documents and books, and archival material from libraries, newspaper morgues, and other sources which came to constitute the Arab American Project. This body of material became the nucleus of what is now the Smithsonian Institution's Arab American Collection and has grown to include over 115 cubic feet of archival data, 500 immigrant artifacts, 2000 photographs, and 400 taped oral history interviews open to students and scholars. The Arab American Project resulted in the publication of my two books: *Becoming American: The Early Arab Immigrant Experience* (Carbondale, Ill.: Southern Illinois University Press, 1985) and *The Arab Americans, from 1880 to the Present* (New York: Chelsea House Publishers, 1988), an illustrated book for young adults.

[2] *Lebanon in History* (New York: Macmillan, 1967), 447. See also A. H. Hourani, *Syria and Lebanon: A Political Essay* (London: Oxford University Press, 1954), 33.

[3] Lucius Miller, *Our Syrian Population: A Study of the Syrian Community of Greater New York* (n.p., ca. 1904), 18.

[4] "Syrian Americans" in *One America: The History, Contributions, and Present Problems of our Racial and National Minorities*, eds. Francis J. Brown and Joseph S. Roucek (Newark, NJ: Prentice Hall, 1952), 283-84.

[5] See for example Alice E. Christgau, *The Laugh Peddler* (New York: Young Scott Books, 1968); Maud Hart Lovelace, *Betsy and Tacy Go Over the Big Hill* (New York: Thomas Y. Crowell, 1942); Lillian Hart Tyron, "Reflections of a Housewife on Buying at the Door," *House Beautiful* 38 (July 1915): 40-42; and Lucille Baldwin Van Slyke, "The Peddler," *American Magazine* 74 (Aug. 1912): 404-414.

[6] Reverend Basil Essey, "Memory Eternal," *The Word* 29 (May 1985): 12.

[7] *Melkites in America: A Directory and Information Handbook* (n.p.: Melkite Exarchate, 1971), 15.

[8] "The Idea of Mixed Clubs," *Syrian World* 2 (Nov. 1927): 51.

THE CONTRIBUTIONS OF ARAB IMMIGRANTS IN NORTH AMERICA TO ARABIC LITERATURE
by Issa J. Boullata

Hundreds of articles and many books have been written in Arabic and in Western languages on the literature that Arab immigrants in the Americas have produced. Fawzi 'Abd al-Razzaq has 1,285 entries in his annotated bibliography of Arabic works on the subject[1] and Francine H. McNulty has 185 entries in her annotated bibliography of works in English and other Western languages.[2] More works have appeared since these two bibliographies were published in 1981.

In English alone, the following are some examples: Hussein Dabbagh's book *Mikhail Naimy: Some Aspects of His Thought as Revealed in His Writings;*[3] Nadeem N. Naimy's book *The Lebanese Prophets of New York;*[4] 'Abd al-Karim al-Ashtar's article "al-Mahdjar;"[5] Issa J. Boullata's articles, "Iliyya Abu Madi and the Riddle of Life"[6] and "Mikhail Naimy: Poet of Meditative Vision;"[7] and C. Nijland's article "Al Rabita al-Qalamiyya: An Arabic Literary Circle in New York."[8]

Therefore, rather than dwelling on oft-trodden ground, this article will concentrate on the innovative literary contributions of Arab immigrants in North America and it will explore the long-term impact which these contributions have had on the Arabic literature of their original homeland.

The Pen Bond
It must be quickly added that these contributions have emanated, in the main, from one specific group of Arab immigrants in North America, namely the *Pen Bond* of New York, known in Arabic as

al-Rabita al-Qalamiyya, which flourished mainly between 1920 and 1931. Not that there were no other significant contributors outside the Pen Bond or in other parts of the United States, or in Canada, Mexico and Central America. But the most powerful literary innovation in North America did come at the hands of the members of the Pen Bond who, together, constituted the first distinct literary school in the history of modern Arabic letters with clearly articulated aesthetic and intellectual aims, fired by a strong vision of social and moral reform.

Established on the 20th of April, 1920, the Pen Bond had ten members, and they were: Jubran Khalil Jubran (1883-1931), its chairman, known in his English publications as Kahlil Gibran; Mikha'il Nu'ayma (1889-1988), its secretary, known in his English publications as Mikhail Naimy; William Catzeflis (1879-1951), its treasurer; Iliyya Abu Madi (1889-1957); Nasib 'Arida (1887-1946); Rashid Ayyub (1872-1941); Nadra Haddad (1881-1940) and his younger brother 'Abd al-Masih Haddad (1890-1963); Wadi' Bahut (d. 1952); and Ilyas 'Ata Allah. The last two were the least active in publication and the others were not all equally prolific or equally prominent as far as literary reputation. Yet they all shared and enthusiastically supported the aims of the Pen Bond. Following the death of Gibran in 1931 and the return of Naimy to Lebanon in 1932, and despite the individual efforts of its members remaining in North America at continued publication, the Pen Bond began to disintegrate as it lost those members to death one after another.

Perhaps the most striking characteristic of the Arabic writings of the Pen Bond members was the spirit of liberation, which exhibited itself in the form that their literature took as much as in the content that it conveyed. Whereas much literature in the Arab world at the time was bound by stultifying literary conventions derived from age-old traditions, the literature of the Pen Bond members was attempting to free itself from such shackling burdens. Its language was simple and direct, its style was fresh and personal, its imagery was new and vivid.

The poets of the Pen Bond writing in verse chose light and sprightly meters, often avoiding the customary monotonous unitary rhyme throughout a single poem and adopting a more sonorous multi-rhyme scheme for it, as they structured their poems in stanzas and strophes. Those like Gibran who wrote prose poems as well as verse were very effective in popularizing an unprecedented literary style by their use of beautiful prose cadences and innovative figures of speech. Still using the classical Arabic, even if simplified, they brought their writing closer to the language of everyday life without being flippant or colloquial.

Some traditionalists in the Arab world accused the Pen Bond writers of lacking sufficient knowledge of Arabic grammar and correct diction. Heedless of such criticisms, the Pen Bond writers continued to forge for themselves a place under the sun in their own creative way, and finally won over the Arabic reading public both in North America and the Arab world.

In the matter of content, liberation as a striking characteristic in the Arabic writings of the Pen Bond members expressed itself in their call for freedom, justice, equality and social reform. It also manifested itself in their concern for religious tolerance and the emancipation of those wrongfully subjugated by the authority of dogma and tradition or by the power of wealth and class. Literary form and semantic content thus combined in the Pen Bond writings to foment rebellious ideas in the minds of Arab readers to the extent that authoritarian and obscurantist religious leaders forbade the reading of Gibran, for example, and considered him and all who shared his views as heretical.

Another salient characteristic of the Pen Bond literary contribution is its meditative quality. While much of the literature of the Arab world of that period was wasted on lavish, vacuous praise of local notables or inane elegies of their dead, the writings of the Pen Bond members tried to delve into the human soul with musings on the human condition. They made an effort to understand life and its purpose, to ask questions about man's place and worth in the universe, and about problems of good and evil that have always bewildered humanity. They did not come out with final or identical answers to the riddles of life but they never ceased pushing the existential frontier in order to explore the mysteries lying beyond it. And many of their positive convictions after such soul-searching exercises were expressed in exquisite poems, insightful essays, thoughtful meditations, moral narratives, and occasional plays dealing with the brotherhood of all human beings, the unity of humankind, the necessity of human cooperation, the ever-powerful effect of love, and the advisability of optimism and a cheerful outlook on life despite the existence of evil.

Associated with the meditative quality of this literature is its lyrical quality. The Pen Bond writers glorified the beauty of nature, found solace in its idyllic scenery, and often adopted it as a symbol of all that is good and conducive to happiness, harmony, and truth. Whether in verse or in prose, they sang the dignity of the human being as the crowning achievement of nature under God, and they posited an ideal existence that is at the disposal of all human beings if they choose the right path leading to it.

Shunning the self-interested materialism of life surrounding them in North America, the Pen Bond writers resorted to nature as a shelter of serenity and spiritual values that specifically reminded them of their simple and happy life in the villages of their origin in Lebanon or Syria. Homesickness and nostalgia for innocent childhood and for the good old days in their Arab homeland redoubled their feelings of alienation in the foreign land to which they had migrated.

To them, their lives in North America became embodiments of the alienation of human beings from heaven, and their condition reinforced their understanding of the necessity of reconciliation between man and God. Search for the path that leads to spiritual invigoration, to self-knowledge and truth, and ultimately to happiness and harmony abounded in the writings of the Pen Bond members. All this was new to the Arabic reading public of the time and was strongly reminiscent of the past glorious days of Oriental mysticism.

Yet, lest it be thought that the writings of the Pen Bond members were all alike, it should be emphasized that each of them retained his own style and personality. One of their principal tenets was that literature was a very personal thing and each writer stamped it with his own individuality, if ever he was a genuine man of letters. They differed from one another as a result of varying social backgrounds, degrees of education, personal predicaments, and natural predispositions and talents. But they all agreed on what was literature and what was not, and had similar ideas on what was good and beautiful in it and what was not. This helped to unify them and, eventually, the Pen Bond became recognized by literary historians and critics in the Arab world and elsewhere as the first movement in the rise of the Romantic school of modern Arabic literature.[9]

Other Arab Writers

Besides the Pen Bond members, there were other Arab immigrants in North America who contributed to Arabic literature such as Amin al-Rihani (1876-1940), Amin Mashriq (d. 1934), Ni'ma al-Hajj, and Mas'ud Samaha (1882-1946). The latter two wrote traditional poetry of some excellence; but the former two were creative innovators and there is evidence that they both were members of the Pen Bond of New York in 1916 along with Gibran, William Catzeflis, 'Abd al-Masih Haddad, Rashid Ayyub, and possibly others, before it was later formally constituted in 1920 with a slightly different membership.[10] Amin Mashriq wrote poetry of delicate sensibility before his untimely death in a car accident.

As for Amin al-Rihani, he was a prolific writer in both Arabic and English and was of great influence on Arabs in North America and the Arab world. Earlier in his life, he wrote Arabic poetry with Walt Whitman as his inspiring model, but later he contributed engaging accounts of his pioneering travels in the Arab world. He also wrote novels and hundreds of articles and speeches dealing with social and political reform in Arab countries and advocating freedom, democracy, modernization, religious tolerance, and a high code of ethics, in addition to authoring a number of works on history and literary criticism. At a time when Arab nationalism was little known or practiced even in the Arab world, he was a believer in its cause and an activist who carried its message wherever he went. Part of this activism consisted of his public speeches and articles in the United States in defense of the rights of the Arabs of Palestine to the land of their ancestors, and part of it also was his strong advocacy of Arab unity and modernization.

Another Arab immigrant and man of letters in North America was the Egyptian poet Ahmad Zaki Abu Shadi (1892-1955), who spent the last nine years of his life in the United States. A medical doctor and professor of bacteriology at Faruq I University in Alexandria, Egypt, before emigrating to America in 1946, he already had an established reputation as a poet, a critic, and a humanist in addition to being a scientist. He was also the founder, in 1932, of the Apollo Group in Egypt, another important literary movement in the rise of the Romantic school in modern Arabic literature. The Apollo Group found expression for its new poetry and thought in *Apollo,* the Group's short-lived monthly journal that Abu Shadi edited in Egypt for three years. In New York, he was literary editor of *al-Hoda* newspaper for a time, lectured at the Asia Institute, was adviser to the Saudi Arabian delegation at the United Nations, contributed as a correspondent to a Cairo newspaper and to Radio Cairo, then joined Voice of America in Washington, D.C., first as a freelancer when it started its radio program in 1950 then as a leading employee in its Arabic section, which he enriched with his prolific literary and cultural contributions.

There were other Arab immigrants in North America who, although not directly contributing to Arabic literature, helped in propagating it and making Arab culture known and understood in the West. These include the noted historian, Professor Philip Hitti, who taught at Princeton University, edited important Arabic historical texts such as *Kitab al-I'tibar* and wrote comprehensive history books in English that now have become indispensable reference works such as his *History of the Arabs, History of Syria,* and *Lebanon in History.*

One would also include, in more recent times, Arab university professors in various fields such as Aziz S. Atiya, George Hourani, Charles Issawi, George Makdisi, Farhat Ziadeh, Majid Khadduri,

Richard T. Antoun, Thomas Naff, Mounah A. Khouri, Najib Saliba, Robert Haddad, Edward Said, Ibrahim Abu-Lughod, Baha' Abu-Laban, George Atiyeh, Su'ad Joseph, Afaf Lutfi al-Sayyid Marsot, Yvonne Y. Haddad, Muhsin Mahdi, Ernest N. McCarus, Hisham Sharabi, and many many others (the list is too long),[11] who published articles and books in English and/or Arabic in their fields of specialization dealing with one aspect of Arab culture or another.

One should also include the Arab journalists in North America who offered the pages of their Arabic newspapers and journals to the creative literary talents of the Arab immigrants in their midst. To name a few, the following are among the founders of newspapers: Dr. Ibrahim and Najib 'Arbili (Arbeely), founders in 1892 of *Kawkab Amirika,* the first Arabic newspaper in the United States or rather in the New World; Na'um Mukarzal, founder in 1898 of *al-Hoda* and his brother Sallum Mukarzal, founder of *Barid Amirika* in 1907 in Arabic, *The Syrian World* in 1927 in English, and other periodicals; Najib Musa Diyab, founder in 1899 of *Mir'at al-Gharb;* Amin al-Ghurayyib, founder in 1903 of *al-Muhajir*; 'Abd al-Masih Haddad, founder in 1912 of *al-Sa'ih;* Mikha'il Zarbatani, founder in 1909 of *al-Shihab;* and Fr. Aftimios 'Ufaysh (Ofiesh), founder in 1910 of *Jaridat al-'Alamayn* with Hafiz 'Abd al-Malik.

Among the founders of magazines and other periodicals, the following may be mentioned: Bishop Rufa'il Hawawini (Raphael Hawaweeny), founder in 1905 of *al-Kalimat;* Sallum Mukarzal, founder in 1910 of *al-'Alam al-Jadid;* Nasib 'Arida, founder in 1913 of *al-Funun;* Bishop Aftimios 'Ufaysh (Ofiesh), founder of *al-Yatim* in 1926 and of *al-Haqq* in 1928; Archimandrite Antony Bashir, founder in 1927 of *al-Khalidat* with Fr. Iliyya al-Hamati; Wadi' Shakir, founder in 1919 of *Fatat Boston;* and Iliyya Abu Madi, founder in 1929 of *al-Samir.*[12]

Writings of Pen Bond Members

Let me now return to the Pen Bond and, in the remaining part of this article, consider some of its members' individual writings that are still being read in the Arab world and continue to be popular and influential in many ways.

Kahlil Gibran

Pride of place will legitimately belong to Gibran's book *al-Nabi,* originally written in English and published in New York by Alfred A. Knopf in 1923 as *The Prophet.* This unique monument of Arabic American literature has been translated into more than fifty languages and it sold about ten million copies in English alone. The Arabic translation was done by Archimandrite (later Metropolitan) Antony Bashir (1898-1966), who also translated other English works of Gibran into Arabic. Although later there were other Arabic translations of *The Prophet,* such as those of Tharwat 'Ukasha (1959) and Yusuf al-Khal (1968), Antony Bashir's Arabic translation remains a pleasantly readable one because of its faithful closeness to the simplicity of the original.

At a time after World War I, when Western literature and thought were busy portraying the collapse of human values as in Oswald Spengler's *Decline of the West* (1918-1922) and T. S. Eliot's *The Waste Land* (1922), and analyzing the fragmentation of human individuality as in James Joyce's *Ulysses* (1922) and Sigmund Freud's *The Ego and the Id* (1923), Gibran was preaching a philosophy of healing, reconciliation, and love through his prophet, Almustafa.

Deeply affected by the Holy Gospel and influenced by the English biblical style of poetic expression, Gibran wanted to transcend what he considered to be the world's temporary ailment under the pressures of modern materialistic life and to address himself to the permanent noble values that are dormant in the human heart and that should be invoked and awakened in order to build a good world. He did not want to be a mere witness to his age, reflecting its ills in his writings, but rather a moral teacher to all ages, calling on the spirituality of human beings of all times and appealing to their good will. The result was this poetic masterpiece of his philosophy entitled *The Prophet.*

After twelve years in a foreign city called Orphalese, Almustafa is ready to leave when his ship finally arrives to take him back to the isle that is his homeland. Heavy-hearted at abandoning the people who had come to love him as much as he loved them, he walks with them through the city to the great square before the temple, where the elders of the city entreat him not to leave. But Almitra, the woman who was the first to believe in him, recognizes his need to return to the beloved land of his birth and she asks that he speak to them and give them his final words of truth. When he accepts to do so, she asks him to speak of love and then of marriage.

Others, in turn, ask him to speak of children, of giving, of eating and drinking, of work, of joy and sorrow, of houses, of clothes, of buying and selling, of crime and punishment, of law, of freedom, of reason and passion, of pain, of self-knowledge, of teaching, of friendship, of talking, of time, of good and evil, of prayer, of pleasure, of beauty, of religion, and of death. And to each of them he gives his words of wisdom on the subject asked about, whether mundane or lofty, weaving his ideas into a wholesome, unitary view of life and the universe. As evening approaches, he walks to the harbour accompanied by the people. He stands on the deck of the ship and speaks one last time to the people of Orphalese, then he bids them farewell as the ship moves eastward and vanishes into the mist. The people cry, then they disperse. Only Almitra is silent as she stands on the sea-wall, pondering Almustafa's last words.

Within this very simple narrative framework, Gibran encapsulated in about a hundred pages the wisdom of a lifetime. He couched it in such a captivating poetic language that the book quickly became a bestseller and continues to be reprinted to this day. His wording is so memorable that it has been endlessly quoted in sermons, songs, formal addresses, and informal conversations. AE, the Irish man of letters whose real name was George William Russell (1867-1935), once wrote of Gibran's *The Prophet:* "I could quote from every page, and from every page could find some beautiful and liberating thought."

Perhaps Gibran was not as impressive a poet when he wrote verse as when he wrote prose. Whether in English or in Arabic, his prose was distinctively poetic and full of imaginative figures of speech and symbols as he expressed his thought in cadences that flowed harmoniously. When he wrote verse in Arabic, he must have felt constrained by the necessities of meter and rhyme. And yet he did write one long poem in Arabic verse consisting of 203 lines, which continues to be read and enjoyed in the Arab world. It is entitled *al-Mawakib* (The Processions), first published in New York in 1919. The well-known, present-day Lebanese singer, Fayruz, has recorded parts of it in a song, adding the mellifluous beauty of her voice to the beauty of Gibran's thought that is to be pondered and enjoyed.

Addressing the old man weary of urban civilized life, the robust young man in the poem invites him to the woods to enjoy the beauty and freedom of nature, and he says:

> Will you, like me, take the woods
> For a home, away from palaces?
> Will you follow the brooks
> And climb up the rocks?
> Will you bathe in fragrance
> And dry yourself with light?
> Will you drink dawn for wine
> In brimful cups of ether?
> Will you, like me, sit in the afternoon
> Amid the grape vines,
> With bunches of grapes hanging
> Like chandeliers of gold:
> Fountains of drink to the thirsty,
> Food for those who hunger,
> Honey and fragrance they are,
> And wine to those who wish.[13]

This is vintage Gibran. "Romantic to the tips of his fingers," as the literary scholar and critic, Dr. Ihsan 'Abbas, says of him.[14] Alienated in a materialistic world which is governed by self-interest and bound by constraining social traditions, cultural conventions, and impersonal relations, he was a rebellious spirit calling for a return to nature and an idyllic life of love and harmony, where everyone would live happily and be unified with God and the universe.

Mikhail Naimy

To a great extent, this was also the view of Mikhail Naimy in his poems composed between 1917 and 1928, and collected in his only volume of poetry entitled *Hams al-Jufun* (Eyelids Whispering) (Beirut, 1943). He developed this view more elaborately in his many prose writings, which include short stories, novels, a play, and hundreds of literary and philosophical essays and meditations published in several volumes.

Like Gibran, he was a pantheist who believed in the unity of all in God; he also believed in the ability of man to rise to the state of divinity. But whereas Gibran was more poetic and lyrical in his writings with regard to the expression of the Unity of Being, Naimy was more rational, analytical, and discursive.

The work in which Naimy epitomized his philosophy was *The Book of Mirdad: A Lighthouse and a Haven.* Published first in English (Beirut, 1948) and later in Arabic (Beirut, 1952), it is the story of a spiritual teacher and his disciples, like Gibran's *The Prophet.* However, Gibran's Almustafa is a prophet who teaches, then departs, but Naimy's Mirdad is a hermit admitted initially as a servant into a monastic group and later becomes its leader who mends the ways of the monks after they have gone astray by involving themselves in the concerns and the riches of the world. Their former leader, called Shamadam, opposes Mirdad's teachings in order to preserve his position but he is finally defeated.

Deriving its basic metaphorical conception from the biblical story of Noah and the flood, *The Book of Mirdad* consists of two parts: the first tells how the narrator of the story obtained the Book of Mirdad, and the second contains Mirdad's teachings in thirty-seven short, sermon-like chapters, each of which comments on events in the monks' lives and on their arguments, discussions, thoughts, even dreams. On the Day of the Ark, the annual festival celebrated by the monks and the people of the neighborhood, Mirdad warns at the conclusion of his mission that a greater flood than that of Noah's time, a flood of fire and blood, will break upon the earth if his message is not heeded and humanity continues to be entangled in material things and neglecting the divine in man.

The essence of Mirdad's teachings is that man can climb spiritually upward to become divine if he does not allow the flood of materialism to drown him. By self-negation, sublimation, and struggle against the flesh, its desires, and worldly interests, he can elevate himself to Godhood and liberate himself from suffering, evil, and death and achieve unity with the universal Absolute. For Mirdad (as for Naimy), "Man is a God in swaddling-bands."[15] He should seek his own Godhood and learn how to free himself from everything in him that ties him to the physical world in order to unite the particular "I" in him with the "I" of the universe, the "I" Absolute, i.e., God.

Despite affinities with Buddhist and, to some extent, Hindu thought, the essence of Mirdad's message is basically Christian with a theosophic twist. Explaining Naimy's thought on this point, his nephew Professor Nadeem N. Naimy says that, for Mikhail Naimy, "Christ was not a God who had descended to man but a man who had elevated himself to Godhood. This is how he was able to do what he did during his lifetime and later to resurrect after death. Christ, therefore, remains the only way to salvation, not as a God-redeemer, but as a human being who has set the example and the final proof that man *can* climb 'the Flint Slope' within him from the human to the divine."[16]

Among Naimy's other influential books still read in the Arab world is his book of literary criticism and theory entitled *al-Ghirbal* (The Sieve) (Cairo, 1923). In this book, he collected his articles published in the United States on this topic, beginning with the first critical article he ever wrote, which was a review of Gibran's novel *al-Ajniha al-Mutakassira* (Broken Wings) published in 1912. The Egyptian writer, 'Abbas Mahmud al-'Aqqad (1889-1964) wrote the introduction to *al-Ghirbal,* supporting Naimy's attack in the book on the literature being written in the Arab world of those days, which both writers considered to be shackled by old literary conventions of traditional form and hackneyed content having little to do with modern life. Al-'Aqqad had co-authored a similar book with the Egyptian writer Ibrahim 'Abd al-Qadir al Mazini (1890-1949) entitled *al-Diwan* (Cairo, 1922). Both books are now considered to have been elemental in opening new horizons for Arabic literature, especially poetry, and helping it become more in tune with modern times regarding its form and language as well as its thematic interest in life and society.

Above all, Naimy wanted literature to be a sincere expression of the writer's inner feelings and frank thoughts, a genuine reflection of his own experience of life that can enrich the life of others and make it more meaningful; he wanted literature to be a means to further the human quest for Truth and Beauty.

Iliyya Abu Madi

In a similar manner, Iliyya Abu Madi's poetry was a continual attempt to express this human quest for Truth and Beauty. In poem after poem, he poured himself out to give vent to his vision of life, often torn by search for meaning. Like other Pen Bond members, his poems show he sometimes found rest from the anxieties of the soul in the woods or in nature, but only for a while. For he repeatedly came face to face with himself in moments of loneliness and deep thought to discover that what he looked for was always within him, as he says at the end of one of his important poems entitled "al-'Anqa'" (The Phoenix).[17] For no matter how arduous the search for Truth is in the human experience of the outside world, only the exploration of one's inner being can bring the fullness of the knowledge of Truth and the comfort of feeling that one is on the right path.

Having arrived at this conviction, Abu Madi does not cease to delve into himself. He comes out with a variety of experiences, basic to all of which is the knowledge that life is what one makes of it. Despite his belief that human beings are essentially slaves of their human condition and instinctively bound to their self-interest,[18] he opts for a positive attitude to life and to humanity. Although he occasionally expresses desperation for improvement in human behavior, his more constant mood in his poetry is that of optimism and faith in the brotherhood of all people, and it is for this major theme in his poetry that he is remembered most in the Arab world today.

Abu Madi's poem "Falsafat al-Hayah" (The Philosophy of Life)[19] sums up his optimism and his call to retain a positive attitude to life, despite the reality of many negative things about it, including the inexplicable fact of lurking death. He ends the poem saying:

> Be a brook that glistens as it runs
> On the earth, watering the fields on both banks,
> Permitting the stars to bathe in it
> And everyone and everything to see their image in it;
> But don't be a receptacle that fetters the water
> And changes it to murky mud.
> At dawn, be a breeze that sniffs
> The flowers one moment, and kisses them the next;
> But don't be a hot wind whirling up dust
> And filling the earth with wailing in the dark.
> At night, be a star that keeps the woods company
> And likewise the river, the hills and the plains;
> But don't be the gloom that hates the world
> And humankind, and casts down dark curtains on all. [20]

His poem "Ibtasim" (Smile), set in the form of a dialogue between the poet and another person, emphasizes the same message. In it he says:

> He said, "The sky is gloomy," and he frowned.
> I said, "Smile. Sufficient is the scowl in the sky."
> He said, "Youth has gone." I said, "Smile.
> Sorrow will not bring back bygone youth."
> He said, "She who was my heaven in love
> Has become the hell of my soul.
> She broke all promises to me after I let her
> Possess my heart. How can I bear to smile?"
> I said, "Smile and be merry, for if you married her
> You would have spent the rest of your life in pain."[21]

Coupled with the idea of optimism is Abu Madi's readiness to be kind and helpful to others. In a poem entitled "Ana" (I), he says:

> If affliction befalls my friend
> I defend him, tooth and nail.
> I lend him my arm when he is weak
> And I cover his body when it is bare.
> I turn a blind eye to his shortcomings,
> Yet I see his merits all over, though unwritten.
> Before he blames me, I blame myself when wrong,
> Yet if he offends me I don't rebuke him. [22]

Abu Madi is determined to be optimistic and cheerful as well as kind and helpful to others, for he wants to make the best of life, knowing fully well that that is what gives it meaning. To him, love for others and a readiness to help them and make them happy are sure roads to one's own happiness and a fulfillment of one's own humanity.

In Abu Madi's view all people share the frailties of the human condition as well as its ennobling potentials. And yet, although they are all made of the same clay, some of them forget this simple truth and tend to treat others as if they were intrinsically of a lesser kind. To these forgetful people intoxicated with their vanity and wealth, Abu Madi wrote one of his more admonishing poems entitled "al-Tin" (Clay),[23] which he ends by saying:

> O human clay, you are not purer or more sublime
> Than the soil on which you tread or lie down....
> The lofty palace you built will collapse
> And the garment you wove will unravel.
> Let not your heart be an abode of enmity,
> My heart has become a temple of love.

Iliyya Abu Madi has five collections of poetry to his name. The first, *Tadhkar al-Madi* (Remembrance of the Past), was published in 1911 in Alexandria, Egypt, where he lived for eleven years after leaving Lebanon and before he emigrated to America. His second collection, *Diwan Iliyya Abu Madi (Volume II),* appeared in New York in 1919 with a preface by Gibran and it exhibited clear tendencies to innovation and to liberation from the traditionalism of his first collection. His third, *al-Jadawil* (The Brooks), was published in New York in 1927 with an introduction by Mikhail Naimy and it contained most of his best poems that established his reputation. His fourth, *al-Khama'il* (The Thickets), was published in New York in 1940 by the press of his own *al-Samir* daily newspaper and it contained several beautiful poems. His fifth, *Tibr wa Turab* (Gold and Dust) was posthumously published in Beirut in 1960.

Some of these collections have been reprinted several times in the Arab world. And because of their popularity they are all available now in one volume published in Beirut in the 1960s.

Although Abu Madi did not write in English like Gibran, Naimy, and Rihani, some of his poetry has been translated into English and other languages,[24] and he is considered by literary critics to be the leading poet of the Pen Bond.

Looking Ahead

The long-term impact which the contributions of Arab immigrants in North America have had on the Arabic literature of their original homeland may be measured by the new horizons of innovation and creativity which they opened for it. In matters of form and content, they offered examples of the desired change that was possible for new writers in the Arab world to adopt. These contributions of the Arab immigrants in North America may not all have been equally influential, but as a body of new literature they had a strong effect on the way many Arabs began to understand literature to be.

Rather than an imitation of past writings in prose and verse, literature came to be understood as an expression of the writer's personal experience of life and human relations. It had therefore to be couched in the writer's own style, free from traditional literary conventions, and it had to express the writer's own thoughts and feelings, free from the mere copying of previous writings. This very important fact that may seem today so obvious was not so in the earlier parts of the twentieth century.

As we come now to the end of this century and look at the various achievements of modern Arabic literature today, we can recognize that these would not have been possible without, at least in part, the innovative contributions of the Arab immigrants in North America. These contributions have encouraged other movements in the Arab world which, in turn, have brought further change and development that have rendered present-day Arabic literature the vibrant literature it is on the eve of the twenty-first century.

NOTES

[1] "Adab al-Mahjar: Bibliughrafiyya li al-Dirasat al-Naqdiyya wa al-Maqalat," in *Mundus Arabicus*, vol. 1, *Arab Writers in America: Critical Essays and Annotated Bibliography* (Cambridge, Mass.: Dar Mahjar, 1981), 89-230.

[2] "Mahjar Literature: An Annotated Bibliography of Literary Criticism and Biography in Western Languages," in *Mundus Arabicus,* vol. 1, 65-88.

[3] Durham: University of Durham, Centre for Middle Eastern and Islamic Studies, 1983.

[4] Beirut: American University of Beirut, 1985.

[5] *Encyclopaedia of Islam*, New Edition, vol. 5 (1986), 1253-1247.

[6] *Journal of Arabic Literature*, vol. 17 (1986), 69-81; see also his article "The Centennial of Iliya Abu Madi," in *The Word* 34 (February 1990): 5-7.

[7] *Journal of Arabic Literature*, vol. 24 (1993), 173-184; see also his article "Mikhail Naimy (1889-1988)," in *The Word* 32 (September 1988): 4-5.

[8] *Bibliotheca Orientalis*, vol. L, nos. 3-4 (May-July 1993), 329-341.

[9] See 'Isa Yusuf Bullata, *al-Rumantiqiyya wa Ma'alimuha fi al Shi'r al-'Arabi al-Hadith* (Beirut: Dar al-Thaqafa, 1960; reprinted Baghdad: Dar al-Jumhuriyya, 1968). See also Ihsan 'Abbas and Muhammad Yusuf Najm, *al-Shi'r al-'Arabi fi al-Mahjar: Amirika al-Shamaliyya* (Beirut: Dar Sadir, 1957).

[10] For more on this former Pen Bond in New York which did not survive, see C. Nijland, in *Bibliotheca Orientalis*, 330-334.

[11] For a fuller list, see the rosters of the Association of Arab-American University Graduates (AAUG), the American Association of Teachers of Arabic (AATA), and the Middle East Studies Association of North America (MESA).

[12] For more on Arabic periodicals in North America, see Philip de Tarazi, *Tarikh al-Sihafa al-'Arabiyya,* vols. 3-4 (Beirut, 1914-1933; reprinted Baghdad, 1968), 406-433.

[13] Jubran Khalil Jubran, *al-Mawakib / al-Bada'i' wa al-Tara'if* (Beirut: Dar Sadir / Dar Gibran, 1981), 15.

[14] Ihsan 'Abbas, *Fann al-Shi'r* (Beirut, 1955), 46.

[15] *The Book of Mirdad*, Chapter IV.

16 Nadeem N. Naimy, *Mikhail Naimy: An Introduction*, 310.

17 See the collection of all his poetic works entitled *Diwan Iliyya Abu Madi* (Beirut: Dar al-'Awda, ca. 1960s), 512-514.

18 See for example his poem "Fi al-Qafr" (In the Wilderness), *ibid.*, 151-152.

19 *Ibid.*, 624-626.

20 *Ibid.*, 624.

21 *Ibid.*, 675.

22 *Ibid.*, 147-148.

23 *Ibid.*, 318-322.

24 See for example A.J. Arberry, *Modern Arabic Poetry: An Anthology with English Verse Translations*, (Cambridge: Cambridge University Press, 1967), 60-63; Mounah A. Khouri and Hamid Algar, *An Anthology of Modern Arabic Poetry* (Berkeley: University of California Press, 1974), 35-36; Salma Khadra Jayyusi, *Modern Arabic Poetry: An Anthology* (New York: Columbia University Press, 1987), 45-48; Gregory Orfalea and Sharif Elmusa, *Grape Leaves: A Century of Arab American Poetry* (Salt Lake City: University of Utah Press, 1988), 65-81.

PART TWO:

Christian Influence on Arabic Civilization

SYRIAC AND ARABIC THEOLOGICAL THOUGHT
by Michel Najim

Syriac Aramaic and *Arabic* have been spoken in a variety of dialects in the Middle East throughout the Christian era.

Syriac originated among the Arameans of Northern Syria and became almost a universal language in the Middle East for over two millennia. Many documents show old Aramaic was in common use until the first century A.D. In succeeding centuries Aramaic split into several dialects.

Throughout history Aramaic has been spoken or written by peoples of different faiths and different ethnic backgrounds. It extended to the west as far as Spain, and to the east as far as India and China. The Syriac language, a form or branch of ancient Aramaic, was extensively used by the Christians of the Middle East. To early writers, Syriac is actually known as "Edessene," an indication it started simply as the local Aramaic dialect of Edessa. Subsequently, it came to be adopted as the literary language of Aramaic speaking Christians all over the Middle East.

Being a Semitic language, Arabic was the language of the dominant tribes including the Christian tribes of the Arabian Peninsula, southern Syria, and Jordan. The expansion of Islam expedited the growth of the Arabic language in many Mediterranean countries. It became the native language of millions in Lebanon, Syria, Iraq, Egypt, Libya, Tunisia, and Mauritania. With this language all these countries developed and transmitted a great civilization which lasted for centuries.

Upon the appearance of Islam, Christianity had already been a vital religion in the Arabian Peninsula. Although the history of Arab Christianity is shrouded in vagueness and incertitude, particularly in its first period, during which the historical texts do not provide us with a clear record of missionary activity, it is quite certain many tribes in the Arabian Peninsula were Christianized in the pre-Islamic period. With the Islamic invasion of Syria and the Middle East, and North Africa, the Arabic language started to replace all the native languages and laid the solid foundation of Arab Christianity, Arabic theology and Arabic Christian literature.

If our task is to undertake an account of Syriac Aramaic and Arabic legacies, this brief presentation can be justified by the desire to present only the general contributions of those two legacies in the history of Christianity, overlooking the details, the persons, and their contributions in the history of Christian religion.

SYRIAC PATRISTIC LITERATURE

Syriac literature is of significant value in its own right since many of the writings of the church fathers were composed in Syriac or translated into Syriac. It is the literature of many Eastern and Oriental churches. Syriac literature was separated into many traditions due to the fact that many churches became separated from each other, or from the mainstream church, in the Roman Empire.

When Nestorius, for example, was excommunicated in the Third Ecumenical Council (431), the first separation took place. The center of gravity of the Nestorian literature lies outside the Roman Empire. The lamentable event, however, took place in the Fourth Ecumenical Council, when the separation of the two sister Orthodox churches — the Chalcedonian and non-Chalcedonian churches — took place mainly as a result of a disagreement on terminological formulations. (Now, by God's grace these two churches are in the process of healing their relationship, reinstating their communion and regaining their kinship.)

These two churches have their own deep roots in the Syriac tradition, although they emerged as separate churches. It is noteworthy to mention that the Antiochian Chalcedonian Church has its own roots in the Syriac tradition, which was replaced gradually by the Arabic tradition.

There are many other churches which are deeply rooted in the Aramaic Syriac tradition. The Syriac Maronites, who now are the majority of Christians in Lebanon, built their own separate church in the seventh century. Sebastian Brock, in his work *The Syriac Fathers on Prayer and the Spiritual Life,* says: "Both (the Maronite and Melkite-Rum) have their roots in Syriac Christianity. The Maronite Church emerged as a separate church in the seventh century as a result of the monotheletic-dystheletic controversy. Whereas the Melkite (Rum) Orthodox Church changed its liturgical language from Syriac to Arabic and its rite from Antiochian to Constantinopolitan in the Middle Ages . . . ."

Under the influence of the Roman Catholic Church two uniate Syriac churches were established: the Syriac Chaldeans (Catholics who branched out of the Nestorians) in the fifteenth century and the Syriac Catholics, in the midst of the nineteenth century. Again, all these Middle Eastern and ancient churches have their roots in the Syriac tradition.

Orthodox churches, however, have the right to proclaim they belong to the Ancient Church founded by Jesus Christ, and to claim by a clear historical evidence that their Apostolic succession comes directly from the Apostles. Since the Syriac tradition is a multi-cultural, multi-ethnic and multi-denominational heritage, it can be regarded as one of the richest heritages in the history of Christianity.

Thus, the Syriac Christian literature is the heritage of several Eastern and Oriental churches, and it can be represented wherever these churches are to be found today in the world — the Middle East, India, Europe, the Americas and Australia.

The earliest major Syriac authors offer us an essentially Semitic form of Christianity. This specifically Semitic aspect of the earliest Syriac literature has been neglected, despite its potential interest for the study of primitive Christianity. The schools at Nisibis and Edessa were typical Semitic schools — most of all they remind one of a Jewish rabbinical school, a "beth-hammidrash."

The Syriac tradition, however, was influenced by Greek thought from the fifth century and onwards. This interaction with Greek thought did not change the structure of the Syriac pattern, but it gave it a new form of expression.

Syriac Christian literature has produced a large number of poets and writers; many of those writers have a genuine originality and a unique spiritual insight. Being a bridge language, however, Syriac translations of the works of the church fathers are of particular interest because the manuscripts are of antiquity. And further, the general area of Antioch provided the most creative liturgical contributions for early Christianity.

Syrian luminaries and theologians were the precursors of many Western theological traditions. They were the first to launch their fabulous knowledge in all fields of theological studies. And they were the first to teach and preach the gospel in Asia, including India and China. Their manuscripts are preserved in many eastern and western libraries, monasteries and museums.

While the European continent was still unenlightened, the one lamp of theological knowledge was set high on a stand in Mesopotamia, Syria, Phoenicia and Asia Minor. This great theological tradition was strictly preserved and sustained from the very beginning in the multitude of the Aramean Syrians' schools, seminaries, monasteries, convents, cathedrals, and churches.

Extreme ascetic theology became the nerve-center of Syrian Christianity. Syriac spirituality is known as the ascetic life of the Sons and Daughters of the Covenant. Asceticism and acquisition of wisdom were the two sides of imitation of Christ. The Sons and Daughters of the Covenant were priests, monks, virgins and holy persons who strove to abstain from all sins and to purify their hearts.

This major contribution of the Syriac spirituality is the result of actual experience of God and the action of the Holy Spirit. This richest contributions of Syriac spirituality were expressed in numerous forms, especially in the exegetical, liturgical and poetic legacies.

The Schools of Edessa and Nisibis

Edessa, the present Urfa, was from a very early date the center of Syriac-speaking Christianity. Its church is thought to be one of the oldest known Christian edifices. Edessa was also most probably the home of the Old Syriac and the Peshitta versions of the New Testament. It was possibly the home of the diatessaron. Edessa was more closely connected with Persia than to the Hellenic world. There, the works of the Greek fathers, hagiographers, and ascetics were translated into Syriac.

The guiding influence of the theological school is connected with the school at Nisibis, which very quickly reached its zenith. Already, by about 535 A.D., Cassiodorus of Vivarium points out that the school at Nisibis and the school at Alexandria are "model" Christian schools. The statutes of the school have come down to us from 496 A.D., but it is not difficult to identify in these statutes the features of a more ancient and traditional system.

The Syriac Translations of the Bible

The Old Testament books were translated into Syriac directly from Hebrew at different times. There has existed an extensive collection of Jewish texts in Aramaic since the end of first millennium B.C. A careful study of the literary text show that the Jewish Aramaic language had two different dialects: the Samaritan Aramaic and the Jewish Aramaic.

Concerning biblical translations, we have two versions of the Old Testament text: the Samaritan translation of the Hebrew Torah and the Palestinian translation of the Aramaic version.

The translation of the Greek Septuagint into Syriac is contained in Origen's *Hexapla,* which was completed in 616-7 by Paul, the Syriac bishop of Tella in Mesopotamia. In addition to these two versions there are many liturgical, Talmudic, homiletical, and exegetical texts in both dialects, primarily in the Jewish Aramaic.

From an early date, Aramaic Syriac was employed in translations of the New Testament. There are several existing versions of the Syriac New Testament of which the oldest is Tatian's *Diatessaron (150-160)*. From that date it circulated widely in the Syriac churches where it became the official text of the gospel until the fifth century.

The earliest surviving Syriac gospel text is known as the *Old Syriac,* and is preserved in two very old manuscripts, the *Curetonia* and the *Sinaiticus.* The standard New Testament version, the *Peshitta,* is a revision of the *Old Syriac,* completed in the fifth century.

Biblical Interpretation

There is also a certain inner similarity between the "historical-grammatical" method of the Antiochian and the rabbinical exegetics of the East. Characteristic of Antiochian theology is a specific and particular method of scholarship which partially calls to mind the *Talmud.* The Nisibisian "statutes" especially cautioned against "speculation" and "allegories." The Scripture was, naturally, the subject taught.

The earliest exegesis of the Bible is attributed to Ephraim while he was teaching in Edessa. Jacob of Sarug's (451-521) principal writing was a long series of metrical homilies, most of them on biblical themes. Philoxenus of Mabbug (440-523) was one of the leading exegetics in Syriac literature; he produced a great number of exegetical works. Biblical exegesis was practiced by many other Syriac scholars such as John ibn Aphtonia, Daniel al-Soulhi, Marotha, Jacob of Edessa, George, bishop of the Arabs, Ibn Khifa, Jacob ibn Salibi, and Ibn al-Ibri.

The Syriac Liturgical Tradition

Most of the liturgical texts were organized in the Syriac tradition. Constantinople adopted much of the practice of Antioch, which was mainly a Syriac tradition. The Egyptian Church also borrowed its eucharistic canons from Antioch.

The Syriac term for Liturgy is either *qurobo,* meaning "to offer" or *qurbono,* "oblation" or "offering." The Liturgy is referred to as the *rozae qadeeshae,* meaning "the holy mysteries," to signify that the bread and wine become the Body and Blood of our Lord Jesus Christ.

The liturgical scheme always consisted of two parts: the Liturgy of the Word and the eucharistic prayer or *anaphora.* The anaphora was based upon the Aramaic prayer used by Jesus himself at the Last Supper.

A great number of Syriac anaphoras survive until our day. Seventy-four existing anaphoras are testimony to the richest heritage in Christian history. After the fifth century schism, both Chalcedonian and non-Chalcedonian churches fully maintained the liturgical tradition established before the schism. Along with the eucharistic tradition, there exists a very rich collection of sacramental literature, and precious commentaries on the Liturgy, sacraments and prayers.

Religious Poetry

Being a poetic and lyrical language, the Syriac writers excelled in religious poetry. The spiritual transparency of Saint Ephraim of Nisibis is unmatched in the history of Christianity. Although Syriac poets seemed to preserve the biblical poetry, they presented their own authentic witness to the maturing of mystical Christian poetry, which transcends all logical definitions. Syriac Christian poetry gives us an example of Orthodox mystical theology. While it presents us with transparent theology, its contribution is the product of sanctity and mystical experience.

Syriac Hagiography

Hagiography has a special position in Syriac literature due to the richness and variety of its literary form. It is divided in two sections: (1) pieces of Syriac origin, such as the life of Alexis, were translated immediately into Greek and Latin and later into Arabic; and (2) pieces that were translated from Greek into Syriac.

Since the Syriac-speaking churches suffered great persecutions in history, the fascinating collections of martyrs came into existence. Hagiography, however, is intimately connected with the monastic movement, and Syriac literature is permeated with the lives and stories of monks, nuns and hermits.

Syriac Writers

Among the great church authors and fathers who wrote in Syriac, the most illustrious names are: Aphraates, Ephraim, John the Solitary (of *Apamea*), Jacob of Sarug, Philoxenus of Mabbug, Jacob Baradeus, John the Ephesian, Bar Hebraeus, Isaac of Nineveh, Stephen Bar Soudaili, Jacob of Edessa and Dadiso Quatraya. Isaac of Nineveh's (eighth century) writings were highly respected in the monastic circles of all Eastern and Oriental churches. We may also cite John of Dalyatha (eighth century) and Jacob ibn Salibi (d. 1171).

There were many other great authors as well. Syriac authors who have been strangely passed over in silence. It is time to re-establish the place of Syriac literature in the larger history of Christian literature. But there are problems. Although the authorities of the British museum were led to believe they had accumulated a magnificent collection of manuscripts, hundreds of them are still in other libraries and monasteries. There is, unfortunately, still no satisfactory up-to-date introduction to, and study of, Syriac literature. The reader has to make the most of what is available.

Syriac literature provides the link between Arab and Greek literature. Familiarity with the Syriac background to Arabic Christian literature is important for another reason as well: it was through Syriac literature that Arab writers became aware of the patristic Greek heritage. Syriac literature gave birth to an Orthodox presence which produced great theologians in the Arabic tradition. This, in turn, was to have a profound influence on European thinking.

ARABIC CHRISTIAN LITERATURE

The use of the term, "Arabic Christian Literature," refers to the body of Christian works produced by Arab Christians, and includes those written by people in the Arabic-speaking patriarchates of the Middle East.

Christianity had been propagated for at least three centuries before the rise of Islam in the Arabian Peninsula, and for six centuries in the regions of Mesopotamia and Syria. When Islam first made its appearance, multitudes of Christians were thriving in the Arabian Peninsula.

The bordering areas to the north were the Christian Arab tribes of the Hira Kingdom of Iraq and the Ghassanid of Syria. The territories to the south were occupied by the Christians of Najrān in the Yemen. There were many Christian groups in the very heart of Arabia as well, not only scattered here and there in small groups, but even in Mecca and Medina.

It was the Najrānites of southern Yemen who concluded the first *dhimi* pact with Muhammad. Subsequently, it was the Arab Christians in Syria who held together the structures and customs which were unfamiliar to newly-arrived Arabs from the various regions of the Arabian deserts. They undertook the setting up of the intellectual apparatus for the development of what was to become known as Arab culture.

In addition, Arab Christians influenced Muslim theology in many ways, mainly through the debates, which influenced the formation of the strictly Muslim discipline of *al-kalam*.

Unfortunately, references to Arab Christians and the Arab legacy appear to today's reader as casual and occasional. Few writers of the past seem to have cared sufficiently to study this legacy carefully. Yet, it is generally believed today that major libraries — ecclesiastical, private, and public located in various parts of the world — contain hundreds or even thousands of manuscripts written by Arab Christians, especially by Antiochians. But only a few of them have been made available. Some have been indexed and critically edited. Even fewer have been made available in European languages. There is today a great urgency to make the bulk of these manuscripts available and usable for historical research and theological study.

In the beginning of this century many authors, both Arabs and Orientalists, began to study and publish segments of the Arabic Christian heritage. Many important contributions have been produced from Syriac, Coptic, Aramean texts such as those in *Patrologia Orientalis,* or in Arabic collections of manuscripts such as the work of George Graf, *Geschichte der Christlichen Arabischen Literatur.*

Many international conferences have been held in the 1980s to uncover this rich heritage.

The theological Arabic tradition falls in two categories: (1) the translated tradition, such as the translation of the Bible to Arabic, or the translation of the Greek, Syriac, Coptic fathers to Arabic; and (2) the theological literature written in Arabic, such as Arabic hagiography, apology and Christianity and Islamic exegetical literature.

It is our task to carry out responsible investigation leading to the discovery of unknown primary sources. Then follows the editing of these manuscripts critically, translating them into western languages, annotating and commenting on them. Then would come the compilation of dictionaries, chronologies and bibliographies; publication of periodicals; organization of seminars and symposia; and writing of monographs, essays, studies and articles.

The temporal extent of Arabic legacy covers the entire period from the beginnings of Islam to the present day, the period from the time when Muhammad preached his first sermon, likely in 710 A.D.; and consideration of how and when he first received a Christian influence. Indeed we must look back even earlier still, to the spread of Christianity throughout the Arab world, from when it engulfed the Arabian Peninsula, penetrating into its heart, preparing and fertilizing it for the birth of Islam. In other words, the Arab legacy goes back to the very beginnings of Christianity in the first century.

As for the geographical space in which Arab Christianity has existed under Islam, it has included all countries and regions that would form what has become known as the Arab world. This embraces the shores of the Maghreb on the Atlantic Ocean to the Arabian Gulf and the Indian Ocean, reaching as far south as the Sudanese-Ethiopian border in the heart of Africa.

To give a true reflection of Christian contributions to Arab culture and civilization, and to give some idea of the richness and complexity involved, it will suffice to recall briefly the major phases of the history of the Arab states and empires. Those Christians, who would become the Arab Christians of the "Arabs-Before-Islam," had behind them an already fruitful and glorious history. The land of Palestine brought us the world's first Christians, those early Apostles and effective disseminators of Christianity. Those who followed the Apostles were the main architects of Orthodox Christian dogma — and of its major heresies and innovations. They were also the significant co-builders of Christianity's clerical and monastic institutions, its ecclesiastical organization, its liturgy, its theology and its literature. All of this occurred under the stimulation and supervision of the three ancient patriarchates of Alexandria, Antioch and Jerusalem — the equals of the other two Christian patriarchal sees, the old Rome and the new Rome at Constantinople — equivalent in authority, prestige and Orthodoxy. By the end of the seventh century, the Arabic-speaking Churches were ripe for comprehensive presentation of Christian faith.

There are several theological branches for Arabic Christian literature, the most important ones are described next.

Ancient Arabic Versions of the Bible

Several versions are known, but there is no complete text to antedate Islam. There are, however, biblical fragments and quotations which definitely predate the Islamic period, and which prove the Bible was translated into Arabic in the pre-Islamic period. The oldest surviving manuscript is the Mount Sinai Arabic codex 151 which was edited and translated into English by Harvey Staal. There are several colophons in the manuscript. The earliest one is on folios 186 and 187 at the end of Hebrews, giving the date of translating the Pauline Epistles as the month of Ramadan, 253 A.H. (867 A.D.).

Arabic Interpretation of the Bible

Throughout the centuries there have always been Arab scholars who have interpreted the Bible, and have laid the foundation for biblical criticism, but they have been disregarded in modern history. It is difficult to imagine a great theological heritage without deep interest in biblical research. In studying the works of the al-Assal family, a scholarly thirteenth century Coptic family, we discover that Arab Christians were the fathers of biblical criticism.

Systematization of the Christian Faith

Systematization is always the fruit of years of doctrinal development. By putting side by side the patristic heritage, systematization is more than a simple repetition of other people's ideas.

The Summa Theologica Arabica was written by Stephen of Ramlah in the year 877 A.D. at the monastery of Mar Chariton in the Judean desert. The Islamic context of this Summa is of great importance because it answers the major intellectual challenges of the Christians in the Arab world. In an Islamic context, Christians had to express their theology under the light of Islamic challenges. The author of the *Summa* concentrates his attention on the oneness of God and Christ's full divinity.

Arabic Apologetics

The primary task of many Arab theologians was to prove the truth of Christianity against the non-Christians. They defended the Christian faith in countless ways.

Although faith is above reason, reason itself might be used to prove the reality of the Christian faith; Christian doctrine is not illogical. The exercise of the mind is required to prove the truthfulness of the Christian faith. The target of their apology was those who have believed after they had studied and understood the faith.

Thus, against the non-Christians, Arab scholars proved Christianity was the only true religion. Arguments were used by Arab theologians to show that true Christianity was founded —

- not by the power of an earthly king, but by God himself

- not out of hardship, but from blessing into enduring the difficult things

- not for glory, but rather from glory to humiliation

- not out of philosophical discipline (it is clear the disciples were not people of tricks, but were uneducated, and simple men), those who received it were not ignorant, but became well-educated

- not out of tribal or kinsmen relationship. Among early Christians, there was little familial relationship.

Muslims were skeptical about Christian monotheism, and therefore Christians were accused of being polytheists. For this reason, there was a great need to defend Christian monotheism. The importance of Christian trinitarian theology for Arabs lies in the fact the Father cannot be separated from his Word (Logos) and his Spirit. Their formula was that God is *Intellect-Intelligent-Intelligible (aqil-Aaqil-maqul)*

Living in an iconoclastic society, many Arab theologians defended the veneration of the icons. For example, Theodore Abou-Kohura addressed the Jews by giving different examples from the Old Testament where the patriarchs and the prophets venerated and prostrated before those persons who should be venerated, specifically the kings. He addressed the Muslims (without mentioning their names), by pointing to the Koranic passage teaching that we should not prostrate ourselves in worship before anyone except God. He quoted these passages from the Koran:

> And behold: We said to the angels: Bow down to Adam: and they bowed down: Not so Satan (Iblis) he refused and was haughty: He was of those who reject faith.

> The brothers of Joseph fell down before Joseph: "And he raised his parents high on the throne of dignity, and they fell down in prostration all before him . . . " (Joseph 12/100).

Arab Writers

Among the great church writers and fathers who wrote in Arabic, the most illustrious names are Theodore Abu Qurrah, Yahia ibn 'Adi, Ibn Mahroumi, Soulaiman Algahzi, Severus ibn al-Moukafah, Abd al-Masih, Bin Ishaq Alkindi, Hunayn ibn Ishaq, Stephen of Ramlah, Qusta ibn Luqa, Abu Bishr Matta ibn Yunis, Bulus al-Bushi.

Conclusion

The significance of this short study is that for a finer awareness of the two great heritages, Syriac and Arabic patrological literature must be given due attention in historical studies. This means editions and modern translations of these two heritages are sorely needed. It is not, however, only parts of these two legacies that are important, but the entire corpus of writings.

Our picture of Christian theologians, now overshadowed by the Greek and Latin fathers, means the study of Syriac and Arabic heritages will make patristics more distinct if those two legacies are studied properly. Even if a part of these two legacies can be shown to be translations from the Greek literature, it may well be that they open up for us the rich tradition of the Church which could be called the greatest patristic school of Christianity.

NOTES

The author's bibliography has been incorporated into the Selected Bibliography at the end of this volume.

SCHISM AND PARALLEL HIERARCHIES: ANTIOCH DURING THE FIRST CRUSADE
by John Lawrence Boojamra

The history of the so-called schism of 1054[1] and its immediate aftermath in the conflict between the Antiochene Patriarch Peter III and Michael I Cerularios,[2] is particularly bizarre given the fact that it was completely ignored by the first crusaders. For their part, the Byzantines were preoccupied by the loss of Anatolia in 1071 to the Seljuk Turks at the battle of Manzikert, who swept across the peninsula between 1071 and 1090, making their capital at Nicea, immediately across the Bosporus from Constantinople.[3] This was the worst defeat the Byzantines had suffered during the eleventh century; the emperor Romanos IV Diogenes (1068-1071) was captured and his army scattered or annihilated.

The Seljuk Turks moved also against the Abbasids, capturing Damascus in 1055, Armenia in 1064, and Antioch in 1084. They established settlements and drove the Christian peasants westwards to the Sea of Marmara, making it clear that they intended to stay. It was this apparent determination to settle in Anatolia that was the origin of the First Crusade. The Muslim Seljuks converted churches into mosques and, in general, aggressively began the transformation of formerly Christian territory into Dar al-Islam. The Byzantines panicked and sought western relief for the return of their former territories, especially the "God-guarded" city of Antioch.

The Crusaders and Alexios

The Byzantines had already made contact with the West for assistance in Anatolia. In 1071 Michael VII Ducas tried to make a deal with Pope Gregory VII (1073-1085) whereby a group of western mercenaries would be sent to assist Byzantine troops in Anatolia to drive out the Seljuks. Gregory completely misunderstood the request, as did future popes; eager to prove the political power of the reformed papacy, he promised an army of fifty thousand men, himself at their head, to liberate the Christian East from the Muslims and free the Holy Land for pilgrim traffic.[4] The agreement was never effected.

Islam during the period just prior to and during the First Crusade was divided among two great and hostile powers, the Seljuks controlling the Abbasids of Baghdad and the Fatimids of Cairo, one Turk and one Arab, respectively. The two hostile Muslim camps met in Palestine and complicated the negotiations with the crusaders.[5] Bohemund of Tarantum proposed an alliance with the Fatimids against the Seljuks. The Fatimids attacked the Turks from the south and west across the Suez. The Fatimids sent an embassy to the Franks at Antioch to propose an alliance by which the westerners would get Antioch and Syria and the Fatimids would occupy Palestine and Jerusalem. Although no agreement was consummated, the Fatimids did occupy Jerusalem and it was they whom the crusaders eventually fought in August 1098.

Preaching the Crusade

Alexios Comnenos (1086-1118) was perhaps one of the most powerful of Byzantine emperors and had a sense that he was dealing with "barbarians," who were Christians but not terribly bright. In 1097 he demanded that all of his territory occupied by the Seljuks be returned to him or held under his suzerainty in exchange for Byzantine military support. There could, however, be no question about the status of Antioch; the gem of the East was never to be negotiable. The Byzantine could "take or leave" much of the rest of Syria or even Jerusalem; they never had the same relationship to it that the West had had, with the possible exception of the emperor Heraclios (610-641).

When Urban II referred to assisting the Eastern churches, he did not intend Maronites, Jacobites, or Armenians, Copts, and Nestorians. He intended the Chalcedonian Orthodox churches. One of the problems of dealing with the area and the period is the nomenclature. The reader is never quite sure who is being referred to. The rapid movement of historical events between the Fatimids and the Seljuks left little place in recorded history for information about the indigenous Christians of Syria, Palestine, Mesopotamia, Cilicia, and Lebanon, as both these people fought over the area to conquer and settle.[6]

The status of the Greek Church or those in communion with Constantinople was not at all clear. It was certainly not clear, for instance, that there was a schism in place since the events of 1054 were all but ignored. At any rate, even had the deteriorating relationship between Rome and Constantinople been taken seriously in 1054, it did not involve Antioch, whose brilliant Patriarch Peter III was a master of moderation, sobriety, and Orthodoxy at the same time.[7] However, Urban needed the prestige of a united effort to help defeat his domestic opponents.

In 1089 he made overture to Constantinople to open the Latin churches in the city, to restore unity, and lift the "excommunications." Something was perceived to be amiss and, if such were not the case, Alexios I would not have asked Nicholas III (1084-1111) to investigate why the popes' names were missing from the diptychs so that he could clear up any obstacle to a common effort against the Turks and Normans. It was this ambiguity that created the fuzzy picture within which churchmen and crusaders had to work, but of which few researchers take note. Antioch fell into this gray area.

The Byzantine council held in 1089 under Nicholas III maintained there had been no earlier synodal action against Rome. Even the findings of Nicholas III in 1089 could only trace the absence of the popes' names from the diptychs when Benedict VIII's was excluded in 1014. Urban was, according to Patriarch Nicholas III, to come in person to make his confession or send a systatic letter to have his name restored.[8] He did not! The council took no action. This is not what Alexios had in mind. Urban sought the good will of the Orthodox Church so he chose a legate sympathetic to the Eastern churches, Bishop Adhemar du Puy. His was obviously a plan to work with the good will of the emperor.

Alexios I needed the situation between Rome and Constantinople normalized since he wanted to control the Normans of south Italy. He also needed assistance from the Pope to regain Anatolia, assistance that had been discussed since the pontificate of Gregory VII.[9] Both sides were operating on mistaken notions, however: Rome that the Eastern Church was controlled by the emperor, and the emperor that the papacy was controlled by the secular powers.

At the same time the Byzantine Church was not aware of the nature of the ecclesiological claims of the reformed papacy; this ignorance greatly affected the nature of ecclesiastical affairs in the eleventh century, including the so-called schism of 1054.[10] On the one hand, the reformed papacy was desperate to establish itself as the locus of an emerging Europe; on the other hand, the pugnacious Normans were eager to establish a Levantine kingdom. The Byzantines had to deal with both agendas.

A Byzantine military commission was sent to the Council of Piacenza in March 1095, from the emperor Alexios to negotiate an alliance to hold off the Turks. The council, called to end the schism between Popes Clement III and Urban II, became an important opportunity for the papacy, whoever occupied it, to consolidate his position.[11] Urban, having learned of the arrival of the Byzantine embassy, invited its members to attend the session of the council and give an account of the dangers threatening the Church in the East.

While it is probable that Alexios requested some form of assistance early in Gregory VII's pontificate, he never expected the numbers and political agendas that the European leaders brought with them.[12] By no stretch of the imagination was Alexios looking for Norman assistance, given the Norman penchant for occupying Byzantine territory from their south Italian holdings and Robert Guiscard's plans for the Balkans, taking the Adriatic city of Dyrrachium in 1081. Alexios never expected all of Europe to respond; he never expected a "Grand Passage."[13]

A famous and highly motivated "pre-crusade" set out early in 1095 under Peter the Hermit with tens of thousands of men and women, almost all socially marginal; the arrival of this rag-tag collection of westerners at the walls of Constantinople greatly impressed the Byzantines who were in general attracted to Peter the Hermit, identifying his lack of cleanliness with "holiness." This undisciplined, albeit pious crew was largely destroyed in Anatolia, with a few making their way back to the West with tales of Christian suffering at the hands of the Muslims, further inflaming the motivation behind the crusade preached at Clermont. Peter the Hermit recounted the bogus story that he had seen the tomb of Christ desecrated by the Turks, when, according to Anna Comnena, he probably never completed his pilgrimages to the Holy Land.[14]

The call for the crusade was repeated at Clermont in autumn 1095 by Urban, where would be better received than in Italy. On November 27, he gathered the people in the cathedral square and gave a speech describing the persecuted Church of the East. What is fascinating is the absence of any hint that any sort of schism had taken place in 1054; clearly no schism or sense of schism was yet fixed in either the pope or the Byzantine emperor, Alexios. Urban explained the importance of Jerusalem and the need to guarantee free access of pilgrims to the Holy Places.

Urban preached the crusade in 1095 made no mention of setting up Latin churches in the Levant. He designated Constantinople as the meeting place and the time of departure as August 15, 1096. Adhemar du Puy, sympathetic to the Orthodox Church, was to lead the crusade on behalf of Urban and pursue Urban's relatively benign policy towards the indigenous churches of the East. Perhaps what Urban was preaching at Clermont was not what Alexios had requested.

Arrival In Constantinople

The leaders of the First Crusade met in Constantinople in the spring of 1097, having arrived by different routes; among them were the infamous Norman duke Bohemond of Tarantum, the son of Robert Guiscard, the Byzantine nemeses who had occupied Byzantine Sicily and south Italy.[15] The emperor welcomed the western armies, albeit with some apprehension and a little confusion over goals and purposes; he wisely shuttled them quickly across the Bosporus into Turkish held Anatolia.[16]

Once in Constantinople, however, the Latin powers took oaths of loyalty to the emperor Alexios. The crusaders were to restore to Alexios all of the territory which had formerly been Byzantine, especially Antioch, and all other territory they would hold as fiefs of the empire. Alexios was concerned about Asia Minor. He manifested no particular concern about Jerusalem and Palestine, a concern so evident among the westerners. No conflict of secular or ecclesiastical jurisdiction was involved, in principle, south of Antioch. It is not at all clear that, as several historians have held, the pope considered all the conquest in the Holy Places as his personal holdings. The entire negotiation process is impossible to understand unless the unique place of Antioch and Syria in Byzantine political psychology is understood. Two different goals were motivating the two differently, neither of which perceived a schism to be in place. The events of 1054 were never mentioned.

Despite the events of 1054 in Constantinople, the East was looked upon as composed of a variety of distinct churches, Orthodox and otherwise, requiring submission in one form or another to a reformed Roman papacy as defined by Leo IX (1049-1054) and Gregory VII (1073-1085). There was no question of the Orthodox being out of communion with Rome, however. The Normans of south Italy, a major portion of the crusaders, albeit Roman Christians, saw the Orthodox East as just another area into which to expand and establish kingdoms as they had elsewhere.[17]

It was the First Crusade which brought the Orthodox and dissident eastern Christians face to face with Latin Christians for the first time in numbers large enough to create the hostile generalities by which both sides began to live. The nature of the reformed papacy was brought home to the Orthodox easterners. How does a Latin Christian, faithful to a reformed papacy, treat the Orthodox? Such a problem became an issue after the crusaders' conquests. Meetings with the crusaders, particularly the Normans, often became confrontations, during which the westerners made no or little distinction between the Christians and the infidels, especially since they all tended to look alike. The issues, however, were not doctrinal but territorial, customary, and structural. The crusaders tended to see all eastern Christians in the same category — dissidents from Roman jurisdictions — which determined legitimacy in terms of jurisdiction rather than doctrine.

It is of note that Islam had traditionally treated Christians and Jews under its hegemony with liberality and kindness, unlike western Christians who had treated both Muslims and dissident, e.g., Orthodox Christians, with disdain and scorn, if not persecution.[18] The Muslims, generally tolerant of their Christian subjects, in response to the crusaders, began to brutalize peasants, pilgrims, churches, and shrines.[19] It was these "abominations" which the western pilgrims reported back in Europe and which fed crusading fervor.[20]

The Crusaders at the Walls

After the capture of Antioch from Yaghi Sinyan, the Franks were in turn besieged by the slow-moving Kerboga of Mosul. The siege of Kerboga in autumn 1098 so demoralized the crusaders inside the walls of Antioch that they had difficulty responding to the call to defend themselves. Adding to the discouragement was the yet unoccupied citadel at the city's heart. One of the things that inspired the tired and bored crusaders, as well as the Orthodox, Armenian, and Jacobite Christians, were the various visions and signs that struck the crusading armies. All sorts of events became signs! In this context occurred the famous dream of Peter Bartholomew who saw St. Andrew telling him where to locate the Holy Lance, which had pierced Christ's side, buried under the floor of the Cathedral.[21] Similarly, and not without producing some jealousy on the part of Peter Bartholomew, was the vision of the priest Stephen of Valence of Christ himself, who urged repentance and fasting to defeat the troops of Kerboga outside the walls and the Citadel inside the city where

Yajhi Sinyan, the emir of Antioch, and his Turkish troops, were holding out.

Adhemar du Puy, the papal legate and titular leader of the crusade,[22] accepted Stephen's vision over that of Peter's, probably because he had recalled seeing the "original" Lance in Constantinople, where the French and Norman crusaders had met earlier in 1097.[23] The interesting aspect of the exchange between Christ and Stephen was its affirmation that the leader of the crusading armies was a bishop, referring to the venerable and brilliant Adhemar du Puy. Adhemar, using Stephen's vision as a rallying point for the soldiers, urged all to stay on and finish the fight for Antioch, most being eager, as might be expected, to move on to Jerusalem.

Adhemar extracted a promise to finish the Antiochian phase of the venture and the city was finally taken on June 27-28, 1098, with Adhemar carrying what he apparently knew to be the bogus "holy lance" into battle against Kerboga, besieging the walls.[24] Who carried "the lance" is debated. The *Chanson d'Antioche* affirming that Adhemar carried it and the *Gesta Francorum* affirming Raymond of Aguilers.[25] The crusaders tended to be ruthless and bloody in completing their battles. After the victory over Kerboga of Mosul, the crusaders sacked the Turkish camp and killed large numbers of people. The Syrian (Jacobite) and the Armenian Christians joined in the massacre in the rural areas, slaying retreating Turks.[26] Once the citadel was captured within the city, the Turks were allowed to leave and many converted, joining Bohemond's army.[27]

Bohemond, the Norman duke of south Italy, however, had his own agenda, and was the first to agree and the most eager to stay on, ready to seize jurisdiction over Antioch as soon as Emperor Alexios of Constantinople (1081-1118) defaulted on his agreement to support the crusaders in exchange for the restitution of all of Byzantine lands occupied by the Seljuks.[28] In order to enhance his position and secure his hold on Antioch, Bohemund actually convinced a goodwill contingent of Byzantine troops to return home after hinting that Frankish animosity could result in a massacre.[29] The conquest of Antioch was complete by June 28, 1098 and by January, 1099, the crusaders were moving on to Fatimid-held Jerusalem.[30] Bohemund stayed behind and the Jerusalem party was led by Raymond of Toulouse.[31] Contrary to this was the Norman desire for a principality at Antioch, but Adhemar, the conscience of the crusade, urged them on to their goal, Jerusalem, in a speech almost worthy of Henry V at Agincourt.[32]

This desire was virtually compulsive Norman behavior, behavior that made them one of the most aggressive and outstanding peoples of the Middle Ages, both western and eastern. If there is teleology in history, then the Normans "had to have kingdoms" and managed to establish them in Scandinavia, France, England, Italy, Sicily, and the Levant, with a major, albeit unsuccessful, thrust in the Balkans during the period under consideration. Bohemund had little desire to move on to Jerusalem.

The crusaders' victory was proof of God's good will and particularly of Bohemond's deserving leadership. All of Antioch was once again in Christian hands after being captured by the Seljuks in 1084; would it be returned to the Byzantines as had been promised by the famous crusaders' oath[33] to Alexios I in Constantinople? The Normans were more than ready to put aside Byzantine claims to both political and ecclesiastical hegemonies in Syria.[34]

Two Points of View

The Byzantines had at best a weak notion of fighting and killing "for the faith." Diplomacy was more their style and so the pejorative term "byzantine" came to be applied to *indirect* maneuvering to accomplish an end. Even in the case of the more aggressive Nicephoros Phocas (963-969) and John Tzmisces (969-976), the closest the Byzantine Empire came to the crusading mentality in the tenth century was content to regain Antioch and accept nominal suzerainty over Jerusalem and Palestine.

Antioch held a completely exceptional and unique place in Byzantine political ecclesiology; without understanding the different place of Antioch in eastern and western thought one can neither understand the Byzantine reaction to Bohemond's "illegal" establishment of a principality at Antioch, nor their nonchalance regarding the political status of Jerusalem.[35] Despite of the belief that the Byzantines were infatuated by the idea of the "Holy Land," very little time and attention are devoted to it in Byzantine literature and politics.[36] For instance, in the seventh century, Heraclios cried over the loss of Antioch to the Arabs and not over the loss of Jerusalem: "Farewell, O Syria, and what an excellent country this is for the enemy."[37]

Popular imagination, rooted in the idea of the Holy Land, did the real work of inspiring western crowds of peasants and lords. There was not only a different approach to the idea of the "Holy Land," but to the "Holy War." Modern literature on both subjects fails to note this distinction between East and West, without which we cannot understand the Byzantine position regarding, and their reaction to, the occupation of Antioch in 1084 by the Seljuk Turks, as well as Alexios' distrust of the Normans and Bohemond, in particular, given their track record in Sicily, south Italy, and the Balkans. It also explains Byzantine lack of enthusiasm for Jerusalem and failure to commit any men and materiel, in spite of Alexios' earlier promise to supply both.[38]

The ideology and theology of the Latin West and the Byzantine East regarding Palestine was radically different. Wilken's work on Jerusalem is an example of the failure to recognize this distinction. The Byzantines, while having an obsession with relics and the tangible manifestations of holiness, were not obsessed with Palestine to the point of crusade. The idea of the "crusade" or "holy war" was rooted in a developed idea of the land as holy. The idea of Palestinian "holy places" came to its fullest expression in the West rather than in the Byzantine Christian East.[39] Alexios wanted two things: Anatolia and the God-guarded City of the East, Antioch, if only for psychological and emotional reasons. In this he was in the tradition of Heraclios, Nicephoros, and John Tzmisces.

The idea of the Holy Land and, in general, the "holy war" was in the tradition of the Latin West and the Latin fathers at the Council of Piacenza paid no attention to the canonical and imperial legislation against soldiers receiving communion or clergy entering battle.

Charlemagne had forbidden clergy to fight in battle but this canon was essentially ignored.[40] The Byzantines had a radically different conception of the Levant and its value, as well as the "holy war." The attitude had less to do with ecclesiology than with culture.

It was Emperor Heraclios (610-641) who came closest to being a Byzantine "crusader," an advocate of a "holy war," and seeker after the "holy land." His lamentation for Antioch we have already quoted, but his concern for Jerusalem, the Holy Cross, and Byzantine hegemony in the area led to a never-ending struggle with the Persians and Arabs.[41] The next major period of the *reconquesta* was the late tenth century, with the "crusading" emperors Nicephoros Phocas and John Tzmisces. It was Nicephoros Phocas who attempted to have all soldiers falling in battle with the Muslims declared a martyr for the faith! It was the Church, in the person of Patriarch Polyeuctos, which absolutely refused the suggestion as blasphemous.[42] Neither of these emperors, however, was obsessed with the Holy Land, or Jerusalem; they were obsessed with Antioch and Syria![43]

The Christians of the East

The crusaders treated the Orthodox as if they were in communion with the Church of Rome; they did not so treat the Jacobites, Maronites, Nestorians, or Armenians. The crusaders, however, wanted to see the Orthodox as heretics, even though there was no formal or effective schism in place. Psychologically the easterners and westerners were different; they looked different, they celebrated and sang differently, they ate differently, and looked more like the Turks and Fatimids whom they were sent to drive out of the Holy Land. The crusaders defeated the Muslim Turks in June 1098; they were not, however, trusted by the Syrians and there was little sympathy for the Franks.[44] The Franks tended to distrust anyone who was different. This, however, did not stop Anna Comnena from praising the bravery of the Normans and Bohemond, but they were barbarians nonetheless![45]

The native Christians could not be trusted from the Frank's point of view, and the indigenous population had little sympathy for the "barbaric" Franks. One need only try to see the Crusades from an Arab Muslim point of view to get the clear impression that they were being invaded by barbarians; they made the same impression on the Christian population.[46]

The westerners were not predisposed to make subtle distinctions among populations they were invading. The pre-crusading movements of Germany and France had been used to release political and emotional pressure, suppressing those who did not confess the Roman faith. Typical of this tendency towards *cleansing* got out of hand in 1073 when a Burgundian crusade combated the Maures in Spain. Pope Alexander II had ordered the Spanish bishops to protect the Jews against these early crusaders, who had confused them with the Muslim population.[47]

Similarly, the episode of the German crusaders en route to Constantinople is particularly instructive to our purpose for what was to happen in Antioch. It expressed itself among minor groups such as those of Volkmar and Gottschalk who sought "vengeance" for the death of Christ and killed off whole Jewish communities, even burning episcopal palaces of bishops who opposed the killing.[48] By the time they reached Bulgaria, they were wasting the Orthodox Christian populations.[49] They made no distinction between Orthodox and heretic.[50]

The westerners, moderated by Adhemar du Puy, confused the relationship among the various Christian groups and maintained a natural disdain for a civilization that was superior to them; everything that was Greek was, in principle, bad.[51] The Greeks returned the feelings. There was little hope for any sort of ecclesiastical settlement that would last in Antioch. It was this hostility, mitigated only by the integrity of Adhemar, which put an end to Orthodox episcopacy and undermined Hamilton's thesis that the Orthodox were recognized as members of the Church of Rome, unlike Jacobites, Maronites, and Armenians.[52] They were recognized as Catholic Christians because the papacy needed them, and the emperor who was their patron while they were under Turkish-Muslim domination.[53]

While Alexios tried to reach agreements with rulers in the West, whether Pope Gregory VII or Robert of Flanders, to save Anatolia, the average and uneducated crusaders, especially without the thoughtful leadership of an Adhemar du Puy, were likely to see every one as an infidel. For the simple, the world was divided between the faithful and the infidel.[54]

The pre-disposition was there to kill haphazardly any dissident or perceived dissident these pre-crusaders found en route or on location.[55] It came to be directed against not just the persecutors of Christians, as the Muslims, but against those who did not profess the faith of the Roman Church. It was only a matter of time before Antioch would fall into the hands of the followers of the reformed papacy, despite the absence of an identifiable schism.

The Taking of the City

Who could the westerners trust? To whom would they turn the city over? Who would control the Church? Thanks to the pious, sensible, and astute Adhemar du Puy,[56] the crusaders' hostility towards the local Christian population was kept under control. Clearly, as long as Adhemar was alive the Orthodox Chalcedonians were in full and complete communion with the Church of Rome, with legitimate clergy in Syria; this clergy, in addition, had jurisdiction over Latin settlers, pilgrims, and crusaders![57] The Church of Antioch was, for Adhemar, the Catholic Church in Syria. While Hamilton sees these as *de jure,* it seems a more likely argument that the *legitimacy* of the Orthodox Churches was *de facto,* rooted in papal need for support for its new-found universality.[58]

After the taking of the city, Chalcedonian Patriarch John was released from prison, where he had been placed by the Seljuk emir Yaghi Sinyan. John IV Oxites and Symeon of Jerusalem, exiled in Cyprus since 1095,[59] were Greeks, like most patriarchs of Antioch and Jerusalem after the Muslim occupation, and in general disliked Roman practices and customs. Bohemond did not trust the Syrian Chalcedonians; in his mind, all eastern Christians were simply non-Romans! The members of the First Crusade were as shocked by the

Byzantines and the Orthodox customs and practices as the Orthodox were shocked by the Latins. The majority of the Christians to be encountered were Orthodox, whether Greek or Arab, since the Jacobites, Maronites, Nestorians, and Armenians were self-contained communities, unlike the Orthodox who had connection directly to Constantinople. This placed them in a qualitatively different situation that had little to do with theology or ecclesiology and a lot to do with power.

In ecclesiastical affairs, Adhemar respected the rights of the Orthodox patriarch of Jerusalem. Hamilton's argument is simple: the Chalcedonian Orthodox Church, in communion with Constantinople, was a "Catholic Church" and therefore not subject to persecution. On the other hand, neither was it left alone, because as a Catholic Church, in contradistinction to the Jacobites, Maronites, Armenians, and Nestorians, it was not allowed to maintain its own hierarchy. This was a subtle though important distinction at the upper end of the ecclesiastical hierarchy, given the fact that the bishop was, for the crusading lords, an administrative and even military official, which he was not for the Orthodox.[60]

The Clerical Hierarchy

The position of the Latin clergy at Antioch under the terms of Adhemar's settlement was analogous to that of the Latin clergy of Jerusalem and Constantinople who had served the needs of western merchants, residents, and pilgrims from the early part of the century. The Latins observed their own rite but acknowledged the canonical authority of the Orthodox patriarchs and bishops. In the case of Antioch, there was no other solution possible, given the political precondition of the oaths taken in Constantinople and Urban II's policies.

In July 1098, Alexios was invited to come to Antioch and take possession. Up to this point the crusade had apparently worked successfully.

Papal policy was clear, albeit never put in writing by either Urban II or his friend Adhemar; the Orthodox hierarchy was to be left in place. Adhemar's treatment of Patriarch John IV Oxites gives further indication of papal policy. At this stage, the crusaders were working in conjunction with the emperor, and, as a corollary, with the Orthodox Church. One of the weaknesses in Hamilton's brilliant work is his failure to see this unique connection to Constantinople as fundamental to the status of the Orthodox Church in a hostile environment. The appointment of a Latin bishop in an Orthodox patriarchate was not in itself a cause of schism, provided he acknowledged, as bishop of Albara, the authority of the patriarchate. In addition, he failed to take account of the appointment of Latin bishops based on political and military necessity, appointments having nothing to do with doctrine or papal jurisdiction. It, however, gave the appearance of a schism.

Bohemund of Tarantum, the Norman leader of the crusade, held on to Antioch, and was the leader of the anti-Byzantine policy that spelled ruin for the existing papal intentions, especially after the death of Adhemar du Puy. Adhemar's premature death on August 1, 1098, put an end to any real cooperation with or acceptance of the Orthodox hierarchy by the western crusaders.

In the principality of Antioch, the Normans began to set up a society like that in the West, the Latin bishops acting as administrators, appointments, for instance, were based on the bishop's role as a political and feudal administrator. In the Orthodox and Byzantine East there was no such need, lay civil service had been a long and well-established tradition.

In the minds of Bohemond and the crusaders, the Orthodox were to become Latin Catholics, subject to the papacy, and a series of new dioceses were created which helped to demonstrate this reality.[61] In September 1098, this first occurred when Raymond of Toulouse captured the important city of Albara, southwest of Antioch. Peter of Narbonne (1098-1110)[62] was appointed by Raymond of Toulouse and consecrated bishop, with half the city and its territory as a fief.

Although Peter was consecrated by John Oxites,[63] his appointment was based on political and military necessity. The appointment did act as a focal point for opposition to the settlement of ecclesiastical affairs at Antioch. Raymond's chaplain did say he was happy to have Latin bishops handle affairs of the Latins. For many crusaders, especially Bohemond, Alexios' abandoning them at Antioch during the siege of Kerboga absolved them from any oath to the emperor.

Albara was significant because it was the first among many new dioceses created as Latin sees within the Antiochian Orthodox Patriarchate. This was not a replacement of an Orthodox Arab or Greek bishop by a Latin bishop, but the immediate appointment of a Latin bishop to administer a new diocese and strategic city en route to Jerusalem, holding the Levantine littoral secure. Following this pattern, the Franks often set up entirely new ecclesiastical organizations where none had existed before. The chief innovation of the Franks was in the dioceses of Syria. The Franks consolidated several Orthodox sees into one Latin see. Aleppo was another diocese created by Bohemund I, not by a patriarch, for political reasons since it was so strategic and played a political and military defense of the crusader state.

In Edessa, Baldwin needed a Latin bishop to oversee the city when he was on campaign in 1098. In 1099, he appointed Benedict.[64] A parallel hierarchy was slowly and methodically growing for political and military, not doctrinal or ecclesiological, reasons.

The conflict became clear after the death of Adhemar when Bohemund sent a letter to Urban II in which Urban is urged to come east and take over his "rightful" patrimony, the Church of Antioch, correctly perceived as the first see of Peter. The appointment of a Latin bishop in an Orthodox patriarchate was not in itself a cause of schism, provided he acknowledged, as bishop of Albara, the authority of the patriarchate. Again, the perception of a schism is as powerful as a clear statement of excommunication. As in Constantinople in 1089, something was perceived to be amiss between the Latin Church and her eastern "sisters."

Urban II appointed Daimbert of Pisa as Adhemar's successor. He reached Syria in September 1099. Not sharing Urban's philosophy or Adhemar's sympathy for the Greek and Orthodox Church,[65] he was hostile to Alexios, having heard rumors of his betrayal of the crusaders.[66] He proceeded to increase the number of Latin hierarchs and, at the request of Baldwin of Edessa and Bohemund of Antioch, consecrated four Latin bishops to sees in Northern Syria — Benedict to Edessa, Roger to Tarsus, Bartholomew to Mamistra, and Bernard to Artah. Since all of these dioceses were in the Patriarchate of Antioch, Daimbert, as papal legate, had exercised supra-metropolitan jurisdiction, and had implicitly rejected the claims of John IV, who was simply ignored.[67]

John Oxites' position became untenable and the situation and crusaders' policy became more directed at Latinization. The situation was all the more complicated by the fact that war broke out in spring 1100, between Bohemond and Alexios, not an unexpected event as the Normans still wanted the Balkan peninsula and control of northern Syria. Bohemund could not trust a Byzantine Greek as head of the Church of Antioch and "second in command" should Bohemond be forced to leave the city.

In the summer of 1100, John retreated to his metochion in Constantinople. The Franks interpreted this as a resignation, freeing them to make their own appointment. A schism was in the works that could have been avoided had Adhemar and Urban lived. Bohemond wrote to Urban II:

> What, therefore, seems more proper in all the world than that you, who are the father and head of the Christian religion, should come to the original and chief city where the Christian name was first used, and bring to a conclusion on your own behalf the war that is yours? For we have beaten the Turks and heathen, but we do not know how to defeat the heretics, the Greeks, the Armenians, and Syrian Jacobites. We, therefore, continually entreat you, dearest father, that you, our father and ruler, will come to the city which is yours, and that you, who are Vicar of St. Peter, will sit on his throne and that you will find in us obedient sons acting, acting rightly in all things, and that you will be able to root out and destroy all heresies, of whatever kind they are, by your authority and strength.[68]

Bernard of Valence, formerly chaplain to Adhemar, was appointed patriarch and consecrated by Daimbert. The Antiochian Chalcedonian bishops chose John V (1106-1137), in absentia. With the appointment of a Latin patriarch, Orthodox patriarchs of Antioch were appointed through 1260 and took up residence in exile in Constantinople. A schism was in place. A parallel hierarchy came into existence in 1100.[69] The ecclesiastical significance of the events of the summer of 1054 in Constantinople were insignificant in comparison to the creation of a parallel or separate Latin hierarchy within the Patriarchate of Antioch and eventually in Jerusalem.

The appointment of Bernard of Valence is interesting since it demonstrates the great gap that existed between the pope and his advisors, on the one hand, and the crusaders, on the other, about the nature of the Church. The crusaders were eager to satisfy their own agendas, agendas blocked by papal interpretation of the Orthodox as Catholics. The definition was bogus, used by the crusaders as long as it served their interests: the support of Constantinople. Hamilton misses the utilitarian point; while each of the other Christian groups, Jacobites, Nestorians, Maronites, and Armenians, was self-contained, it was the Orthodox who had connections, potentially useful to crusader policy in Constantinople. It was this Constantinopolitan connection that made the difference. Once it was perceived as useless, then the catholicity of the Orthodox became expendable.

It was, however, the need for military and administrative support for the newly-forming crusading "kingdoms" that forced the appointment of Latin bishops to established and newly created dioceses where they might serve as administrative as well as military support for the crusaders. A schism was effectively in place. For the first time, we have a schism that can be identified and dated. The pope ratified the appointment of a Latin patriarch by sending him a pallium (Greek = omophorion). Bernard's successor, Ralph, did not wait for papal approval of his position and simply wore the pallium directly from the altar.[70]

After this, Greek and Orthodox titularies were appointed from Constantinople and usually remained in the imperial capital, where life was more congenial. Most of these appointees were of little consequence and of little note, spending their time bored at Constantinople, participating in ceremonies, and conspiring in the capital, usually against the ecumenical patriarch. By 1165, however, Manuel I Comnenos (1143-1180) managed, after a major military victory, to negotiate the restoration of an Orthodox patriarch to Antioch, Athanasios II, a Constantinopolitan.[71]

The people of Antioch hardly took note and he died in 1170 in an earthquake, only to be replaced by a Latin. (In general the Orthodox faithful of the patriarchate were unaffected; indeed, in the rural regions Orthodox population and clergy were often left alone. Who their bishops were often made little or no difference to them, having primarily political and military significance for the Latin kingdom.)

Orthodox parish priests and monasteries retained religious freedom and were in full communion with the Orthodox Church, though subject to the canonical authority of the Latin bishops. No conclusions can be drawn from this fact, except that confusion allows us to establish no historical precedent. Certainly the Latin hierarchy made no effort to Latinize the Orthodox faithful or clergy and were content, for practical reasons, to simply exercise political and military jurisdiction when necessary. They were prepared to leave in office any cleric who did not occupy a central place in secular government or constitute a threat to their security and who exercised no spiritual authority over the Franks.

The papacy and the crusaders did play free and easy with the traditional boundaries of the Patriarchate of Antioch, leaving few decisions to the patriarch as to which dioceses actually belonged to Antioch as Jerusalem expanded into Beirut, Acre, and Sidon. Pascal's grant of all bishoprics within the Kingdom of Jerusalem to the Patriarchate of Jerusalem had upset the balance of the traditional structure of the eastern patriarchates. Jerusalem's essentially honorary position in Byzantine political ecclesiology was radically altered by the crusading notion of the Holy Land and the Holy War.

By July, 1138, Innocent II had formally transferred the obedience of Tyre to Jerusalem.[72] The implications of these transfers are clear: Antioch did not have the same place in crusading politics and mythology as it had in the Byzantine. The transfer was clear proof that Jerusalem held an emotional place in the crusader's minds which it could never have in the Byzantine. For ecclesiastical purposes, the integrity of the Antiochian See had been clearly violated.

If anything of note happened in 1054, it was not recorded or effective in consummating a schism between the churches of the East and the West. Far more significant were the identifiable political and military implications of the crusader's establishment of a feudal ecclesiastical structure, involving a parallel hierarchy or an exclusive Latin hierarch, in the venerable and great Church of Antioch and Syria. It was in the East, in Antioch and Syria, in 1100 that an ecclesiastical schism was consummated between the Church of Rome and the Orthodox Churches of the East.

NOTES

[1] George Ostrogorsky, *History of the Byzantine State* (New Brunswick, NJ: Rutgers University Press, 1969), 336-340.

[2] John L. Boojamra, *Church Reform in the Late Byzantine Empire* (Thessalonica, Greece: Patriarchal Institute for Patristic Studies, 1983), 91-96.

[3] Ostrogorsky, 364.

[4] Steven Runciman, *A History of the Crusades* (Cambridge: University Press, reprint 1987), I: 98-99.

[5] Rene Grousset, *The Epic of the Crusades*, translated by Noel Lindsay (New York: Orion Press, 1970), 22-24.

[6] The western notices give little information of Christian churches enroute to battle, but we do have information from Byzantine chroniclers and Michael the Syrian. During the papacy of Innocent III (1196-1216), the Roman Church tried to reach better terms with the different Oriental churches and during the final decades of the occupation tried to keep more detailed records. See Rocjhrade Rose, "Vita of St. Leontios," *Catholic Historical Review,* July 1987.

[7] Ostrogorsky, 337.

[8] A.A. Vasiliev, *History of the Byzantine Empire* (Madison,WI: University of Wisconsin Press, reprint, 1982) II: 475. What is clear is that no sense of schism was founded and that the only real development that can be documented is a sense of "growing apart" and differences in intellectual and customary practices.

[9] Ostrogorsky, 362-364; he actually received assistance from Robert of Flanders. See F. Ganshof, "Robert le Frison et Alexis Comnene," *Byzantion*, 31 (1961): 57-59.

[10] Runciman, *The Eastern Schism* (Oxford: University Press, 1935), 71-72.

[11] Runciman, *Crusades*, 104-105.

[12] Runciman, *Crusades*, 116-120. It is unlikely, as Peter Charanis maintains, that the Byzantine emperor launched a crusade at the request of Urban II; see P. Charanis, "Byzantium, the West, and the Origin of the First Crusade," *Byzantion,* 19 (1949), 17-19. The Byzantines did not have interest in the Holy Land to invite a host of westerners, especially Normans, to cross their territory.

[13] Alexios issued a general invitation to assist eastern Christians in a letter to Robert of Flanders, this tradition source of the First Crusade is reliable as is found in Henri Pirenne, "A propos de la lettre d'Alexis Comnene a Robert le Frison, comte de Flandre," *Revue de l'Instruction Publique (*1907), 225.

[14] Anna Comnena, *The Alexiad of Princess Anna Comnena*, translated by Elizabeth Dawes, 1928 (Reprint, London: Routledge and Kegan Paul, 1967) II: 207.

[15] Ostrogorsky, 342, 357-359; Runciman, *Crusades*, 68-69.

[16] Joan Hussey, "Byzantium and the Crusaders, 1081-1204," in Kenneth Setton, *The History of The Crusades* (Madison, WI: University of Wisconsin, 1969), II: 126.

[17] Timothy Baker, *The Normans* (New York: Collier Press, 1969), 166.

[18] John L. Boojamra, "Christianity in Greater Syria After Islam," *St. Vladimir's Seminary Quarterly,* 35 (1991): 223-241.

[19] Runciman, *Crusades*, 78-79.

[20] Samuel Moffett, *A History of Christianity in Asia* (San Francisco: Harper, 1993), I: 383, 387; the accounts of the activities of the mad Fatimid caliph al-Hakim had inspired a sense of a need for action as early as the second decade of the eleventh century. Al-Hakim and the legends surrounding his mysterious disappearance are the source of the Druze Muslim sect.

[21] *Gesta Francorum et Aliorum Hierosolymitana,* ed. and trans. by R. Hill (London, 1962), IX, 26, 136; as well as Lewis Sumberg, *La Chanson d'Antioche* (Paris: Editions A. et J. Picard, 1968), 285-289.

[22] J. A. Brundage, "Adhemar of Puy: the Bishop and His Critics," *Speculum,* 34, (1959): 201-212.

[23] *Gesta Francorum*, IX, 24, 128-32. See J. Ebersolt, *Les Sanctuaires de Byzance.* (Paris, 1921), 24, 116. Also Runciman, "The Holy Lance Found at Antioch," in *Analecta Bollandiana* (Melanges P. Peeters, 1950), 68: 197-209. No great role accredited to it and it did little to lift the morale of the army. It became important only after the taking of the city.

[24] Only Lewis Sumberg, 293, makes this claim.

[25] *Gesta Francorum,* IX, 28, 146-150.

[26] Sumberg, 306; *Gesta Francorum*, IX, 29, 150-158.

[27] Sumberg, 307.

[28] For a description of the oath-taking, see Runciman, *Crusades*, 151-152.

[29] Grousset, 22.

[30] Runciman, *Crusades*, 272.

[31] Grousset, 28.

32 Sumberg, 307-308.

33 Ostrogorsky, 363.

34 Ostrogorsky, 357-9; the Byzantines were hard-pressed to put together a consistent "foreign policy" that would meet the needs of the empire and Syria.

35 See review by J. L. Boojamra, of Robert Wilken, *The Land Called Holy: Palestine in Christian History and Thought* (New Haven, Conn.: Yale University Press, 1992), in *St. Vladimir's Theological Quarterly*, 38 (1994): 120-124.

36 See Robert L. Wilken, *The Land Called Holy* (New Haven: Yale University Press, 1992), 172 for a typical overstatement on the role of Jerusalem in Byzantine thought; the review of the work by John Boojamra.

37 Quoted in Philip Ḥitti, *Makers of Arab History* (New York: Harper and Row, 1968), 31.

38 Theodore Scutariotes, *Anonymous Chronicle*, ed. K. Sathas, in *Bibliotheca Graeca medii aevi*. (Paris, 1894), 7: 184-185, where there is a description of Alexios' promise to supply support assistance to regain the Holy Sepulchre, yet in the hands of the Seljuks. This the chronicler says was a "heaven-sent pretext" to get their assistance for Anatolia. Quoted in Deno J. Geanakoplos, *Byzantium: Church Society, and Civilization* (Chicago: University of Chicago Press, 1984), 269.

39 See Wilken, 172, where he exagerates this treatment of Jerusalem to the point of claiming that had it not been for the Muslim conquest, Jerusalem would have challenged the ecclesiastical authority of Rome! Wilken, a brilliant scholar, with great sensitivity for the Orthodox Churches, misses this completely; he further claims that a hostile army's occupation of Jerusalem threatened Byzantine liturgy and worship! See Wilken, chapter 6.

40 Boojamra, *Church Reform*, 168 n, 80; John L. Boojamra, *The Church and Social Reform* (New York: Fordham University Press, 1993), 63 n, 45, 64 n, 46. See also C. Erdmann, *Die Entstehung des Kreuzzugsgedankens* (Stuttgart, 1935). Comnena, 256-59, where she describes the movements of armed fighting men, including clergy and bishops, who serve the Eucharist with one hand and carry a bloodied sword with the other.

41 Ostrogorsky, 92-112.

42 Ostorgorsky, 290.

43 For a general treatment of the idea of the Holy War and war, see Boojamra, *Church and Social Reform,* 63 n, 64 n. Also the important Vitalien Laurent, "L'Idee de guerre sainte et la tradition byzantine, *"Revue Historique du Sud-est europeen* 23 (1946): 71-98.

[44] Runciman, *Crusades,* 236.

[45] Comnena, 17, 23.

[46] Amin Maalouf, *The Crusades Through Arab Eyes* (New York: Schocken Books, 1985).

[47] See Sumberg, 146, who quotes the papal document of Mign, P.L. 146, 1387. The rights of Jews were defined for the first time by Pope Callistus II 1119-1124. See Gavin Langmuir, "*Judei nostri* and the Beginning of Capetian Legislation," *Traditio*, 16 (1960): 203-239.

[48] See Jacob Katz, *Exclusiveness and Tolerance: Studies in Jewish-Gentile Relations in Medieval and Modern Times* (New York, 1961); see Sumberg, 146-147, which is filled with references to avenging the Lord's death.

[49] Runciman, *Crusades*, 236.

[50] Sumberg, 147.

[51] Sumberg, 176.

[52] Bernard Hamilton, *The Latin Church in The Crusader States* (London: Variorum, 1980), 1-18.

[53] It is interesting that attacks on Constantinople were part of every crusade's planning process, even before the distraction of the Fourth Crusade by the Venetians trying to collect on unpaid bills. See Sumberg, 177.

[54] See I. Langmuir, "*Judei nostri* and the Beginning of Capetian Legislation," *Traditio*, 16 (1960): 203-239 on the application of crusading principles in Europe before the Council of Clairmont. A trail of blood was left across Europe by the hordes, such as those of Gottschalk and other leading small groups, who murdered numerous Jews in Germany and burned episcopal palaces of bishops who opposed this killing. The Manichaeans were so done away with in Macdeonia.

[55] Occasionally, as the crusading idea degenerated after the First Crusade, it came to serve papal political interests and achieved total bankruptcy as a religious movement, even in the West. See Sumberg, 145-146.

[56] Runciman, *Crusades*, 236.

[57] J.A. Brundage, "Adhemar of Puy: the Bishop and his Critics," *Speculum* 34 (1959): 201-212.

[58] Hamilton, 4.

[59] V. Grumel, *Traite d'Etudes Byzantines, I. La Chronologie* (Paris, 1958), 452.

[60] Hamilton, 9-12.

[61] A conclusion which Hamilton refuses to draw.

[62] Hamilton, 10-11.

[63] *Gesta Francorum*, X, 31; Hill, 75. William of Tyre notes that Bernard of Valence, John IV's Latin successor, did the consecrating; see William of Tyre in *Willelmi Tyrensis Archiepiscopi Chronic,* ed. R. Huygens, (Turnholt, 1986), VII: 8.

[64] Hamilton, 16, 24.

[65] Hamilton, 15.

[66] Daimbert was carried east by a much-needed Pisan fleet, which managed to attack Greek Orthodox islands en route. As archbishop of Pisa he had also to be aware of Constantinople as a competitor of his home town.

[67] Hamilton, 16.

[68] H. Hagenmeyer, ed., *Die Kreuzzugsbriefe aus den Jahren 1088-1100* (Innsbruck, 1901), 141-142. Runciman, *The Eastern Schism*, 102.

[69] William of Tyre VI, 23.

[70] Hamilton, 16-17.

[71] Hussey, 176.

[72] Peter Elburg and John Rowe, *William of Tyre, Historian of the Latin East* (New York: Cambridge University Press, 1984), 119-120.

"THERE WERE ALSO MANY WOMEN THERE:" WOMEN AND THE FOUNDATION OF THE CHURCH
by Susan Ashbrook Harvey

"There were also many women there." With these words, the evangelist Matthew closes the scene of the crucifixion.[1] The words state a situation even as they tell a story: at every moment of Christian history — from the conception and birth of Jesus the Christ, through his ministry and travels, at the scene of his death, at the place of his tomb, at the revelation of his Resurrection — there were also women there.

Nor would this situation change. Gathered in the upper room at the Ascension, in the missionary work of the apostolic period, as evangelists, as consecrated widows and virgins, as deaconesses, and as martyrs; as parish workers, choir members, pilgrims, mothers, and nuns; as scholars, teachers, founders of monastic institutions, hospital workers, workers among the poor and homeless; as devotees and as saints — in the history of Christianity — women are also there.

Yet, if we look more closely at the history of women in the church, difficulties arise at every point. There is much general evidence to tell us, as the evangelist did, that women were there. Beyond the generality, details are too often lacking. More problematic is the nature of the evidence itself. For the most part and for many centuries — especially during the patristic era, the focus of this article — the evidence that survives was written by men. Women's own voices are rarely heard. A tension is often evident between the actions described and the words used to describe them; where there were clashes between cultural expectations and women's vocations, the writings often curtailed the full impact of women's work or omitted their presence altogether.

Nonetheless, the history of women in the church remains a profound witness to the power of faith. In this study, I would like to survey the outlines of what we *can* know about women's presence in the first centuries of Christian history (roughly, up to the seventh century). I will not treat the case of Mary the Theotokos, for her story in Christian history, theology, and devotion is unique and demands a separate study.[2] My concern is to reconstruct the stories, situations and work of early Christian women,[3] with particular reference to the tradition of the greater Syrian Orient.[4] We may lack women's own words by which to tell their history, but that history compels our attention even so.

Women in the New Testament

It is clear from our sources that earliest Christianity was a movement of both women and men, and one that granted women considerable scope for religious activity. In the Gospels, Jesus did not preach specifically on the subject of women, but his actions spoke clearly.[5] He addressed women with the same respect he accorded the men who came to him, as equals and as persons responsible for their own lives in relation to God. Such behavior on his part was sometimes at odds with social convention no less than Jewish religious custom. He spoke respectfully to the Samaritan woman at the well, whose ethnic identity, quite apart from her irregular marital situation, rendered her anathema to Jews.[6] He refused to condemn the woman taken in adultery,[7] or the sinful woman (whose sins are not named in the gospel story).[8] He healed Peter's mother-in-law by touch and accepted the touch of the hemorrhaging woman in order to heal her, despite the violation of Jewish purity codes this involved.[9] He praised Mary of Bethany for having chosen the "better way" over her sister Martha, when she left the traditional women's work of serving men and instead sat attentively among the followers as a disciple.[10]

The Gospels tell us that women reacted to Jesus' ministry by heeding his call to discipleship. Jesus declared that those who would be his disciples must leave their homes and families, their livelihood and worldly ties, to follow him.[11] Women responded to that call. They were part of the group that traveled with Jesus and they provided much of the financial support for his band of followers.[12] They participated as disciples rather than as serving women.[13]

Mary Magdalene

The most prominent example among the women disciples is Mary Magdalene, who is called in Orthodox tradition, "Equal to the Apostles." The Gospels preserve for us only four pieces of information about this woman named Mary, from the town of Magdala: first, that Jesus healed her of a great sickness;[14] second, that she became his disciple and travelled with Jesus and the other disciples;[15] third, that she stood at the foot of the cross at his death;[16] fourth, that she went to his tomb, and there became the first person to see and know the Risen Lord.[17] In these four things she was not the only woman disciple, but in the final scenes, at the cross and at the empty tomb, Mary of Magdala's name is first among the women.

Of all those mentioned in the Gospels, Mary Magdalene alone is presented as the one who truly fulfilled Jesus' stark call to discipleship. She alone of the women is named by herself— Mary of Magdala — with no identifying details about her family, her marital status, or her social class. Indeed, we know absolutely nothing about her life situation. Other disciples are named in relation to someone else: for example, James and John were the sons of Zebedee, Simon and Andrew were brothers (and Simon had a mother-in-law whom Jesus healed). The women are named in relation to their husbands, fathers, brothers, or sons: Mary the betrothed of Joseph and mother of Jesus, Mary and Martha the sisters of Lazarus, Mary the mother of Clopas, Joanna the wife of Chuza Herod's steward. By contrast, Mary of Magdala is identified only by the place she left in order to follow Jesus.

More than this, Mary Magdalene was the only disciple who remained publicly faithful to Jesus throughout the gospel acounts. The men lapsed or fell away. Judas betrayed his Lord, Peter denied him;

in fear, the men left Jesus alone at the cross, hid themselves behind closed doors, and refused to believe the news of the Resurrection. Thomas refused the witness of his own eyes until the Risen Christ bid him to touch his wounds.[18] But Mary Magdalene was there at the cross and at the tomb, despite the dangers of being known as a follower of a condemned criminal. According to the gospel of John, when she encountered the Risen Lord in the garden outside the empty tomb, she believed even when he forbade her to touch him.[19] Her report to the other disciples was at first dismissed as foolish.[20] Constancy and singularity of purpose are the sole characteristics of her gospel presentation.

Mary Magdalene is not mentioned again anywhere else in the New Testament. A few scattered references from other early writings, apocryphal accounts not included in the canonical scriptures, suggest that Mary continued to live with the other disciples, and that she held particular authority as a teacher because of her unique relationship with Jesus. These accounts indicate conflict within the apostolic community over the issue of authority, with Peter especially opposing the right of a woman to teach, and others supporting Mary's place among them.[21] These apocryphal stories, like the gospel accounts, end without telling us what happened to Mary Magdalene. Silence surrounds her work.

So troubling was the loss of Mary Magdalene's story even for the early church, that people gave her a story. Where other women disciples in the Gospels were unnamed, people took these unnamed women to be Mary of Magdala. She became the sinful woman who washed the feet of Jesus with her tears and wiped them with her hair, and whose many sins Jesus forgave because she had loved much. Although the gospel story never identifies the particular sins of this woman, in time it was decided that Mary Magdalene must have been a prostitute. This legend grew especially in the West, where by the sixth century her story was fused in part with that of Mary of Egypt, so that Mary Magdalene became the great penitent harlot of Christian tradition.[22] In the western version of her legend, she served as missionary in France before turning to the solitary life of penance in the desert.

Although Orthodox Christianity never accepted this elaborate legendary portrait of Mary, and indeed holds no official teaching of Mary as a penitent harlot nor as the sinful woman of the gospel account, yet in popular tradition the identification can still be found.[23] Nonetheless, in granting her the title "Equal to the Apostles," Orthodoxy has chosen to stress Mary's role as the first to receive the Risen Lord and the first to preach the Resurrection. It is her Paschal role as first among the Myrrh-bearing Women that marks Mary Magdalene's presence for the Eastern Church.

Mary Magdalene presents the model for all subsequent Christian holy women. Christ's call to discipleship was taken to be the defining call, regardless of political or social dictates; it was a call demanded equally of all believers, women and men. There is evidence both inside and outside the canonical New Testament that women not only received the Good News of salvation through Christ, but were also active participants in the emerging church. Their houses were offered as house churches; they held leadership positions in the earliest Christian communities; they assisted Paul in his missionary efforts (he referred to certain of the women as his "co-workers"); they were teaching, prophesying, and sometimes baptizing converts.[24]

But our sources also indicate a strain imposed by this situation, between the kinds of work women perceived to be their vocations or callings and the normative social and political structures that defined their daily lives in the Roman Empire. The New Testament letters, for example, with injunctions that women be silent and submissive,[25] conflict with other Christian sources earlier, contemporary with, and subsequent to those letters, portraying women as active and authoritative agents within the growing Christian body — women such as Priscilla (Prisca), who taught with Aquila and corrected the false understanding of Apollos.[26]

Although the church insisted from the start that women and men stood equal before the Lord — citing Paul's statement that in Christ there is neither male nor female[27] — this teaching was not used to question the existing Roman social order wherein women's roles and positions were tightly constrained.[28] At the same time, the urgency surrounding the work of earliest Christianity — of setting the church on its firm foundation, of gaining converts and instructing the faithful, of gaining a legitimate place in the hostile political order — required all the help that could be had. Normative social roles could not be given precedence over the searing need to establish the church in circumstances both dire and dangerous. The early church needed missionaries and it needed believers willing to declare their faith even to the point of death as martyrs; the two roles were often one and the same. Women no less than men rose to this challenge.

Martydom

From its inception with Jesus' own death on charges of political insurrection, Christianity was an illegal religion in the Roman Empire, punishable by death.[29] Because it was classed as a crime of treason, the death penalty was generally an aggravated one, accompanied by torture.[30] Outright persecutions happened sporadically — some governing officials were more lenient than others — but martyrdom was a constant possibility for every Christian until at last legalization came under the Emperor Constantine in the year 313.

It is important to understand that the context of these persecutions was not one of religious decadence, as is so often portrayed in stories and legends. Rather, the Roman Empire was a vast entity held together by an intricate webbing of religious and political structures. The exclusive claims of Christianity did not allow for the religious tolerance required by the Roman polytheistic system.[31] Judaism had been granted a special legal exemption for its beliefs, but this was not extended to Christianity.

For roughly the first three hundred years of Christianity's existence, then, the public interrogation, torture, and death of Christians were often the experiences that framed and defined church communities. The church remembers this traumatic period of foundation in the Acts of the Martyrs.[32] These accounts carry harrowing portraits of the women who also died for the faith.

To mention but a few: around the year 112, Pliny the Younger, governor of Bithynia, tortured two unnamed slavewomen deaconesses to death when they would not admit Christianity to be a crime.[33] In 117, the slavewoman Blandina in the city of Lyons endured tortures for such an extended period that even her torturers wearied and wished she would die.[34] At the turn of the third century, around the year 203, the young noblewoman Perpetua in the city of Carthage gave up her nursing infant son to face the executioners with her fellow Christians; her companion the slavewoman Felicitas gave birth in prison and released her newborn to the care of others so that she, too, could die with her companions. The Roman audience in the stadium was horrified at the sight of such young mothers being put to death; in the end Perpetua had to guide the unsteady hand of her own executioner's sword.[35]

The company of martyrs from Roman persecution is filled with named and unnamed women such as these.[36] When legalization finally came within the Roman Empire, Christians beyond those borders often found themselves endangered in persecutions provoked by international political tensions. The fourth century Acts of the Persian Martyrs and the sixth century eyewitness reports of the Christians martyred in the Arabian city of Najrān contain strikingly fierce accounts of women who died for the faith. To cite but a few: Martha in Karka d-Ledan, who refused an offer of marriage that would have saved her life; the noblewoman Ruhm of Najrān whose face had never been seen in public before, but who took her daughters to the town square to join her in martyrdom rather than face compromise; the women of Najrān who jumped into the fires in which their husbands were dying.[37]

The situation of persecution and martyrdom allowed women a dramatically public role in the propagation of the faith. Necessity required leadership from all who could offer it. Moreover, the church glorified those who died, women and men alike without distinction, as the true saints of the community. Persecution ironically provided women with prominent roles of authority and deep veneration by the faithful. That situation was one of two factors significantly affecting the place of women in the early church. The second was Christianity's exaltation of virginity as a religious vocation.[38]

Celibacy

Marriage had been the only life available for women in the ancient world.[39] In advocating the celibate life of service to God, the apostle Paul may well have been motivated by pragmatism.[40] But early Christians heeded his words together with the model of Christ's own singularity: singlehearted devotion to God allowed service unimpeded by any other demands. Furthermore, the marriage parables of the Heavenly Kingdom gave rise to the image of Christ as the Heavenly Bridegroom and each believer as His betrothed.[41]

The vocation of virginity in the early church was not a denial of sexuality, but a redirection of it — sexual faithfulness to one's true spouse, Christ. At the same time, there were enormous cultural implications to the meaning of celibacy. Across the Mediterranean world, marriage and families were the means of perpetuating society: children were the physical establishment of a future generation; inheritance and family financial dealings were the means by which the economic and political structures maintained themselves. There was no place for the unmarried.

In the Persian Empire as well as the Roman Empire, the Christian vocation of virginity evoked tremendous distress among non-Christians; in both empires, marriage was a sacred institution, representing religious order no less than social, political, and economic order. Virginity therefore signified the removal of one's body from this "divinely" instituted and all-pervasive order, rendering one's physical life utterly beyond the domain of the state.[42] It was because Christians paid little apparent heed to the future of this world that Romans held them in disdain. Christians, however, had their eyes focused not on the future welfare of the Roman Empire or any other political entity, but on the Eschaton.

For women, virginity held profound practical implications. Paul had noted the necessary distractions when life involves a spouse and children to care for, thereby suggesting that virginity was a more expedient route for service to God. From a strictly physical point of view, the nature of ancient medical technology was such that pregnancy was a dangerous condition. Mortality rates in childbirth and in early childhood were high. Freed from these responsibilities and dangers, women who chose to serve the church through a life of virginity also found themselves freed for entirely new vistas of activity.

Like Mary Magdalene, the celibate Christian woman defined herself not by a relationship to father, brother, husband, or son — the relationships governing her legal situation in the Roman Empire — but solely in relation to God. As a result, women could and did travel as missionaries and later as pilgrims. They could and did develop rich friendships with men, based not on the sexual codes of a marriage-oriented culture, but on common faith and devotion to God. The spiritual friendships between Christian women and men became a hallmark of early Christianity, made possible by valuing the individual apart from her or his sexual identity.[43] At the same time, virginity bestowed considerable honor on its adherents; here, too, women benefited by the respect and admiration accorded the celibate life.

Early Saints

The impact of virginity on the lives of Christian women is vividly demonstrated in the "Acts of Thecla," the legend of Paul's famed companion and co-worker.[44] Thecla was a young noblewoman betrothed for marriage, who was converted to Christianity and to the life of virginity when the apostle Paul preached in her town of Iconium. To the horror of her family and fiancé, she left them to follow Paul and assist in his work of evangelization.

Thecla set off as missionary, sometimes in the company of Paul and sometimes on her own, eventually baptizing herself. She survived attacks, imprisonments and tortures, on charges of Christian faith as well as impiety against the sacred institution of the family. She finally escaped altogether when the women of Antioch contrived to subdue the wild beasts to whom she had been thrown for the death penalty — the women lulled the animals to sleep with a massive shower of flowers and spices. Despite severe hardships, Thecla carried on her work. Legend claims thousands of converts by her efforts.

Her story identifies her virginity as a physical condition in measure of her soul's purity of faith, but further as the situation that allowed her the freedom to travel as missionary. Unlatched from the obligations of family and society, she was free to heed her holy calling. Orthodoxy has granted Thecla the highest titles possible for a woman saint: she is hailed as "Apostle," "Equal to the Apostles," "Great Martyr," and "First Martyr." Her cult grew during the patristic period to become one of the most prominent devotions of Byzantine and Christian Arab cultures.[45] To this day, she remains the subject of pilgrimage and intense piety, not only in the Middle East but also at her shrine at the Antiochian Village in Ligonier, Pennsylvania.

Thecla's model can be seen in the accounts of the great virgin martyrs of the church, figures such as Barbara, Irene, and Catherine of Alexandria. These three are stories of daughters of nobility, beautiful and learned, who decided for themselves to embrace the Christian faith and who were betrayed by their own families for execution. Catherine's intellectual brilliance destroyed the arguments of the greatest philosophers of the day gathered to debate with her, bringing public humiliation on paganism. Barbara coolly traded witticisms with her tormentors. Irene converted thousands both in Roman territory and in the Persian Empire.

All three died spectacular deaths. All three presented the model of women who chose for themselves the life of Christianity, opposing their families, friends, and legal obligations (for the Roman aristocracy, a weighty matter indeed). They are also presented as women whose choice of virginity freed them for intellectual and theological study of rigorous dimensions — an element portrayed with particular force in Catherine's story, but present for Barbara and Irene as well.[46] In a society that saw little value to the education of women, the Christian vocation of virginity was repeatedly presented as one that enabled women to pursue scholarship at the service of theological ministry, a situation that led to great achievements in the later patristic era once the threat of persecution had passed.

Thecla's model made its impact directly on women's stories and in women's lives. In the legend of St. Eugenia, the saint was converted to Christianity by reading the story of St. Thecla.[47] When Gregory of Nyssa wrote the account of his holy sister, the *Life of St. Macrina*, he noted that Macrina's secret name was Thecla, after the great saint, and that Macrina in imitating Thecla's model became the model for others.[48] Thecla was summoned as model and guide in the epic romance about St Febronia,[49] and in the account of St. Olympias, friend and sustainer of St. John Chrysostom.[50]

The church's glorification and remembrance of its saints meant that stories of holy women as well as holy men were told and retold as time went by. These stories were the constant reminder that women, too, were required for God's work; they provided models for women to follow in their own lives. Stories of Christian holy women were a serious force for social change, teaching women to measure their vocations according to God's will alone and to refuse the trappings of a worldly life that would hinder their ability to fulfill the call to discipleship in whatever form it might take.[51]

In legends, the actions of holy women were spectacular: Thecla outfought men who attacked her and slew wild animals with a single glance; Mary of Egypt levitated and walked on water. In daily life, the work of holy women was no less spectacular (albeit, perhaps less histrionic). Women founded and ran monsteries for both women and men;[52] established and conducted social service networks for whole cities;[53] ran underground railways for religious refugees;[54] fought the Roman Senate[55] and if necessary the emperor himself;[56] were notable scholars[57] and teachers;[58] wore iron chains for ascetic discipline so heavy that men could barely lift them, and followed ascetic regimes so severe that men were jealous.[59]

Sometimes the considerable impact of these women stemmed from high social status and wealth; sometimes women earned their positions of authority and influence by the sheer quality of their spiritual lives.[60] In fifth century Constantinople, St. Matrona's many friends in high places — including two empresses — seem to have been gained by the simple force of her teaching and works.[61] In the sixth century, a young Persian girl ran away from her noble family, changed her name to Susan, and entered a convent in Palestine in poverty and anonymity. Years later, under extreme conditions of religious persecution, Susan was recruited against her will to direct a monastic community of women and men in Egypt: the monks and nuns desired her leadership because of her profound spiritual accomplishments, not because of any knowledge of her privileged past.[62]

More pointedly, the holy woman Euphemia and her daughter Maria worked for their living in the city of Amida (modern Diyarbekr in eastern Turkey). Maria spun yarn which Euphemia sold to feed the hungry and provide for the sick. Some of the citizens complained, among other reasons, because Euphemia left her daughter alone all day to spin while she herself went out to work among the poor.[63]

There is no question that such women created tension within the church no less than within the social order. In Amida, church officials complained that people honored Euphemia and Maria "more than they did the bishops".[64] We see such issues even in the accounts of the martyrs. In the "Acts of Thecla," for example, the apostle Paul appreciated Thecla's work but attempted time and again to restrict her activity, "pondering whether another temptation was not upon her."[65]

Still, the women we hear about seem genuinely concerned with answering God's call to their particular vocation. It was not a sense of self or self-worth that led them outside their normal boundaries, but rather the sense that God had called them and they must answer. Thus Susan, the unwilling monastic leader of men and women, hid her face completely from men throughout her career, fearing both that she might cause harm to a man and might suffer it herself; yet one day she explained to a discouraged monk how she found the strength to battle demons: "I am aware that the strength of the Lord surrounds my weakness like a wall of bronze, and there is no other power that can rise against it."[66]

So, too, did Euphemia explain why she and her daughter would not accept help with their work, or an easier occupation: "God gives me strength, and that poor girl who is with me, so that we may work for our own needs and minister to our brothers according to our strength."⁶⁷ What mattered was not that one was a woman, but the vocation to which one was called.

Evangelism

The impact of women's faithful example was not restricted to other women. In the early church, the most effective missionaries were often sisters, wives and mothers, converting their non-Christian brothers or husbands, or raising their children as Christians whether or not their spouses might approve. Indeed, this kind of evangelism, away from the public eye, was a considerable factor in Christianity's early growth.⁶⁸

The role continued, with prominent examples from the fourth century. Augustine of Hippo's mother Monica profoundly shaped his faith, overriding his father's lack of religious conviction.⁶⁹

The two Cappadocian brothers Basil of Caesarea and Gregory of Nyssa had the example of their devout mother Emmelia (four of whose children are canonized saints of the church), and of their remarkable sister Macrina.⁷⁰ Gregory credited Macrina with influencing Basil away from the secular career of his early adulthood, and with initiating the great monastic structure that was part of Basil's legacy to the church. Gregory presents Macrina as the philosopher and theologian most influential for his own life.⁷¹

Their friend Gregory of Nazianzus in like manner credited his father's conversion to his mother Nonna's stalwart faith,⁷² and presented his sister Gorgonia, a mother of five children, as another such example.⁷³ In his discussions of Nonna and Gorgonia, Gregory stresses their pious "silence" — echoing the New Testament injunctions against women's speech.⁷⁴ Yet he describes both as women whose lives give us serious pause for thought: devoted wives to their husbands and mothers of numerous children, they both also served for many years as spiritual advisors for their Christian community, as well as overseeing the distribution of funds and goods for the poor and the sick in their cities. We must understand Gregory's term "silence" as other than literal, indicating sound teaching rather than unspoken or empty words.[75]

Again, we are often told that men were led to holy careers as monks and as bishops under the inspired guidance of holy women they had known as children. In the sixth century, Cyril of Scythopolis wrote that two Palestinian monastic leaders, Theodosius and Theognis, were led to their holy careers by female spiritual mentors (whose names he does not report); a third young man, in Cyril's account of John the Hesychast, was brought to the religious life by a pious nun Basilina (to whom John would not grant an audience).[76] Cyril himself was brought to his ecclesiastical vocation by the piety of his mother,[77] as was Theodoret of Cyrrhus in the early fifth century.[78] The seventh century East Syrian monastic writer Martyrios (Sahdona) was dramatically influenced by a local holy woman of his village named Shirin. While he does not refer to Shirin as a nun, he describes in moving terms her role as spiritual guide for the monks as well as the laywomen of the region.[79]

Roles for Women in the Early Church

The earliest Christian communities had developed defined positions for women, first as widows, deaconesses, and virgins, and later as consecrated lay women and as nuns.[80] These were at some point all forms of holy orders, consecrated offices with specific ministries and duties to be performed. Sometimes their focus of ministry was among the other women of the parishes: widows had responsibilities to teach the younger women; deaconesses were required for catechizing women converts and assisting in the baptismal sacrament when performed for women. But the types of duties could also be much broader.

Syrian Christianity by the third century had developed the lay order of the Sons and Daughters of the Covenant (Bnay and Bnat Qyomo), which lasted well into medieval times. These men and women took vows of poverty and celibacy, lived in separate households within the Christian community, and worked to assist the parish priest or bishop.[81] The Daughters of the Covenant were responsible for chanting Psalms and *madroshe* (sacred hymns of the church); indeed, in Syria, women's choirs may have been a form of ministry. The Daughters of the Covenant also worked in the women's hospital run by the Church of Edessa. They assisted the clergy in both villages and cities.

In the fifth century, Bishop Rabbula of Edessa legislated the particular responsibilities of the different consecrated offices.[82] He dictated that the Daughters of the Covenant must not be "compelled by force" to weave garments for the clergy, indicating the need to safeguard the religious nature of women's ministry, which clearly at times could be reduced to little more than housekeeping.[83]

Such positions granted women a recognized but restricted status in the larger church structure; the ordination of women was an issue in the early church.[84] At the same time, these positions acknowledged the wide range of women's activities in the Christian community. However, when the ecclesiastical hierarchy settled into place following its legalization in the fourth century, women's official ministries became increasingly limited. The offices of widow, deaconess, and Daughter of the Covenant gradually disappeared. Celibate women were encouraged to live in enclosed religious communities that did not carry the kinds of public ministries among the poor and sick so common in the patristic period.[85] Under Islamic domination in the Middle East, convents virtually vanished.

Ironically, the early church gave women greater official authority and a wider range of ministries than they have held at any time since, to this day. The ancient offices have not been revived. These offices, as well as the nature of ancient women's religious communities (whether for consecrated lay women or nuns), had been the major vehicle for women's education during the early Christian centuries. Education for women in the secular sphere tended to be available only among the wealthy until modern times. The teaching ministry of women's religious offices, and the emphasis on the study of theology and the lives of the saints among women's religious communities, made learning available to women across social and economic classes in the early church. This valuing of women's intellectual roles within the church was a feature of the early and patristic periods, and seriously diminished later.[86]

Numerous accounts of women's many and varied vocations survive to us in ancient Christian texts. Yet social stereotypes continued to bear upon the image of women presented in Christian teaching: in sermons and treatises, women were often presented as weak of will and intellect, sexually promiscuous, and greedy.[87] Saints' lives present women from both views, according to cultural stereotypes and according to the gospel model that called women as well as men to full discipleship in the service of the Lord.[88]

Two final examples of Christian holy women illustrate the broader situation of women in the early church. The fifth century account of St. Pelagia, famed courtesan of Antioch, became one of the most beloved stories of the Christian middle ages, both in the East and the West.[89] Unrivalled in beauty, wealth, and independence, Pelagia was converted suddenly and in spectacular fashion by Bishop Nonnos. Pelagia received baptism, freed her slaves, gave her wealth away, and secretly departed disguised as a monk. She lived out her days in the guise of a eunuch recluse named Pelagius on the Mount of Olives in Jerusalem, a spiritual teacher especially venerated for his holy way of life. At her death, Pelagia's true identity was discovered amidst mingled cries of horror and astonishment. "Praise be to You, Lord," the bishops marvelled, weeping, "how many hidden saints you have on earth — and not just men, but women as well!"[90]

Various stories developed around the motif of holy women disguised as monks; in these, the emphasis most often lay on the saint's life in disguise and what wondrous deeds derived from the pretense.[91] But in Pelagia's story, the starting point of this theme in hagiographic literature, little is said of her adopted life: only that she became holy, served the faithful accordingly, and died undiscovered then to be revealed. The story's accent and detail come in its first part, concerning her life as a prostitute and the spectacle of her conversion.

Pelagia's reform and subsequent transformation express a meaning similar to that in the story of Mary of Egypt, or indeed of Mary Magdalene, as a former prostitute: the powerful image of the reformed harlot.[92] For all biblical teaching, both Old and New Testament, the harlot has been the image of love gone astray: not of sexuality as a sin, but of love turned away from God. The penitent harlot is one who turns back to God, back to faithfulness, back to love truly given and truly received — a love we can only know when we give and receive it in the presence of God.

In the case of Pelagia, her transformation was so complete that only a change in her total identity could measure it; her achievement of holiness was so great that it transcended the boundaries of social expectations, of gender, and of any human judgement. Even the most abhorred of women could find redemption in the power of Christ. A woman could symbolize this mighty truth of Christian salvation with particular force precisely because of the social prejudices regarding women's nature.

Nonetheless, the image of women saints is more often one that continues the model of the gospel women, of Mary Magdalene, and of early martyrs and missionaries like Thecla: women whose intellectual and physical strengths were matched only by the courage with which they lived in witness to Christ. St. Febronia was a Syrian nun, said to have been martyred around the year 302 by Roman officials.[93] Febronia was raised from birth in a convent near Nisibis, renowned for the erudition and wisdom of its sisterhood. Within this community, Febronia grew to hold a special place on three accounts: for her surpassing ascetic labors, for her capacity to teach others, and for the fact that she had never seen a man or been seen by a man. Both by the women of the convent and the women of the city, Febronia was considered truly blessed. The arrival of Roman soldiers on the scene, however, led to her imprisonment and death by slow torture, much of it sexual, as a warning to other Christians in the area.

The scenes of mourning amongst the women of the region — Christian and pagan, married and unmarried — are hauntingly evoked. The women mourn as much for the loss of their cherished one, as for the invasion of her life by men, from whose eyes and whose evils Febronia had always been protected. Her life had been seen as one of true freedom in Christ, not restricted by society's dictates, but devoted instead to education, contemplation, and friendship. In fitting tribute, her story claims to have been written by a woman — an event remarkable in itself in antiquity — Febronia's spiritual sister Thomaïs, who became abbess of the convent soon after the saint's death. Women saints are often presented as individuals who are exceptions to the rule of their own kind. Febronia, by contrast, is presented as a special woman among many fine women. The story does justice to the impact of early Christianity on the lives of women in the church. Her cult was popular, and remains so to this day.[94]

The history of women in the church is both powerful and empowering. Whatever their circumstances — in times of severe oppression by state or by society, in situations of hardship or hopelessness — Christian women have repeatedly responded in faith with strength, courage, and leadership. They have done this out of their own initiative, and not because men have carried the burden for them. In an age when we see women gaining their true equality in society for the first time, it is important to remember that women have known that equality through the empowerment of the Spirit throughout the history of the church, even when conditions would obscure its meaning. This is a history to be remembered. Above all, it is a history to be continued.

NOTES

[1] Matt. 27: 55-56. Compare Mk. 15:40; Lk. 23:29; Jn. 19:25. All Biblical quotations in this article are taken from the Revised Standard Version. In this article I employ the following abbreviations: BHG = F. Halkin, *Bibliotheca Hagiographica Graeca*, 3rd ed., Subsidia Hagiographica 8a (Bruxelles: Société des Bollandistes, 1957) and idem, *Novum Auctarium Bibliothecae Hagiographicae Graecae*, Sub. Hag. 65 (Bruxelles: Société des Bollandistes, 1984); BHO = P. Peeters, *Bibliotheca Hagiographica Orientalis*, Sub. Hag. 10 (Bruxelles: Société des Bollandistes, 1954); BHL = *Bibliotheca Hagiographica Latina Antiquae et Mediae Aetatis*, Sub. Hag. 6 (Bruxelles: Société des Bollandistes, 1949) and *Bibliotheca Hagiographica Latina Supplementi*, Sub. Hag. 12 (Bruxelles: Société des Bollandistes, 1911).

[2] For a summary of the major Marian themes, see H. Graef, *Mary: A History of Doctrine and Devotion* (Westminster: Christian Classics, 1985). While Graef includes the eastern Christian traditions, another insightful discussion relevant to the present article is E. Behr-Sigel, *The Ministry of Women in the Church*, trans. Steven Bigham (Redondo Beach, CA: Oakwood Publications, 1991), 181-216.

[3] The study of women in early Christianity has produced an enormous bibliography in recent years. Major primary source documents are conveniently available in translation in R. S. Kraemer, *Maenads, Martyrs, Matrons, Monastics: A Sourcebook on Women's Religions in the Greco-Roman World* (Philadelphia: Fortress Press, 1988) and E. A. Clark, *Women in the Early Church* (Wilmington, Del.: Michael Glazier, Inc., 1983). For the former, a helpful commentary on the sources that sets early Christianity in the context of traditional Greco-Roman and Jewish religions, can be found in R. S. Kraemer, *Her Share of the Blessings: Women's Religions Among Pagans, Jews, and Christians in the Greco-Roman World* (New York: Oxford University Press, 1992). No work on women in early Christianity can be done without reference to the fundamental study of Elisabeth Schussler Fiorenza, *In Memory of Her: A Feminist Theological Reconstruction of Christian Origins* (New York: Crossroad, 1983). A convenient survey is M. Alexandre, "Early Christian Women," in G. Duby and M. Perrot, eds., *A History of Women in the West*, Vol I: *From Ancient Goddesses to Christian Saints*, ed. P. S. Pantel, trans. A. Goldhammer (Cambridge, MA: Belknap Press, 1992), 409-444. For an Orthodox consideration of the early Christian evidence regarding women, see the singularly important study by Behr-Sigel, *Ministry of Women in the Church*.

[4] Syria, Lebanon, Palestine, Mesopotamia, and eastward into Persia. There are some distinct patterns to the history of Christianity in the Syrian Orient. For a general survey with respect to women, see S. P. Brock and S. A. Harvey, *Holy Women of the Syrian Orient* (Berkeley: University of California Press, 1987); S.A. Harvey, "Women in Early Syrian Christianity," in A. Cameron and A. Kuhrt, *Images of Women in Antiquity*, rev. ed. (London: Routledge, 1993), 288-98, 312.

5 My primary concern in this study is with the images of women the church has preserved; my treatment of New Testament material is necessarily abbreviated. See Fiorenza, *In Memory of Her* and Kraemer, *Her Share of the Blessings*, for detailed analyses of how Biblical scholarship underlies any effort to reconstruct the historical picture of women in earliest Christianity.

6 Samaritan woman: Jn. 4: 7-30.

7 Jn. 8:1-11. In the ancient manuscripts, this periscope is sometimes placed at the end of the Gospel of John, or after Luke 21:38, with some variant readings.

8 Lk. 7:36-50.

9 Peter's mother-in-law: Matt. 8:14-5, Mk. 1:30-31. Hemorrhaging woman: Mk. 5: 25-34; Lk. 8:43-48.

10 Lk. 10:38-42.

11 Lk. 14:25-33; Matt. 10:37-39. This is also represented in the calling of the first disciples: Mk. 1:16-20; Matt. 4:18-22; Lk. 5:1-11; Jn. 1:40-42. Compare Matt. 6:25-34 and Lk. 12:22-30 (the lilies of the field); or Lk. 18:18-30, Matt. 19:16-22, and Mk. 10:17-22 (Teacher, what must I do?).

12 Luke 8:1-3, 10:38-42; Mk. 15:40.

13 The critical analysis remains that of E. S. Fiorenza, *In Memory of Her*, 97-159.

14 He cast out seven demons: Lk. 8:2. The seven demons are often interpreted to indicate that Mary suffered from epilepsy.

15 Lk. 8:1-3; Mk. 15:40-41; Matt. 27:55-56; Lk. 23:49.

16 Mk 15:40-41; Matt. 27:55-56.

17 Lk. 23:55-24:11; Mk. 16:1-11; Matt. 27:61, 28:1-8; Jn. 20:1-18.

18 Jn. 20:24-29.

19 Jn. 20:1-18.

20 Mk. 16:11; Lk. 24:8-35; Jn. 20:1-10.

21 Gospel of Thomas, Logion 114; Gospel of Phillip, ch. 63-4. Both are translated in B. Layton, *The Gnostic Scriptures* (Garden City, NY: Doubleday and Co., Inc., 1987), G Thom, 114: 399, G Phil, 63-4: 339 (here as sec. 48); Gospel of Mary (Magdalene), trans. in J. Robinson, *The Nag Hammadi Library in English*, 3rd ed. (San Francisco: Harper and Row, 1988), 523-7.

[22] B. Ward, *Harlots of the Desert: A Study of Repentance in Early Monastic Sources* (Kalamazoo: Cistercian Publications, 1987), 10-25. For western medieval versions of her legend, see D. Mycoff, *The Life of Saint Mary Magdalene and of her Sister Saint Martha* (Kalamazoo: Cistercian Publications, 1989); Jacobus de Voragine, *The Golden Legend: Readings on the Saints*, vol. 2, trans. W. G. Ryan (Princeton: Princeton University, 1993). For her cult in the West, see above all V. Saxer, *Le Culte de Ste. Marie Madeleine en occident des origines a la fin du moyen age* (Auxerre-Paris, 1959).

[23] The Bridegroom Matins for Holy and Great Wednesday commemorate the sinful woman, culminating in the exquisitely wrought hymn by Kassione. *The Lenten Triodion*, trans. Mother Mary and Archimandrite Kallistos Ware (London: Faber and Faber, 1977), 534-41. While the service and hymnography do not name this woman as Mary Magdalene, many a priest has done so in the evening sermon and many parishioners assume that identification to this day.

[24] E.g., Acts 9:36-40; 12:12; 16:1, 13-5; 17:4, 12; 18:2-3, 26; 21:9. Rom. 16:1-15; 1 Cor. 16:19; Phil. 4:2-3; Col. 4:15. Kraemer, *Her Share of the Blessings*, 128-90; Fiorenza, *In Memory of Her*, 160-241; Alexandre, "Early Christian Women."

[25] 1 Cor. 14:33-35; 1 Tim. 2:11-14; Titus 2:3-5; Eph. 5:22-24. See the discussion in Fiorenza, *In Memory of Her*, 251-84, and compare Behr-Sigel, *Ministry of Women in the Church*, 61-72, 151-3.

[26] Acts 18:18, 24-26; I Cor. 16:18; Rom. 16:2. Cf. Kraemer, *Her Share of the Blessings*, 136, on the relationship between Priscilla and Aquila.

[27] Gal. 3:27-28.

[28] H. Chadwick, *The Early Church*, 58-59.

[29] W. H. C. Frend, *Martyrdom and Persecution in the Early Church: A Study of a Conflict from Maccabees to Donatus* (Oxford: Basil Blackwell, 1965); G. de Ste. Croix, "Why were the Early Christians Persecuted?" *Past and Present* 26 (1963): 6-38. See also E. Ferguson, "Early Christian Martyrdom and Civil Disobedience," *Journal of Early Christian Studies* 1 (1993): 73-83.

[30] E. Peters, *Torture* (Oxford: Basil Blackwell, 1985), 18-36.

[31] R. Wilken, *The Christian as the Romans Saw Them* (New Haven, CT: Yale University Press, 1984) is a helpful study on how Christianity appeared in the eyes of their persecutors.

[32] The earliest documents are edited and translated in H. Musurillo, *The Acts of the Christian Martyrs* (Oxford: Clarendon Press, 1972).

33 Pliny, Ep. 10.96, To Trajan; ed. and trans. W. Melmoth and W.M.L. Hutchinson, *Pliny, Letters* (New York: The MacMillan Co., 1915) 2 vols.

34 "The Martyrs of Lyons and Vienne" (from Eusebius, *Eccl. Hist.*, v.1.3-63); ed. and trans. in Musurillo, *Acts of the Christian Martyrs*.

35 "Perpetua and Felicitas," ed. and trans. in Musurillo, *Acts of the Christian Martyrs*. This extraordinary text incorporates Perpetua's haunting and brief prison diary, the oldest diary by a woman extant in any language. In the past, this text has carried the aspersion of representing the deaths of heretical Montanists, although no one in the text is identified as a Montanist. A recent commentary by M. Tilley offers sound argument for rejecting that attribution and rather understanding the visions and prophecies as those of a mainstream charismatic Christian context. M. Tilley, "The Passion of Perpetua and Felicity," in E. S. Fiorenza, ed., *Searching the Scriptures: A Feminist Ecumenical Translation and Commentary* (New York: Crossroads, 1994).

36 In addition to Musurillo's edition of the early texts, a fine collection is available in English that draws on a variety of sources: *The Lives of the Holy Women Martyrs: An Orthodox Martyrologion of Spiritual Heroines*, trans. Holy Apostles Convent (Buena Vista, CO: Holy Apostles Convent, 1991).

37 Translated with commentary and bibliography in Brock and Harvey, *Holy Women of the Syrian Orient*, 63-121.

38 The monumental study by P. Brown, *The Body and Society: Men, Women, and Sexual Renunciation in Early Christianity* (New York: Columbia University Press, 1988), is crucial to any study of the topic.

39 Celibacy was a route for women only under rare circumstances: the Vestal Virgins (who could marry after their thirty year term of service), certain of the philosophical schools, and for Judaism perhaps the Essenes and Therapeutae.

40 1 Cor. 7.

41 Matt. 22:1-14; Lk. 14:15-24.

42 P. Brown, "The Notion of Virginity in the Early Church," in B. McGinn, J. Meyendorff, and J. Leclerq, eds., *Christian Spirituality: Origins to the Twelfth Century* (New York: Crossroad, 1985), 427-43. For the Persian situation, see Brock and Harvey, *Holy Women of the Syrian Orient*, 63-99.

43 See esp. E.A. Clark, *Jerome, Chrysostom, and Friends: Essays and Translations* (Lewiston, NY: Edwin Mellen Press, 1979); R. Rader, *Breaking Boundaries: Male/Female Friendship in Early Christian Communities* (Ramsey, NJ: Paulist Press, 1983).

44 "The Acts of Paul" in *New Testament Apocrypha*, 2: 322-90 (trans. 352-90), esp. 330-33, and 353-64 (trans. "the Acts of Thecla").

45 The second century account of the The Acts of Thecla was expanded in the fifth century, and became the basis for the subsequent flowering of her cult in the Christian East. Thecla: BHG, 1710-1722; BHO, 1152-56; BHL, 8020-8025. The essential work is G. Dagron, *Vie et Miracles de Sainte Thècle: texte grec. traduction et commentaire*, Subsidia Hagiographica 62 (Bruxelles: Société des Bollandistes, 1978).

46 Irene: BHG, 952y-954d; BHO, 538; BHL, 4467. Barbara: BHG, 213-218q; BHO,132-134; BHL, 913-971. Catherine of Alexandria: BHG, 30-32b; BHO, 26; BHL, 1657-1700. The legends of Barbara, Catherine, and Irene appear late and unreliably in their textual witness; cf. H. Delehaye, *Les Passions des Martyrs et les Genres Littéraires*, Subsidia Hagiographica 13B (Bruxelles: Société des Bollandistes, 2nd ed. 1966). The Byzantine traditions for all three are presented in *The Lives of the Women Martyrs:* Barbara, 528-42; Catherine, 491-520; Irene, 180-86.

47 Eugenia: BHG, 607-608; BHO, 281-284; BHL, 2666-2670. She was said to have been martyred under Diocletian (284-305).

48 Gregory of Nyssa, *Vita S. Macrinae*, ed. V. W. Callahan, in *Gregorii Nysseni Opera*, ed. W. Jaeger, Vol. 8, pt. 1, *Opera Ascetica* (Leiden: E.J. Brill, 1952), 347-414; trans. in V. W. Callahan, *Saint Gregory of Nyssa: Ascetical Works*, Fathers of the Church 58 (Washington: Catholic University Press, 1967), 161-91. Macrina lived c. 327-80; her brother composed her vita not long after she died.

49 Febronia: BHG, 659; BHO, 302-303; BHL, 2843-44. The earliest form of the text is the Syriac version, ed. P. Bedjan, *Acta Martyrum et Sanctorum*, vol. 5 (Paris/Leipzig: O. Harrassowitz, 1895; repr. Hildersheim: Georg Olms, 1968), 573-615; trans. in Brock and Harvey, *Holy Women of the Syrian Orient*, 150-76 (for Thecla, see sec. 19 on p. 163).

50 *Vita S. Olympiadis*, 1. Ed. in A.-M. Malingrey, *Jean Chrysostome: Lettres à Olympias*, 2nd ed., Sources Chrétiennes 13 bis (Paris: Les Editions de Cerf, 1968), 393-449; trans. in Clark, *Jerome, Chrysostom, and Friends*, 127-44.

51 S. A. Harvey, "Women in Early Byzantine Hagiography: Reversing the Story," in L. L. Coon, K. J. Haldane, and E. W. Sommer, *'That Gentle Strength': Historical Perspectives on Women in Christianity* (Charlottesville: University Press of Virginia, 1990), 36-59.

52 Prominent founders are Melania the Elder, Melania the Younger, Paula, Macrina, Olympias, Matrona, and Caesaria.

⁵³ See below for the examples of Gregory of Nazianzus' mother Nonna and sister Gorgonia (below, nn. 72 and 73) and for Euphemia and Maria in Amida (below, n. 63). Compare the works described in the *Life of Olympias* (above, n. 49), or, e.g., Palladius, *Lausiac History*, sec. 67; ed. C. Butler, *The Lausiac History of Palladius* (Cambridge, 1898-1904), trans. R.T. Meyer, *Palladius: The Lausiac History*, Ancient Christian Writers 34 (New York: Newman Press, 1964).

⁵⁴ John of Ephesus, *Lives of the Eastern Saints,* 12, ed. E. W. Brooks, in *Patrologia Orientalis* 17-9 (1923-5), 166-86; trans. Brock and Harvey, *Holy Women of the Syrian Orient*, 124-33; Palladius, *Lausiac History*, secs. 63-4.

⁵⁵ Palladius, *Lausiac History*, secs. 46, 54 (Melania the Elder).

⁵⁶ *Life of Olympias*. Anastasia: BHG, 79-80; BHO, 242; the Syriac is translated in Brock and Harvey, *Holy Women of the Syrian Orient*, 142-49.

⁵⁷ Melania the Elder (Palladius, *Lausiac History*, sec. 55) and Melania the Younger (*Life of Melania the Younger*). The sixth century patrician Caesaria, in John of Ephesus, *Lives of the Eastern Saints*, ch. 54 *Patrologia Orientalis* 19 (Paris 1925), 185-91.

⁵⁸ The case of Gregory of Nyssa's sister Macrina is gaining increasing scholarly interest. See below, n.70. Febronia, as discussed below, was venerated as a teacher of religious and lay women. For the example of St. Matrona, see E. C. Topping, "St. Matrona and Her Friends: Sisterhood in Byzantium," in *Kathegetria: Essays Presented to Joan Hussey*, ed. J. Chrysostomides (London: Porphyrogenitos Press, 1989), 211-24. Matrona: BHG, 1221-1223.

⁵⁹ Theodoret of Cyrrhus, *History of the Monks of Syria*, ch. 29, 30, ed. P. Canivet and A. Leroy-Molinghen, *Théodoret de Cyr, Histoire des moines de Syrie*, Sources Chrétiennes 234 and 257 (Paris: Les Editions du Cerf, 1977-79), trans. R. M. Price, *Theodoret of Cyrrhus, A History of the Monks of Syria* (Kalamazoo: Cistercian Publications, 1985); Palladius, *Lausiac History*, 20; John of Ephesus, *Lives of the Eastern Saints*, 12, 27, 54.

⁶⁰ Consider the important studies in E. A. Clark, *Ascetic Piety and Women's Faith: Essays on Late Ancient Christianity* (Lewiston, NY: Edwin Mellen Press, 1986).

⁶¹ See Topping, "St. Matrona and her Friends."

⁶² John of Ephesus, *Lives of the Eastern Saints*, 27, *Patrologia Orientalis* 18, 541-58. Trans. in Brock and Harvey, *Holy Women of the Syrian Orient*, 133-41.

⁶³ *Ibid.*, 12. (Texts above in n. 54).

64 *Patrologia Orientalis* 17, 174-5; Brock and Harvey, *Holy Women of the Syrian Orient*, 128.

65 *Acts of Paul and Thecla*, sec. 42, Hennecke and Schneemelcher, *New Testament Apocrypha*, 2: 364. He was particularly alarmed about her decision to cut her hair and dress like a man — actions that would have made her travels as missionary much easier. *Acts of Paul and Thecla*, sec. 25, 42.

66 Brock and Harvey, *Holy Women of the Syrian Orient*, 140.

67 *Ibid.*, 128.

68 Cf., for example, A. Harnack, *The Mission and Expansion of Christianity in the First Three Centuries*, trans. J. Moffat (New York 1908), Bk. 4, chap. 2.

69 Saint Augustine, *Confessions*, trans. H. Chadwick (Oxford: Oxford University Press, 1991).

70 Both are discussed at length in Greg. Ny., *Life of Macrina*.

71 Macrina is gaining increasing attention from scholars on just this point: J. Pelikan, *Christianity and Classical Culture: The Metamorphosis of Natural Theology in the Christian Encounter with Hellenism* (New Haven: Yale University Press, 1993) presents her as "the fourth Cappadocian." The study of R. Albrecht, *Das Leben der heiligen Makrina auf dem Hintergrund der Thekla-Traditionen* (Gottingen, 1986) is crucial.

72 Gregory of Nazianzus, Oration 18, "On His Father," sec. 8-12, 21, ed. J.-P. Migne, *Patrologia Graeca* 35 (Paris 1886) cols. 985-1044. Trans. L. P. McCauley, in *St. Gregory Nazianzen and St. Ambrose, Funeral Orations*, Fathers of the Church 22 (New York: Fathers of the Church, Inc., 1953), 119-156.

73 Gregory of Nazianzus, Oration 8, "On his Sister, St. Gorgonia," Ed. Migne, *Patrologia Graeca* 35, cols. 789-818; trans. McCauley, in *St. Gregory Nazianzen and St. Ambrose, Funeral Orations*, 101-18.

74 Oration 8, "On Gorgonia," sec. 11; Oration 18, "On his Father," sec. 10.

75 R. Darling Young, "Gorgonia's Silence: The Married Woman as Ascetic in the Thought of Gregory of Nazianzen," (unpublished paper) presents a nuanced and sophisticated analysis of Gregory's use of "silence" for these two women, one which suggests that more is at stake than the rhetoric of social control for women's lives — although that, too, is an element at work here.

76 Cyril of Scythopolis, *The Lives of the Monks of Palestine*, Theodosius, sec. 1; Theognius; John the Hesychast, sec. 23-4, ed. E. Schwartz, *Kyrillos von Skythopolis*, Texte und Untersuchungen zur Geschichte der altchristlichen Litertur 49, pt. 2 (Leipzig: J. C. Hinrichs, 1939), trans. R. M. Price, *Cyril of Scythopolis: The Lives of the Monks of Palestine* (Kalamazoo: Cistercian Publications, 1991).

77 Cyril mentions this at various points: *Lives of the Monks of Palestine*, Saba, sec. 75; John the Hesychast, 30.

78 Theodoret, *History of the Monks of Syria*, 9, 13.

79 The text is translated in Brock and Harvey, *Holy Women of the Syrian Orient*, 177-81.

80 The literature on the development of women's offices is extensive. Helpful guides are Kraemer, *Her Share of the Blessings*, 174-90; and Alexandre, "Early Christian Women," at 421-38.

81 See esp. G. Nedungatt, "The Covenanters of the Early Syriac-Speaking Church," *Orientalia Christiana Periodica* 39 (1973) 191-215, 419-44.

82 "The Rules of Rabbula for the Clergy and the Qeiama," ed. and trans. in A. Vööbus, *Syriac and Arabic Documents Regarding Legislation Relative to Syrian Asceticism*, Papers of the Estonian Theological Society in Exile 11 (Stockholm: Este, 1960), 34-50. On the Daughters of the Covenant see esp. canons 20, 23, 27, 29, 37. The *Vita S. Rabbulae*, composed soon after Rabbula's death, offers some expansion of the canons; ed. P. Bedjan, *Acta Martyrum et Sanctorum* IV, 396-450. Page 444 refers to the Daughters of the Covenant working in the women's hospital of Edessa. There is a tradition associating women's choirs with the work of St. Ephraim the Syrian; see K. McVey, *Ephraim the Syrian: Hymns* (New York: Paulist Press, 1989), 28.

83 "Rules for Clergy and Qeiama," canons 3, 4, 9, 10, 11, 19, 28.

84 St. John Chrysostom, "On the Priesthood," III.9 evidences unease among the Christian community regarding the exclusion of women from the priesthood in his time. *Jean Chrysostome, Sur le Sacerdoce (Dialogue et Homélie)*, ed. A.-M. Malingrey, Sources Chrétiennes 272 (Paris: Les Editions du Cerf, 1980); trans. G. Neville, *St. John Chrysostom, Six Books on the Priesthood* (Crestwood: St. Vladimir's Seminary Press, 1984), 78. See Fiorenza, *In Memory of Her*, 285-342; and compare Behr-Sigel, *Ministry of Women in the Church*, 81-92, 149-80.

85 One already sees this happening in e.g., Theodoret of Cyrrus, History of the Monks of Syria, ch. 29, 30. In his chapters on holy men, Theodoret praises an extremely extroverted, publicly exercised ministry; in these final two chapters on holy women, he exhorts women religious to remain enclosed, silent, and passively

contemplative. The irony is that the lay populace, even as Theodoret describes them, do not view holy women as having such an introverted role to play. And contrast the women religious, for example, in John of Ephesus, *Lives of the Eastern Saints*, where it is clear that any number of circumstances could easily impel women into more public kinds of ministry. See the discussion in S. A. Harvey, *Asceticism and Society in Crisis: John of Ephesus and the Lives of the Eastern Saints* (Berkeley: University of California Press, 1990), 108-33.

86 The developing situation for the western churches is well sketched in the two now classic studies: *Religion and Sexism: Images of Women in the Jewish and Christian Traditions*, ed. R. R. Ruether (New York: Simon and Schuster, 1974) and *Women of Spirit: Female Leadership in the Jewish and Christian Traditions*, ed. R. R. Ruether and E. McLaughlin (New York: Simon and Schuster, 1979). For the development in the Byzantine Empire, see the outline and bibliography in J. Herrin, "In Search of Byzantine Women: Three Avenues of Approach," in Cameron and Kuhrt, *Images of Women in Antiquity*, 167-89, 307-9. The history of Christian women under Muslim rule has yet to be written.

87 E.g., the texts gathered in Clark, *Women in the Early Church*, are representative of the larger situation.

88 Harvey, "Women in Early Byzantine Hagiography."

89 Pelagia: BHG, 1478-1479; BHO, 919; BHL, 6605-11. See above all, P. Pelitmengin, ed., *Pélagie la Pénitente: métamorphoses d'une legende*, 2 vols. (Paris: Etudes Augustiniennes, 1981-4). I follow the oldest version, extant in Syriac, trans. in Brock and Harvey, *Holy Women of the Syrian Orient*, 40-62.

90 Brock and Harvey, *Holy Women of the Syrian Orient*, 61.

91 The roots can be traced back to Thecla's decision to cut her hair and dress like a man. See esp. E. Patlagean, "L'histoire de la femme déguisée en moine et l'évolution de la santeté féminine à Byzance," *Studi Medievali* 17 (1976), 597-623; and the discussion of this motif in Harvey, "Women in Early Byzantine Hagiography," 46-48.

92 See the insightful discussion in Ward, *Harlots of the Desert*.

93 See n. 48 for texts. Although tradition places her martyrdom ca. 302, the earliest extant text dates from the sixth century and the descriptions of convent life are more representative of that period.

94 E. Gülcan, "The Renewal of Monastic Life for Women in a Monastery in Tur Abdin," *Sobornost* 7 (1977): 288-98.

THE MARTYRDOM OF EARLY ARAB CHRISTIANS: SIXTH CENTURY NAJRĀN[1]
by Irfan Shahîd

The six centuries or so that elapsed before the rise of Islam in the seventh century are not well documented for the history of the Arabs. This is especially true of the history of Christianity as it spread among them in this period. But enough sources have survived to suggest that Christianity played an important role in their life and history, both in the first half of it during the period of the pagan Roman Empire, and in the latter, the three centuries from the fourth to the seventh, during which the Arabs lived in the shadow of Byzantium, the Christian Roman Empire, Christian since the conversion of the emperor Constantine.

This latter period was indeed the golden period of Arab Christianity. It is better documented than the previous one, and a close examination of the extant sources reveals that Christianity was a vital force in the history of the Arabs before the rise of Islam, and that the converted Christian Arabs in their turn contributed to the fortunes of Christianity, a role practically unknown to ecclesiastical historians. This has relegated to obscurity their place among the peoples of *Oriens Christianus,* such as the Syrians, the Armenians, the Copts, and the Ethiopians.

The Arab sector in the circle of *Oriens Christianus* is the most neglected and the least understood; its history remains to be written.[2] This article is a contribution in that direction; it is limited to one aspect of Arab Christianity in this Byzantine period of its history, namely, Arab martyrdom in the sixth century.

During this sixth century, the three great centers of Arab Christianity were: (1) Ḥīra on the Euphrates, the capital of the Lakhmid dynasty. Although the Lakhmids converted to Christianity officially only towards A.D. 590, their city had been for some three hundred years the great center of Arab Christianity before the rise of Islam.[3] Ḥīrā was full of churches and monasteries, and it was hence that the Christian mission reached out to the Arabs of the Persian Gulf and eastern Arabia; and it was here that, according to tradition, the Arabic script or one version of it developed. (2) In the western half of the Fertile Crescent there was no one single city that could be considered the counterpart of Ḥīrā as a Christian center that was diffusing Christianity. But al-Jābiya, the capital of the Ghassānid Arabs, the Arab allies of Byzantium in the sixth century, may be considered the closest approximation to Ḥīrā. It was situated in the Jawlān, and its kings and rulers, the Ghassānids, were zealous Christians who promoted the spread of that faith both in Bilād al-Shām and in the Arabian Peninsula.[4] (3) Najrān, an Arab city in southwestern Arabia,[5] an important oasis and caravan city, was converted in the fifth century. It became the most important Christian center first in South Arabia, and then in the whole of the Arabian Peninsula after the extraordinary events of ca. A.D. 520, the theme of this article.

Around this date, the then king of the Ḥimyarites, Yūsuf, who apparently was possessed by a great missionary zeal, wanted to convert to his Jewish faith the South Arabian region including Christian Najrān. He therefore laid siege to it, and when the city opened its gates to him after a promise of no forced conversion, he faced its inhabitants with the two choices of conversion or death. Many of them chose the latter and were thus killed, including their *sayyid,* the chief of the city, al-Ḥārith ibn-Kaʿb, known to the Greek speaking world of Byzantium as Arethas, and also Ruhayma/Ruhm,[6] the leading woman in Najrān.

News of the martyrdoms soon spread throughout the Christian Orient and in Byzantium. Shortly after, the Christian Ethiopian Negus, Ella-Asbeḥa/Caleb, led an expeditionary force against Ḥimyar in South Arabia, Byzantium contributing the fleet that transported the Ethiopian host. The Ethiopians defeated Yūsuf and the Ḥimyarites, avenged the martyrdoms of the Christians of South Arabia, and made of it an Ethiopian dependency. This resulted in the evangelization of South Arabia, and the country remained Christian until the advent of Islam.

During this period of a century or so, Najrān became the great religious center in the Arabian Peninsula until its inhabitants emigrated to the Fertile Crescent sometime in the caliphate of Omar, A.D. 634-644.[7]

The history of Christian Najrān is a passionate drama in the story of Arab Christianity in this period, its golden period. It has many facets and dimensions, but only one will be treated here, namely the martyrdoms. An account of them will be given with special reference to the two chief martyrs, Arethas and Ruhayma, and then the significance of these martyrdoms for Arab Christianity will be marked.

Fortunately the history of these martyrdoms can be written, based not on late secondary sources, but on primary contemporary ones, that derive from documents of eyewitnesses of these events. They have survived mostly in the Syriac language and in a Greek hagiographical text, the *Martyrium Arethae*.[8] The details may be consulted or read in these sources. What is more profitable in this context is to hear the martyrs themselves speak.

— I —

The Syriac sources have preserved the actual speeches of the two chief martyrs, and it was natural that these speeches should have been "retouched" by hagiographers. The substance, however, of the two speeches is genuine. They are buried within the folios of the volumes that tell the story of Najrān, but this is an occasion to have them exhumed from that obscurity or inaccessibility when presented in this new context as the live voices of two Arab martyrs who died for their faith some fifteen centuries ago.

Ḥārith/Arethas

This was the chief or *sayyid* of Najrān, who had fought the Ḥimyarite rulers of South Arabia and had refused to entertain the overtures of King Yūsuf when he besieged Najrān. However, he was

The Martyrdom of St. Arethas
(Vatic. gr. 1613, f. 135)

overruled, and Yūsuf entered the city and faced its inhabitants with the two hard choices.

Among those who refused to renounce their Christianity was Ḥārith/Arethas, whom the Ḥimyarite king stripped naked before he offered him the choice. On the refusal of Ḥārith to accede to the king's request, he was decapitated. The speech that he delivered before the king is not preserved in its entirety, since one entire leaf was torn off the codex in which the account of the martyrdoms was included. But enough of it has survived to give a true picture of this Arab martyr of the sixth century.

It opens with Arethas' reply to Yūsuf's jeer that the former stood naked before those who used to consider him their chief so that he might be disgraced in his old age before them. It reads as follows: [9]

> "Truly, if the raiment I have on were made visible to you, you would not be saying this word to me. But since it is not visible to you, you imagine that I am standing naked. Truly I say to you that in this moment my soul has grown great in my eyes and I am not ashamed of the nudity of my body. For Christ knows that I am finer than you inwardly and outwardly, and taller than you are; that I am more fit than you, that my body <is stronger> than yours and my arm is mightier than your arm. No scar from arrow, spear, or sword is <to be seen> on my back, only on my breast; for never have I shown <my> back in war as a runaway <would>. In many wars I was victor by the power of Christ; and the brother of him that sits on your right hand <and> who is your paternal first cousin, him did I kill in war."

> The king said to him: "So then it was on these that you relied and also revolted against me. I am advising you now to spare your old age. Deny that Christ, <that> deceiver, and his Cross and so live; if not, you

shall die a grievous death, you and your companions and all who will not deny Christ and the Cross."

(ḤRTH) <Ḥārith> said to him: "Do (remember) the oaths (you swore) to us by the God of Abraham, Isaac, and Israel, and by your Torah and the Tablets and the Ark."

The king said to him: "Leave these aside and deny Christ and the Cross."

The old man said to him: "Truly I am grieved for all my Christian companions, (who were) with me in the city, because I counselled them, but they did not listen to me. For I was prepared to go out against you in war and to fight with you for the sake of the people of Christ, and either you would have killed me or I would have killed you, and I was trusting in Christ, my Lord, that I would vanquish you; but my companions (did not) let me do this. I also sought to lead out only my family and my slaves and go out against you for an encounter; but my Christian companions locked the gates of the city and did not (let me) go out.

"And I also told them (to watch over) the city and not open the gates (for you), and I was trusting in Christ, my Lord, that the city (would not be subdued) by you because it lacked nothing; and in this, too, my companions would not listen to me. And when you sent them your word, your oaths, I counselled (them not) to believe you and told (them) you were a liar and that truth (does not) reside in you, but my companions would not be persuaded (to listen to me).

"And now (in my old age you tell) me to deny Christ, my God, and become a (Jew like you. Perhaps) I will (not) live (one hour or a single day after I have uttered my denial, and yet) you (want) to (alienate me from Christ), my God, in my old age. (Truly) you have neither (spoken nor) acted as a king; (for a king) who lies is not a king (for I have seen) many kings (but I have not seen) kings that were (liars. As for me), I (hold sway over my own) self, (and I will not be false in my promise to Christ). Far be it from me (to deny Christ...)"

Ruhayma/Ruhm

Ruhayma was the most distinguished woman in Najrān, as is evident from her speech. Her husband 'Arabī had been killed or martyred by the Ḥimyarite king, three days before she herself had her encounter with him. She too met the same fate as her husband after refusing to renounce her Christianity. Her speech was delivered at the market in the middle of Najrān before the women of the city, who had assembled there.

Unlike that of Arethas, her confessional speech has been preserved in its entirety, and it reads as follows:[10]

> O women of Najrān, my Christian, Jewish, and Pagan companions, hearken. You know that I am a Christian, and you know my lineage and family and who I am; and that I have gold and silver and slaves and handmaids and field produce and that I lack nothing. And now that my husband has been killed for the sake of Christ, if I desired to marry another, I should not be lacking a husband.
>
> And here I am saying to you that on this very day I am in possession of forty thousand *denarii*, sealed and placed in my treasury apart from the treasury of my husband, and jewellery and pearls and jacinths; and there are among you women who, together with their daughters, have seen these in my house. And you

know, my (companions), that a woman (has no days) of joy comparable to the days (of her wedding); and from the wedding (onward it is all grief and) groans: when she gives birth (to children) she (does so) with anguish and wailing; (when she is) deprived of them she is (in pain and) distress and when she buries her children, she does so with weeping and lamentation.

But from this day onward, I am free from all these <cares>, continuing to rejoice in the days of my first wedding. And here are my three virgin daughters, since they are not betrothed to men, I have adorned them for Christ.

Look at me, for twice you have seen my face: at my first wedding, and now at this second one also; with unveiled face before all of you I went over to my first spouse, and now <again> with unveiled face I am going to Christ, my Lord and my God, and the Lord and God of my daughters, just as He himself came to us. Look at me and at my daughters, for I am not less beautiful than you are, and here in my beauty I am going to Christ, my Lord, uncorrupted....

And this, my beauty, will be a witness for me before my Lord that it was unable to lead me astray into the sin of denying Christ, my Lord. My gold, my silver and all the jewellery of my adornment, my slaves and handmaids and all I possess will be a testimony for me that I did not, for the love of them, deny Christ. And now the king has sent <word> to me to deny Christ and <so> live, but I sent <word> back to him that if I denied Christ, I should die, but if I did not deny Christ, I should live.

Far be it from me, my companions, far be it from me that I should deny Christ, my God, Him in whom I believed, in whose name I was baptized and had my daughters also baptized, whose Cross I adore, and for whose sake I shall die, I and my daughters, as He died for us. Behold! The gold of the earth is abandoned in the earth. Whosoever wishes to take my gold, let him take it; whosoever wishes to take my silver and my jewellery, let him take it, for I have abandoned everything of my own free will, in order to go and receive from my Lord a recompense.

Blessed are you, my companions, if you listen to my words. (Blessed are you, my companions), if (you know the truth for which) I and my daughters are dying. Blessed are you, my companions, if you love Christ. Blessed am I and my daughters because we are journeying to such blessedness.

From now onward, peace and tranquillity will <reign> among the people of Christ, and the blood of my brothers and sisters who have been killed for Christ will be a wall to this city, if it abides <faithfully> by Christ, my Lord. Behold how with unveiled face I am going out of your city in which I have lived as if in a temporary dwelling, so that I may journey, I and my daughters, to the other city, because it is to that place that I have betrothed them.

Pray for me, my companions, so that Christ, my Lord, may receive and may forgive me for having remained alive three days after the father of my daughters <had been killed>.

— II —

Arethas and Ruhayma/Ruhm, the distinguished citizens of Najrān, were only two out of at least some three hundred Najrānites, men and women, who died around A.D. 520. Detailed accounts of the martyrdoms of some of these have survived.

In a short article such as this one, there is no room for a more detailed treatment of these martyrdoms, and accounts of them may be read in the sources. But at least their names should be made known, obscured as they have been by the fame of the pair, Arethas and Ruhayma.

In the order of saintliness, however, all the martyrs of Najrān are equal. The case for listing them in this context is therefore necessary and called for, especially as their names have been buried in tomes that are accessible to only a few scholars, and they do not even appear in the martyrologies, menologia, and synaxaria that celebrate the 24th of October as the Feast Day of the Martyrs of Najrān. It is therefore well that at least their names should be made known to a larger reading public, especially that of the Arab Christian Churches.

As the reader will notice, their names are resoundingly Arab, with the exception of one or two in the lists of the martyrs. The list is taken from the most reliable and complete contemporary source that has recorded these events.[11] The number of male martyrs is slightly less than two hundred, while that of the female martyrs is less than one hundred.[12]

The List of Martyrs[13]

Ḥārith, Ḥumāma and 'Amr, Tamīm and Add and Jabr and Ḥārith, his brother, Tha'laba, their nephew and Ghanam and 'Abdallāh and Ḍabb, he who was for a time a judge and a persecutor but afterwards became a true Christian and was deemed worthy even to the stage of martyrdom for the sake of our Lord, and 'Amr and Jabr and Bar Ḍabb, and ẒWRBN and 'Abdallāh and Malik and S.........(four lines missing) and Abū

'Afr and Bar Ḥuzaiqa and Nuʿmān and Saʿd and Ḥārith and ʿAuf and Sergios and Muʿāwiya and 'YZD and Baddā and 'BYSh and Busr and ʿAbd YWFR and 'BYSh and Muʿāwiya and Qaʿbān and Dhuhl, his son, and Dhib and Haufāʿamm and Shalim and Dhuhl, his son, and ʿAbdallāh and Salima and Asad, the son of his sister, and LYLWB and Faʿmān and ʿAmr and Dhuhl, his brother, and ʿArbai and Sār and ʿAbdallāh and Samurah and Kuraib and ʿAbd and Nuʿmān and KF and KYTWL', his brother, and Asfar and ʿAuf and Ḥumāma, his brother, and ʿAbdallāh and Habīra, his son, and Malik and ʿAbd and Jadan and NʿMrah and Azmam and HB and Ashab and Māzin, his brother, and Nuʿmān and Yazīd and Nuʿmān and Jarīr and ʿAbdallāh and ʿAbdallāh and Malik and Nuʿmān and ʿAmr, brethren, and Ḥārith and Taim and ʿAmr, brethren, and Nauf and Ghanam and Azfar, his sons, and Nuʿmān, son of Ruhm, daughter of Azmaʿ, and Azraq and Abraq and Shalima and Qais, his brother, and Ḥārith and Nuʿmān, brethren, and ʿAmr and Ḥabīb and ʿĀmir, his brother, and Duwaid and Kalīl and Ḥārith and ʿQD and Ḥārith, brethren, and Nuʿmān and ʿAbdallāh and his little baby-brother, whom he carried on his shoulder and who was killed, and Nuʿmān and Aswar, his son, he to whom the king said: "Deny and I will make thee my son," but he would not and was killed in a good confession, and Aswar and ʿAmr and Busr, his son, and ʿAbdallāh and Aḥmam and 'DKY' and MḤWYN and Abraham and Hāni and MKRDY and Muʿāwiya and Dhuhl and Busr, his son, and ʿAbdallāh and Muʿāwiya, his son, and Wā'il and Muʿāwiya and Dhuhl and Baddā and ʿAmr, his brother, and Haufaʿamm and Namirah and Aus and Malik and Rabīʿa and ʿAlā…r and SRHB and Jarīr and Yazīd and Kalīl and ʿAmr and ʿAlā'u and Kāhf and ZFRY and

Nu'man and 'Auf and Ḥārith and Hāni and ḤYRM
and Aswar and Azraq and Taimai and Qais and Ḥuldai
and 'L..ā and 'Abd and Duwaid and Jarīr and M...
and LYL and Tamīm and Shalimah and Mu'āwiyah
and ...YN and Busr and 'ṢRY and Dhuwāb and
Mu'āwiyah and Wā'il and Tha'laba and Karib and
MKR[DY] and Marthad and Ḍabb and DY' and Dhuhl
and Sha'd and 'RḤB and Malik and Jabr and Shalimah
and Ḥāritha and Ḥannah and Ḥiṭṭān.

The List of Martyresses[14]
Humāma and Ruhm and Arqas and Thummal(i)ki and
Ruhm and her three daughters and Ama and Jabrah
and Aumah and her daughter, and Ruhm and Ushana,
her sister, and their mother, and Ḥayya and Aumah
and her four sisters, and Ḥubba and 'Uzāfa and Aqṭam
and Waddah and her daughter, and SRHB and Aqṭam
and Salmā and 'Yla and her three daughters, and
SLWma and 'Auṣa and Ma'na and TMNya and Ṭaibah
and Ḥamdah and 'Auda and Ummu Busr and Ṭaibah
and YHWbah and Ḥabībah and 'Auṣa and Durrah and
'Amma and HBB and Hinṭ and Ḥubbah and
Thummal(i)ki and Ama and Māriya and Asmā' and
Ummu 'Amr and Asmā' and Māwīya and Jadīda and
Māwīya and Hasana and Ḥinṭ and Ḥasana and Khalīla
and Alhān and Ummu Bayya and Asmā' and Kabsha,
HLH and Jaushanah and HWLH and Ḥayya and Ḥinṭ
and 'Auṣa and Durrah and Namlah and Maḥmida and
Mayyah and Ḥamdah and Ḍabbah, YHyah and Ummu
Busr and Ummu Jabala and Umayya and Aumah and
Ḥabība and Jadīda and Ama and Fāṭima and Ummu
Shalshala and Hinṭ.

There is a list too of martyred clerics, which, like the lists of the
lay martyrs, is not recited during the celebration of the Feast Day on

the 24th of October, but its clerics deserve to be remembered. As has been said before, the sources are scanty for documenting the ecclesiastical history of the Arabs in Pre-Islam, or rather what has survived of the sources is such, but luckily those for Najrān are unique — *inter alia* — for their preservation of the names of the martyred *clerics*.

The list, therefore, is a precious document because it is informative on the structure of this Arab Church, and it is the one, solitary, extant document that does just that for an Arab church in this period in its entirety. None has survived for the Arab churches in the Mesopotamian region of Ḥīra or for the Jābiya of Bilād al-Shām.

The sources elsewhere record the name of Najrān's bishop, Paul II, and that of a deaconess, Elizabeth.[15] They also testify to the existence of the Order of the Sons and Daughters of the Covenant.[16] As to the list of clerics, they are presented in hierarchical order, consisting of archpresbyters, archdeacons, and arch-subdeacons. Noteworthy is the existence of the order of arch-subdeacons, nowadays nonexistent.

The List of the Martyred Clerics[17]
The names of the archpresbyters who were burnt in the church of Najrān: SRGYS (Sergios), the Roman presbyter; JBRĀYL <Gabriel>, the Najrānite presbyter; ILYĀ <Elias>, the presbyter from Ḥīra of Nu'mān, who in former times had been the pupil of the blessed Mar Nu'mān, son of MKĀYL <Michael>, who was laid to rest in the holy convent of Dayr Mār Bass in ḤWRYM <Ḥārim>; Abraham, the Persian presbyter.

The names of the archdeacons: ḤNNYA <Ananias>, the Roman archdeacon; YWNN <Jonas>, the Cushite deacon; SHLMWN <Solomon>, the Najrānite deacon; MWSHĀ <Moses>, the Najrānite deacon, son of MZN <Māzin>; MWSHA <Moses>, the deacon who was killed by the sword.

The names of the arch-subdeacons: Abraham, son of M'WYĀ <Mu'āwiya>; M'WYH <Mu'āwiya>, son of THWNH; QYWS <Qays>, son of SHLMN <Salmān>.

— III —

These martyrdoms, nowadays hardly remembered, were of great significance in the history of Najrān amd Arabia, of *Oriens Christianus*, and of the Arabs in pre-Islamic times.

– A –

Before they took place, Najrān was a key caravan city as well as an agricultural/industrial center in western Arabia on the spice route, the *via odorifera* of the ancient world and of Late Antiquity. It had been an important Christian center in Arabia since its conversion in the fifth century, but after the baptism of blood around A.D. 520, it became a Holy City.

(1) It immediately was transformed into a city of martyrs, a true martyropolis, as deserving of that appellation as Martyropolis,[18] the capital of Armenia IV. In Najrān was built the famous *martyrion*, called Ka'bat Najrān, well-known in pre-Islamic times and remembered by its poets, such as al-A'shā who visited it.[19] This *martyrion* quickly became a pilgrimage center for the Peninsular Arabs, and also a place of refuge. And this gave Christianity and its propagation in Arabia the impetus that it needed in the struggle of rival religions for supremacy in that Peninsula; the martyrdoms signalled the turn of the tide in favor of Christianity.

(2) The Arab tribal group that ruled Najrān, Banū-al-Ḥārith ibn-Ka'b, otherwise called Balḥārith, enjoyed a powerful presence in pre-Islamic Arabia, militarily and otherwise. But the martyrdoms of their chief, who was also called al-Ḥārith ibn-Ka'b, and of other members of this group considerably enhanced the prestige of Balḥārith, and within them that of the leading clan, Banū-'Abd al-Madān. As custodians of the Ka'ba of Najrān, they emerged as protectors of Christianity in the sixth century among the Arabs of pre-Islamic times

in much the same way as the Ghassānids of Bilād al-Shām, who were related to them through affiliation to the larger tribal group, al-Azd.

Banū-'Abd al-Madān and the Balḥārith retained their prestige even in the early Islamic period. One of them, a lady, Rayṭa, was married to the father of the first 'Abbāsid caliph, al-Saffāḫ: hence the reference to Balḥārith as al-A<u>kh</u>wāl, the maternal uncles of the 'Abbāsids.

– B –

In the history of the early church, the martyrdoms in Najrān were unique. Christianity brought with it a new set of ideals sharply contrasting with those of the pagan world with its traditional heroes. The new heroes of Christianity were the priests, the monks, the confessors, and the martyrs.

But the highest Christian virtue was that displayed by the martyrs, who were canonized and thus became saints. Such were the Arab saints of A.D. 520. But these were distinguished, even in the history of martyrdom, by the fact that their passions took place *after* the Peace of the Church, when during the reign of Constantine the Edict of Milan was promulgated in A.D. 313. After that date, the persecutions ceased and with them disappeared the band of martyrs and confessors.

During the two hundred years or so that elapsed from the Edict of Milan to the persecutions of Najrān there were almost no martyrs within the empire or in its sphere of influence;[20] this was a period that witnessed the rise of the cult of martyrs, their veneration and pilgrimages to their *martyria,* beginning with the memorable pilgrimage of Helena, Constantine's mother, to the Holy Land. The persecutions and martyrdoms of A.D. 520 returned the Church to the world of the pagan Roman Empire, when Christianity was a persecuted religion, and it jolted the sensibilities of the Christian *oikoumenē* both in Byzantium and in the Orient, especially as these martyrdoms were not few in number.[21]

Those whose names have been preserved came to about three hundred, more than the martyrs of Lyons who numbered forty-eight. Needless to say, these martyrdoms gave an impetus to the cult of relics in the entire Christian Orient, already in great vogue in the fifth and sixth centuries.

– C –

Finally, these martyrdoms had a special importance in the spiritual history of the Arabs, since it put the Arabs indelibly on the ecclesiastical map of the Universal Church. These martyrs belonged mostly to the Monophysite doctrinal persuasion, but their Monophysitism was not of the extreme type such as that of the Julianists/Docetists. It was the Severan type, so close to the theology of Chalcedon.[22]

Moreover, Chalcedonian Byzantium gave full support to the common Christian effort to avenge the martyrs of Najrān when it contributed a fleet for the transportation of the Ethiopian expeditionary force across the Red Sea to South Arabia. Thus these martyrs were canonized and were considered Saints of the Universal Church. Their feast is celebrated on October 24.

Martyrdom was a new experience to the Peninsular Arabs.[23] These, known to us principally from what remained of pre-Islamic Arabic poetry, had other sets of ideals, expressed through the Arabic term *murū'-a*, the ideal of a man, *mar'*, Latin *vir-tus*. This was a capacious term within which were subsumed, among others, such virtues as courage in war and hospitality in peace. But dying for Christianity was not one of them, and *shahīd* in Arabic, even in the Koran, does not have the meaning of *martyr* but rather that of witness, exactly what the Greek word *martys* had meant before it came to mean *martyr* in the Christian acceptation of the term. With the martyrdoms of Najrān, a new ideal appeared among the set of ideals venerated by the Arabs, namely, laying down one's life for the sake of one's religious persuasion, and of course the term itself, *shahīd*, underwent the corresponding semantic development.

Although the martyrs of Najrān advertised Arab Christianity in the entire world of the Christian *oikoumenē* in the East and in the West, it was in the East, in the Orthodox Christian Church and in the

Orient, peopled by the Armenians, the Syrians, the Copts, and the Ethiopians, that Najrān and its martyrs made the deepest impression.

The Arab contribution to the history of Christianity was assured by the blood of these martyrs, and Najrān, Arab Najrān, took its place as one of the Holy Cities[24] of the Christian Orient, alongside Etchmiazin, Edessa, Abū-Minā, and Axum, holy for the Armenians, Syrians, Copts, and Ethiopians respectively.

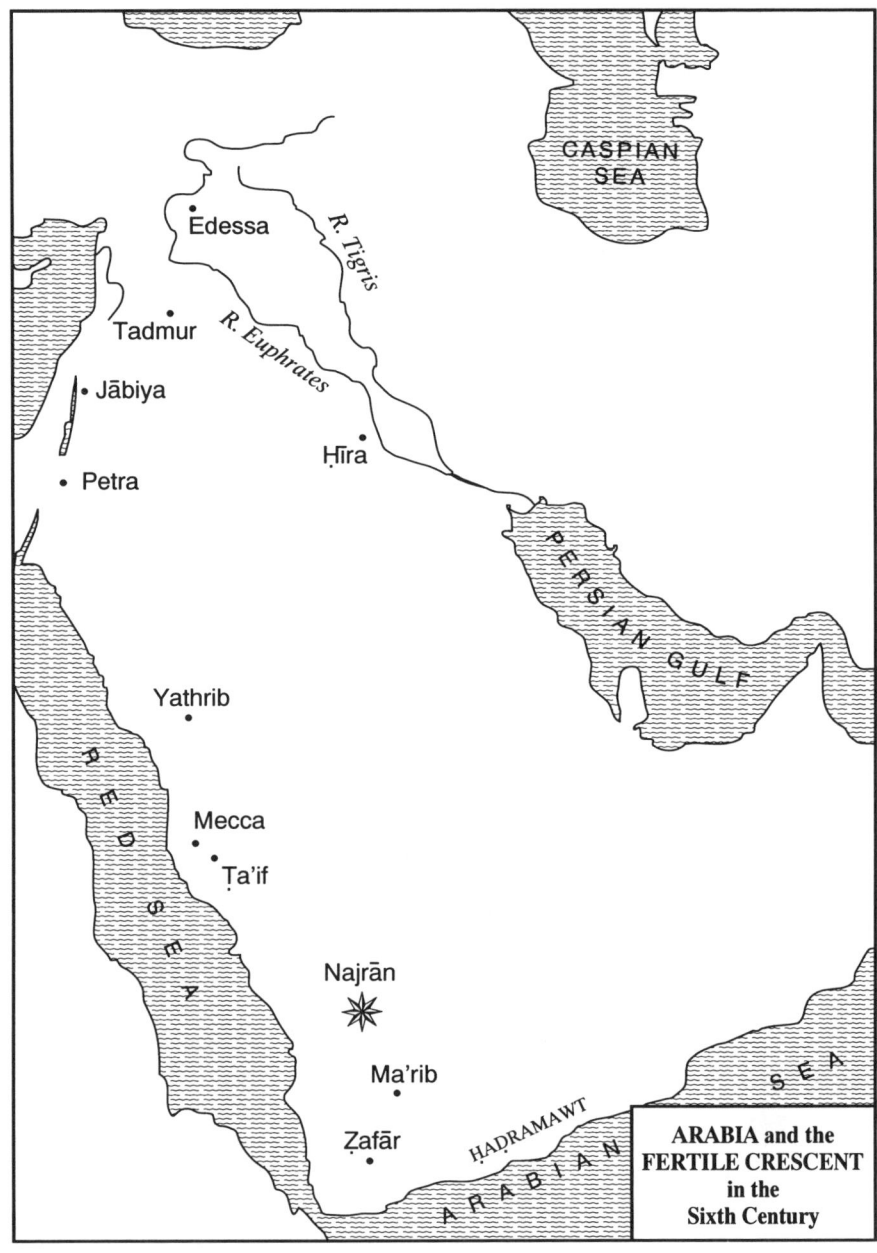

NOTES

I should like to thank warmly the Société de Bollandistes, especially the Reverend Fathers Paul Devos and Ugo Zanetti, for permission to reproduce the long quotations from my book, *The Martyrs of Najrān,* published as No. 49 of their series, *Subsidia Hagiographica,* and Monsignor Paul Canart, Biblioteca Apostolica Vaticana, for permission to reproduce "The Martrydom of Arethas" from a miniature in the Menologium of Basil, Vat. gr. 1613.135.

[1] The choice of the theme of this article is in response to the request of the Most Reverend Metropolitan PHILIP that I write on the Arab martyrs.

[2] The Jesuit priest Louis Cheikho devoted practically all his life to writing the history of Arab Christianity, especially in the pre-Islamic period. As he wrote in Arabic, his work has remained known only to the few western scholars who could read Arabic, and most of them considered that he did not proceed critically in his reconstruction of Christian Arab history. The criticism is justified up to a certain point, but the vast *oeuvre* of this dedicated priest/scholar will remain a mine of information out of which a history of Arab Christianity may be written. The most recent comprehensive work on Arab Christianity in this period is J.S. Trimingham, *Christianity Among the Arabs in Pre-Islamic Times* (London, 1979), but it is only a short survey, and, useful as it is in some respects, it is open to many objections: see the present writer's review of it in *Journal of Semitic Studies* 26 (1981): 150-153. Readers of this article may, however, consult it as background reading.

[3] To Ḥira may be added such Euphratesian towns as 'Ayn al-Tamr and al-Anbār, where Christianity also flourished.

[4] On the Ghassānids and their role in the service of Christianity, see the present writer's, *Byzantium and the Arabs in the Sixth Century.*

[5] Najrān was in the fifth and sixth centuries an Arab city, situated in the largely non-Arab south, dominated by the Ḥimyarites, who were a Semitic people, cognate with the Arabs but distinct from them. The Ḥimyarites were converted to Judaism in the fifth century, or so they are said to have done, according to some South Arabian scholars. See accompanying map.

[6] Her name was either Ruhm or Ruhayma. A version of this name may have survived in *Rihām*, still applied to Arab women in modern times.

[7] For the history of Najrān in this period, see the present writer's "Byzantium in South Arabia," *Dumbarton Oaks Papers* 33 (1979), 23-94.

[8] The Syriac sources are represented by *The Book of the Ḥimyarites*, ed. and trans. Axel Moberg (Lund, 1924), hereafter referred to as *Book*, and the *Letters* of Simeon, the bishop of Bēth-Arshām in Mesopotamia. The most recent work on his *Letters*

is *The Martyrs of Najrān* (Brussels: Société des Bollandistes, 1971), hereafter referred to as *Martyrs*.

[9] For this speech, see *Martyrs*, 50-51. For certain words in this speech and the one which follows, enclosed within brackets and parentheses, see *ibid.*, 43.

[10] For Ruhayma's speech see *ibid.*, 57-58.

[11] The *Book*.

[12] The number of martyrs was apparently more than those in the two lists, since the author in various parts speaks of other martyrs whose *names* did not reach him: see *Book*, p. ciii, no. xxiv; p. cxvii, lines 13-14, 20-21; p. cxxi, lines 18-20. The names of the martyrs are transliterated from the Syriac text; hence the correct pronunciation is not always clear in the transliteration which sometimes gives only the consonantal skeleton of a name (in capital letters).

[13] *Book,* cxvi-cxvii.

[14] *Ibid.*, cxxi.

[15] *Martyrs*, 46, 47.

[16] *Ibid.*, 250-251.

[17] *Ibid.*, 64.

[18] Modern Silvan in Turkey. According to a late tradition, the relics of the Christian martyrs of Persia, who died in the fourth century during the reign of Shapur II, were buried in its walls.

[19] See "Byzantium in South Arabia," (*supra* n.7), 70-74.

[20] Arabia was a sphere of influence for Byzantium through the powerful presence of its Arab allies in that Peninsula, such as the Salīhids of the fifth century and the Ghassānids who superseded the former as the principal allies of Byzantium in A.D. 502. The Christians of Persia, however, provided the Church with martyrs, but that was, mostly, in the fourth century during the reign of Shāpūr II.

[21] According to the pre-1970 Roman Martyrology of the Catholic Church the number was 340.

[22] See J. Lebon, *Le monophysisme sévérien* (Louvain, 1909); R. Chesnut, *Three Monophysite Christologies* (Oxford, 1976), 1-56.

[23] The two most celebrated Arab martyrs of the Pagan Roman Empire, St. Cosmas and St. Damian, were not *Peninsular* Arabs.

[24] Echoes of the holiness of Najrān are audible in the Muslim sources, which will be treated in the second volume of *Byzantium and the Arabs in the Sixth Century*.

ANTIOCH AND ALL THE EAST: INDIAN SCIENCE AND THE EARLY SYRIAN FATHERS
by George Saliba

Introduction

In the context of a centennial celebrating the spread of Antiochian Orthodoxy to the New World, this article may seem out of place.

Yet, on second thought, in the spirit of this festive occasion, it is not at all inappropriate to reflect, albeit briefly, on the history of Antiochian Christianity and on the role its founding fathers played in the development of human civilization, way before there was any New World, and before their descendants ever set foot on the shores of that world. For by understanding the richness of the tradition those descendants inherited, they will be better equipped to appreciate the cultural role their forefathers played.

This article will not even attempt to trace the very long and illustrious history of the Antiochian See, for that has already been done most elegantly by the very competent historian of that see, Asad Rustum, in his monumental multi-volume work, *Kanīsat Madīnat Allāh Antākia al-'Uzmā* (The Church of God's City, the Great Antioch).[1] Suffice it to say here that it was in the Antiochian See that the disciples were first called Christians,[2] together with what that meant for the history of Christianity.

This article will focus on the early life of the Antiochian See, especially in connection with its eastern orientation, just to add some more meaning to the phrase *"sā'ir al-mashriq"* (All the East), usually added to the title of the patriarch of Antioch, who is formally referred to as the "Patriarch of Antioch and All the East." Therefore, the period covered will range from the early third century, before the time of the official Christianization of the Roman Empire, to the early ninth, when the Christian East had by then come under the hegemony of the Islamic civilization.

In between those two dates the Antiochian area witnessed a variety of theological currents that engulfed eastern Christianity and led to the multiple schisms whose echoes are still heard up till our own days. Those innovative, and sometimes even heretical voices, were mainly focused around the city of Antioch, and by extension the area of northern Mesopotamia, the natural realm of the See of Antioch, and less importantly around the city of Constantinople, the seat of Imperial Rome, and around the city of Alexandria in Egypt. Our concern of course centers around the domain of Antioch.

Not addressed here are the inner theological issues of the church, interesting as they were and are. Instead, some of the works of the early church fathers will be examined, for the theological tracts contained therein disclose some evidence for the secular scientific doctrines that were current in their time within the Antiochian See. With that I hope to illustrate the importance of the cultural role played by the intellectuals of that see during the period, who, almost without exception, happened to be the clergy.

I also hope to demonstrate that the geographical location of Antioch did not only force it to become a bridge between the major empires of the time, namely the Persian and the Roman (Byzantine), but that it also turned it into a conduit for intellectual currents coming from as far east, or say southeast, as India. Since some of India's scientific thinking did originate in the Mesopotamian region, it is at times hard to determine whether the said intellectual currents were coming from India or flowing back into it.

Whatever is the case, it is important to note that the Antiochian domain was always in the middle. And when we remember that some of the same Indian scientific currents played a crucial role in the scientific formation of the Islamic civilization (which became the heir of earlier empires), we can better appreciate the mediating role played by the intellectuals of Antioch in that civilization, and in the civilizations that came to inherit it in turn, such as our very own civilization in the New World.

All the East

The focus of this paper is on the scientific doctrines, now identified as Indian, which can be documented in the works of the church fathers who lived in the region of the Antiochian See. In that narrow sense it is an attempt to explore the secular relationship between that see and India.

However, the question of the location of India during the period under discussion is not a trivial one. The preserved sources include several references to India or Indian that cannot be readily identified with the country of modern-day India in southern Asia. One need only refer to the place of origin of the fourth century ecclesiastic and Byzantine envoy, Theophilus Indus, to appreciate the difficulty of locating "India" in this period.[3]

Similarly, the debate concerning the mission of Saint Thomas to India, and the origin of the document describing that mission, point to a close relationship between the Antiochian See, especially through Edessa (al-Ruhā), and India.[4] Whether the country India in southern Asia is intended in the said document or not, one is not sure.[5]

Modern scholarship now tends to affirm that the same document giving the details of Saint Thomas's mission to India was in fact written by the famous Aramean philosopher, Bār Daiṣān (d. 222),[6] who lived in Edessa before the Nicean Council, and to whom we shall soon return. All the stories connected with the evangelization of India by Saint Thomas, apocryphal or otherwise, indicate a close connection between Indian Christianity and the land of Mesopotamia. As a result it is not surprising to find that the modern Syrian church of India still traces its roots to that area, and was always affiliated with the See of Baghdad which was usually occupied by a Catholicos.

The extent of the connection between India and Mesopotamia is attested in the historical sources originating mainly from the early Islamic period, but continuing well into later medieval times. In those sources, several localities in the region of the modern-day Persian

Gulf are referred to as the port of India, or the land of India. The ancient city of Ubulla, incorporated by the modern-day Basra in the lower Iraq region, was explicitly referred to in early Islamic times as the "land of India."

Yāqūt al-Ḥamwī, the author of the most famous medieval geographical dictionary, has preserved an anecdote from the time of the early Islamic conquest, in which he recounts how the second Caliph 'Umar Ibn al-Khaṭṭāb had ordered Sa'd Ibn Abī Waqqāṣ, who had conquered the area around Ḥirā in the same region, to send 'Utba b. Ghazwān "to the land of India" for the latter had "occupied an important position in Islam and was among the fighters at the battle of Badr."[7] Yāqūt quickly adds parenthetically "for Ubulla at that time used to be called *arḍ al-Hind.*"[8] The whole story is quoted by Yāqūt under the entry for Basra itself.

There is a long tradition therefore that may have gone back to early Christian times according to which the area around the Persian Gulf was thought of as being within the intellectual and cultural domain of India. Frequent trade and the actual presence of Indians in the region, as documented by Ṣāliḥ 'Alī,[9] may have accounted for that association. In that context, it is quite natural to expect a continuous flow of ideas back and forth between Mesopotamia and India proper.

Intellectual Contacts with India

The kind of references available in the preserved sources documenting these contacts is not very elaborate. In fact it is rather fragmentary, sometimes in the literal sense of the word. This is mainly because such references to Indian ideas were only incidental to the main purposes of the said sources, or were at best used in such contexts that did not require the much desired elaboration. But fragmentary as they are, they still are helpful to show the level of contacts that must have existed between the two regions, and which is reflected in those sources.

A. The Cosmological Works of Bār Daiṣān[10]

Not much is known about Bār Daiṣān himself. Even his name is disputed, for most people think that he acquired it from being born by the river Daiṣān which flowed through Edessa. He was apparently of distinguished pagan descent, for all the sources seem to agree that he was a childhood mate of Abgar (ruled 179-214), king of Edessa. At some point in his youth Daiṣān converted to Christianity. But his pagan origin never seems to have left him, and may have tainted his standing in his acquired faith. One senses that later church fathers were at times too quick to accuse him of heresies even when the nature of these heresies was not very well defined.

He is also credited, even by his critics, as having been one of the most eloquent figures of Syriac literature. Some attribute to him the invention of Syriac poetics, and that through his poetry he was able to gather around him the youth of Edessa, and thus lead them astray as the church fathers were quick to point out. None of that poetry seems to have survived. But we are told by the same sources that Saint Ephraim the Syrian (d. 373), to whom we shall soon return, composed his poetic refutations of Bār Daiṣān's doctrines in the same meter and rhyme. What concerns us of this author is his obvious acquaintance with ideas that are usually associated with India.

One of the earliest surviving sources which definitely seems to have been authored by Bār Daiṣān, namely, his *Book of the Laws of Countries,* gives a clear indication that the customs and laws of India proper were well known to Bār Daiṣān in northern Mesopotamia by at least the end of the second century if not before.[11] Bār Daiṣān spoke of the customs of the Brahmans and non-Brahmans of India in the following terms:

> There is a law among the Indians for the Brahmans, which many thousands and tens of thousands of them are, not to kill, to worship no idols, to commit no fornication, to eat no meat and to drink no wine. And among them not one of these things takes place, and behold, these people have been living for thousands

of years already according to that law which they have established for themselves. *Another law in India:* There is another law in India, and in the same territory, which obtains for people who do not belong to the caste of the Brahmans and are not followers of their doctrine. According to this law they may worship idols, commit fornication, kill and do other evil things that the Brahmans do not approve. And in the same part of India there are people who are accustomed to eat human flesh, as other peoples eat the flesh of animals. And the malign stars have not forced the Brahmans to do evil and impure things, neither have the benign stars induced the other Indians not to do evil things....[12]

In the same section Bār Daiṣān goes on to say that "All Hindus, when they have died, are burnt with fire."[13]

The context of Bār Daiṣān's references to the laws of the Indians is his attack against the doctrine of the astrologers. The latter made the claim that man's destiny was controlled by the stars and thus man had no free will, a position that would obviously exempt the sinner from the consequences of his sins. Bār Daiṣān disagrees with the astrologers on this issue for he argues, like a good Christian, that such a position would impinge on God's justice.

He goes on to say that human laws are indeed much more important in determining human behavior than the stars, and man must have a free will to make such laws and to counter them as well as to counter the laws of the stars, and thus must bear the responsibility for his deeds. For that reason he calls his book the *Laws of Countries*.

The references to Indian customs contained in the *Laws of Countries* are in themselves a clear indication that Bār Daiṣān was well acquainted with the mores of India proper, for such practices as the ones described in this work are not known from the Mesopotamian region, nor are they reported as taking place among the Indians who probably lived in that region. The routes of contact that could have supplied Bār Daiṣān with that information point to India proper, either directly or through the land routes over Persia. This should not be surprising for the sources documenting such contacts along both of these routes are too numerous to recount here.

These contacts were not restricted to hearsay reports about the habits and customs of the Indians, but also included the very important scientific ideas that originated in India. Among these ideas was that of the decimal system, which is still used to carry out calculation all over the world. This system seems to have originated in India, and was apparently first encountered outside India proper by the early church fathers who lived in the Mesopotamian region. Their references to this system indicate that it was known in their region long before it was later appropriated by the Islamic civilization, which passed it on to the rest of the world. The numerals used in that system, despite their Indian origins,[14] are still referred to in the western culture of today as Arabic numerals.

Going back to Bār Daiṣān, it is unfortunate that more of his religious works did not survive. For on the basis of the very reasonable and orthodox position that he held in his extant work, the *Laws of Countries,* it is hard to understand why he was branded as a heretic by the early fathers.[15] All other references to his religious ideas, such as his association with Mazdeans and Zoroastrians, come from his detractors, or his sworn enemies who lived centuries after him, and who zealously tried to contain the spread of his ideas among his followers from the youth of Edessa.

The little known of his other beliefs definitely indicates his acquaintance with the customs of a variety of nations was quite extensive, and demonstrates quite clearly that the Mesopotamian region in which he was active, the hinterland of Antioch, was quite a cosmopolitan domain from the earliest times of Christianity. In that sense, it is not at all surprising to find that most of the dynamic ideas that rocked the church in its earliest times had come from this same region. Most importantly, it is in that environment that the early fathers of the Antiochian See, especially those who lived along the Euphrates valley, came in contact with the secular thought of India.

Other indirect references to the works of Bār Daiṣān illustrate clearly that the Aramean Philosopher, as he was often called, was not merely interested in theological issues in the strict sense of the word or in matters of ethnography and ethnographic customs. Other writings of his, as cited by other authors, seem to have earned him the reputation of an astronomer, which at that time would not have been distinguished from an astrologer. But from his own attack against the astrologers, he was probably one of the first people to draw a distinction between astronomy and astrology.

A work by the later Mar Ephraim (or Saint Ephraim the Syrian d.373),[16] has as its subject a severe attack against Bār Daiṣān.[17] Being one of the most gifted church fathers, the "cither of the holy spirit,"[18] as Mar Ephraim was called by Saint John Chrysostom, the attack of this fourth century teacher of the famous School of Nisibin must be taken very seriously. For it means that Bār Daiṣān most likely held these ideas, or was at least perceived as having held them.

It also means that such ideas were still current in northern Mesopotamia about a century and half after Bār Daiṣān's death. Most importantly, this attack also means that Bār Daiṣān's teachings were still very attractive—otherwise one would be hard pressed to explain why the most gifted poet of the Syriac language, and most eloquent of the early church fathers would take the pain to respond to them.

What is of concern here is not the actual theological content of Bār Daiṣān's ideas that were found to be so dangerous, but his ideas that seem to have been connected to the Indian tradition. In his attack against Bār Daiṣān, Mar Ephraim presents Bār Daiṣān's ideas first, and then turns around and attacks them by listing all the objectionable things he found in them. In that context, while summarizing the ideas of Bār Daiṣān, he says the following:

> LXVIII. When the resurrection comes to pass – this comes to pass as the result of it; – and if every one had been raised ... – **** LXIX. ... in Adam ... all ... were dying – though as yet they were not born, – from the womb ... *** LXX. *** LXXI. The second Adam

also – ... and was raised up in Sheol, – He brings all that are [there], – in Him they were living secretly, – and when their resurrection drew nigh – there sprang upon them the voice of ... – in that as a dead man made the living die – the voice of resurrection makes them alive. LXII. For that first Thousand – is the type of that last Thousand, – in that as the death of Adam put to death – all those that that Thousand [*had brought to life*]... delivered – one that flew away and one that was rescued.

LXXIII. Our Lord also in the last Thousand – raises the Dead by His resurrection – in that all the Dead are found in His Thousand, – and there comes the Deluge of Fire – in the midst of which the Wicked sink – and the Righteous in it are delivered; – like Enoch the living [are] snatched away, – in the manner of Noah the Dead are rescued.[19]

Admittedly, this fragmentary text does not make much sense as it now stands. In fact it is surprising any sense could come out of it at all, since the original manuscript on which it is based, namely, British Museum manuscript Addenda 14623, is itself a palimpsest — i.e., it was intentionally erased and overwritten most likely in order to save on parchment. Under those conditions, one cannot hope for much better text.

But fragmentary as it is, this text still gives us a sense of what Mar Ephraim thought of Bār Daiṣān's doctrine. According to Mar Ephraim, this doctrine involved some belief in a world that was apparently created in cycles of thousands of years, i.e. millennia. Since the "Adams" are referred to in such terms as the "second Adam," each millennium presumably had its own Adam. This points to such types of cycles of re-creation that are very well known from the Indian traditions. And since the time of the Resurrection of Christ is designated by Bār Daiṣān as the Deluge of Fire, one can presume that Bār Daiṣān's doctrine recognized as well the famous astrological shifts that are also known from later astrological sources.[20]

According to the doctrine of planetary conjunction shifts, the two superior planets, Saturn and Jupiter, conjoin[21] approximately once every 20 years (called a small conjunction). Each time they repeat this conjunction, they do so when they meet at a point along the Zodiac which is about 242;30°[22] from the point where they met before.

Since the zodiacal signs are arranged according to the elements Fire, Earth, Air and Water, they form triplicities among themselves such that every four of them that are separated by 240° from one another would have one Element in common which would give its name to the triplicity. Since Aries, Leo, and Sagittarius that are separated from one another by 240° are all Fire signs, they would all form the Fire triplicity. Taurus, Virgo, and Capricorn would form the Earth triplicity, and so on.

Now, if Saturn and Jupiter were in conjunction at the beginning of such a triplicity, say at 0° Aries, they would meet again after a small conjunction, i.e., in about 20 years, at Sagittarius 2;30°, which is a point in the same triplicity at 242;30° away from the previous conjunction as we said before. The third time they meet they will meet at 5° of Leo, and so on. That means that their successive meetings creep forward in the triplicity by about 2;30° each time they meet in a small conjunction of 20 years.

Since the zodiacal sign is only 30°, several successive meetings would push the conjunction out of the sign. In fact, after 12 such conjunctions, i.e., 30÷2;30 = 12 times, the signs of the triplicity would be exhausted, and the two planets would begin to meet in the next triplicity. Therefore, after some 240 years, i.e., 12 x 20, the conjunctions would shift from one triplicity to the next, and the period of 240 years (called the middle conjunction) marks the shift among the triplicities.

Since there are altogether four triplicities, then a grand period of 240 x 4 = 960 years (called a grand conjunction) would bring the series of conjunctions back to the beginning, as if bringing the whole order of creation back in full cycle. Note that 960 years is very close to one thousand, and thus could have given rise to the millenary concept of re-creation every thousand years or so. This is only the cycle of conjunctions of Saturn and Jupiter. Other cycles were also computed, in which the conjunctions of all other planets were taken into consideration, and at times even their apogees and nodes were included.

By considering only the conjunctions of Saturn and Jupiter as we have demonstrated, and by computing backwards, one could re-arrange history in accordance with such major millenary cycles, which have embedded in them those triplicity shifts from Fire to Earth to Air and to Water.

The age of the Flood, for example, was computed as having taken place when the shift from Air to Water occurred. The commonly accepted date for that shift is usually dated in the Indian sources to the year 3102 B.C., February 17/18, for several traditions assert that the conjunction of the two superior planets, Saturn and Jupiter, had indeed shifted into the zodiacal sign of Cancer in the water triplicity during that year.[23]

In addition, all the other planets were supposed to have formed a grand conjunction during that year as well, i.e., the Kaliyuga of the Indian tradition.[24] Hence a new cycle of creation is marked at that year. It is cataclysmic events of this scale that are usually marked by such shifts, and this date itself could very well be taken as the cosmological beginning of a new age.

In the text of Bār Daiṣān, which was attacked by Mar Ephraim, the concept of the Thousands was clearly indicated, and the concept of re-creation, a rebirth of a new Adam, could also explain the fragmentary hints that we saw before. The whole arrangement may indeed have been accepted as such by Bār Daiṣān in his theory of Thousands. But the fragmentary nature of the text does not allow any more guesses with any confidence.

By returning to the astrological doctrines, we also find that the Resurrection of Christ happened during the shift from Water to Fire. In fact one medieval source states explicitly that "[t]he eighth small conjunction of the middle conjunction in which the birth of Christ occurred, [was] in the fire triplicity."[25] This means that according to this medieval tradition, the planets Saturn and Jupiter had been meeting in the Fire signs for seven successive meetings, and on the eighth, Christ was born. They would still meet for another four times in the same Fire triplicity.

The reference to the Deluge of Fire by Bār Daiṣān, during the time of the Resurrection, could very well be a reference to these meetings in the triplicity of Fire during the time of Christ, which indeed took place. In fact both Saturn and Jupiter were on the same degree in the Fire sign Leo, on the 20th of March in the year 35 of the Christian Era,[26] which puts this conjunction very close to the date of the Resurrection.

Could this be the reference to the Deluge of Fire that Bār Daiṣān was talking about, or was he talking about the end of a world that would not live for more than six thousand years? By his time the world was already in its sixth millennium according to the Christian reckoning, which was later adopted by Byzantium.[27] George, the bishop of the Arabs (d. 724), who also knew of the works of Bār Daiṣān, assumed in his turn that Bār Daiṣān was indeed advocating such eschatological ideas.

So far I have been referring to these ideas of millenary cycles, major and minor conjunctions, as well as shifts of triplicities as Indian in nature. Others have referred to them as Zoroastrian, Persian, and the like.[28] Other more medieval sources, however, actually locate these ideas in Babylonia itself, around the same area where Bār Daiṣān lived.[29]

More importantly, these same medieval traditions credit the "Persians and some of the Babylonians," with the definition of the World Year (i.e., a cycle such as the ones described) as requiring the conjunction of all the planets, without their apogees and nodes, in contradistinction to the Indians who did require the conjunction of everything. The famous medieval chronographer, Abū al-Raiḥān al-Bīrūnī (d. ca. 1054) states unequivocally that the era of the Deluge originated in Babylonia, and not in Persia and India, for the latter two actually "deny" it.[30] Bīrūnī goes on to say that "the astrologers have tried to correct these years, beginning from the first of the conjunctions of Saturn and Jupiter, for which the sages among the inhabitants of Babel, and the Chaldeans have constructed astronomical tables, the Deluge having originated in their country."[31]

Therefore, the question whether the doctrines advocated by Bār Daiṣān, regarding millenary conjunctions and shifts of triplicities, came from India or Persia, or whether they were native to Babylonia, cannot be answered at this stage, and much more research needs to be done in that regard before it can be settled. But since Mar Ephraim's reference is clearly to the ideas of Bār Daiṣān, and by extension Bār Daiṣān himself predates any Persian or even Indian references, it can be assumed tentatively that this specific cosmological astrological tradition was indeed developed by Babylonian astrologers, the famous Chaldeans of antiquity, and from them went to the Persians, and after some further modification to the Indians. This situation illustrates the difficulty of determining the direction of the influence between India proper and Mesopotamia.

The fact that Bār Daiṣān was indeed interested in such millenary concepts and in the recurring conjunctions of all planets, without their apogees and nodes, is attested in at least one other source. The source in question is now lost but was luckily quoted directly by later authors such as Severus Sebokht (fl.660 A.D.), the professor at the monastery of Qinnesrin on the eastern part of the Euphrates and the bishop of that monastery, and George, the bishop of the Arabs, who was apparently a bishop to the Arabian tribes in the same area of Mesopotamia. Fortunately, the preserved fragment of this work of Bār Daiṣān is in a much better shape than the text cited by Mar Ephraim.

The quotation from Severus Sebokht[32] appears in the context of a letter addressed by Severus Sebokht to a priest called Basil of Cyprus, who had apparently asked about the possibility of the conjunction of all the planets.[33] In the response, called by Sebokht "A chapter regarding the occurrence of the conjunction of the seven planets in times past and that such [conjunctions] will take place in the future," Sebokht indicates that from Basil's question it was obvious that many people in his region (i.e., Cyprus) had quarreled much about this problem. They probably thought that the end of the world was coming once more in the wake of these conjunctions. Sebokht took it upon himself to set them straight on this matter.

In order to illustrate his point, he states that such a conjunction of the seven planets had indeed taken place in the year 245 of the era of Diocletian (i.e., 529 A.D.), and gives the positions of the planets for that time as he calculates them by using the standard *Handy Tables* of Ptolemy (fl. 150 A.D.).[34] He then continues to say:

> That you should know that such was not only known to the foreigners (literally those who are outside, probably meaning pagans if not Greeks) but that it was also known by people from among the Syrians who had been instructed by the Christian faith. I mean Bār Daiṣān, the one called "the Aramean philosopher", a man much versed in all such matters, and well acknowledged for the fact that many such things were in his grasp. This [man] wanted to demonstrate that during the six thousand years, which he attributed to the age of the world by his time according to the old traditions, there had been one hundred conjunctions of these 7 planets. That is because Saturn completes its revolution in thirty years approximately. Jupiter in 12 years. Mars in one year and a half. The sun in one year. Venus in ten months. Mercury in six months. And the moon in one month.[35] Each one of them is approximate as we said before. For the computation of their conjunctions we proceed thus: Two revolutions of Saturn are sixty years, five revolutions of Jupiter are sixty years, forty revolutions of Mars are sixty years, sixty revolutions of the sun are sixty years, seventy-two revolutions of Venus are sixty years, one-hundred-and-twenty revolutions of Mercury are sixty years, and seven-hundred-and-twenty revolutions of

the Moon are sixty years. And this is one of their conjunctions all together, namely the time it takes for them to be in conjunction all at once. Similarly, one hundred conjunctions such as this one take place in six thousand years as such: Two hundred revolutions of Saturn are six thousand years, five hundred revolutions of Jupiter are six thousand years, four thousand revolutions of Mars are six thousand years, 6 thousand revolutions of the Sun are 6 thousand years, 7 thousand and two hundred revolutions of Venus are 6 thousand years, 12 thousand revolutions of Mercury are 6 thousand years, and 72 thousand revolutions of the Moon are 6 thousand years.

He thus spoke and made the computation so that you would know that neither among the Greeks nor among the Barbarians was there any doubt about these matters for those who occupy themselves with these things in any degree.[36]

One can sense that Sebokht wanted to assert that the phenomenon of conjunctions was a natural phenomenon, hence should not be interpreted in an eschatological sense. He also believed that Bār Daiṣān, for whom he seems to have had much respect, also carried out these computations of conjunctions for the same purpose. Incidentally, Sebokht seems to include Bār Daiṣān within the Christian flock, as having been "instructed in the Christian faith." He certainly takes some pride in his association with him as a fellow Syrian. In the context of Sebokht's sensitivity to the claims of Greek superiority in astronomical sciences, as we shall see below, Bār Daiṣān was once more welcome by Sebokht to the bosom of the community.

The importance of the quotation, however, is that it confirms the hints encountered in the text of Mar Ephraim, in that it shows beyond any doubt that Bār Daiṣān was interested in such issues as cycles of conjunctions. Whether he was interested in them because he believed in them, or whether he studied them in order to refute them, as he did with the astrologers' doctrines is hard to tell.

The tone of Sebokht's quotation is rather positive, and I would tend to agree with him that Bār Daiṣān was in all likelihood proving to the doomsday preachers of his days, probably from among the ranks of the Chaldeans, that such phenomena occur rather often, and that they had already occurred one hundred times during the six thousand years of the world and nothing happened. I even suspect that he may have even doctored up some of the planetary periods just to make these conjunctions work in the manner he wished to employ them.

The second quotation preserved in one of the works of George, bishop of the Arabs, is in fact a section of the same text just cited by Severus Sebokht, and one would think that Sebokht was in all likelihood the source for George.[37] A closer look, however, reveals some editorial variations, as well as some subtle differences in the language, that could indicate an independent source for the bishop of the Arabs. For the sake of comparison, the following is from the translation of Cureton. George, the bishop of the Arabs said:

> Bardesan, a man of antiquity, and renowned for the knowledge of events, has written in a treatise composed by him touching the synods [meaning conjunction] of the heavenly luminaries with one another, saying thus: Two circuits of Saturn are 60 years; 5 circuits of Jupiter 60 years; 40 circuits of Mars 60 years; 60 circuits of the Sun 60 years; 72 circuits of Venus 60 years; 150 circuits[38] of Mercury 60 years; 720 circuits of the moon 60 years; and this is one synod of them all, that is to say, the time of one synod of them; so that hence it appears, that for 100 such synods there would be six thousand years, in this manner: 200 circuits of Saturn 6 thousand years; 500 circuits of Jupiter 6 thousand years; 4 thousand circuits of Mars 6 thousand years; six thousand circuits of the Sun six

thousand years; 7 thousand and 200 circuits of Venus 6 thousand years; 12 thousand circuits of Mercury 6 thousand years; 72 thousand circuits of the moon 6 thousand years: and Bardesan made these calculations when he was desirous of shewing that this world would stand only six thousand years."[39]

We note immediately that we are dealing with the same text, with slight variations. And as noted before, the same nonsensical numbers of planetary periods are used here again. But because of such nonsense, we are in a much better position to assert that the original text which was quoted by both Sebokht and George, the bishop of the Arabs, was indeed authentic. In fact the same text seems to have also inspired the later Byzantine Greek text which we said was cited in the *Catalogus Codicum Astrologorum Graecorum* (CCAG) in the note above. At times, mistakes and false doctrines are much better indicators of cultural transmission of ideas.

The presence of Bār Daiṣān's text in the Byzantine Greek manuscript listed in *CCAG* deserves some attention. At the very least, it indicates that scientific ideas were not always flowing from Greek into Syriac and Arabic, but at times, even when they were of no real scientific consequence, flowed back into Greek from those languages. Bār Daiṣān's text is an excellent illustration of this process.

To sum up, there is evidence of a widespread belief in cosmological astrological doctrines in upper Mesopotamia, during the first three centuries of Christianity. These ideas were well known to the church fathers, and were sometimes disapproved of. At some point these same ideas seem to have migrated east into Persia, slightly modified, and then went south into India, only to come back during Islamic times and from there into medieval Europe. The traffic may have moved in the opposite direction, but in both cases the centrality of the Antiochian region is obvious.

But cosmological doctrines are not the only evidence of contacts between upper Mesopotamia and India. Other evidence, some of which is much clearer than the few fragments examined so far, can be solicited at this point.

B. Theory of the Five Elements

The Hellenistic doctrines regarding the nature of the Elements that are the four building blocks of the world, Fire, Earth, Air and Water, are well known. The addition of a fifth element, is of undoubted Indian provenance and deserves some attention.

The same Parisian manuscript (Syriac 346) in which the text of Severus Sebokht was preserved, has another section by Severus Sebokht dealing with the directions of winds in which he claimed that he was deriving his information from Olympiadorus? (sixth century).[40]

At the end of that treatise (fol. 63v), Sebokht reports that "there are those among the Indians (*hendwāye*) who say that wind is a fifth element. But that is a falsehood and an untruth (lit. a lie), for there are only four elements and not five."

In fact Indian doctrines do claim that there are five elements.[41] But whether one should equate wind, as mentioned by Sebokht, with the ubiquitous Indian concept of *ākāśa*[42], is not clear. What is sure, is that there were reports circulating in northern Mesopotamia towards the middle of the seventh century, when Severus was writing, that the Indians had a doctrine about the elements different from that of the Greeks, and that the Indian doctrine advocated five elements instead of the Greek four.

C. The Decimal System, and Indian Numerals

The same Parisian manuscript, an understudied mine of information, contains yet another text by Sebokht towards the end (beginning on folio 168v), which was first noticed by François Nau.[43] The text is a separate chapter in which Sebokht tries to demonstrate the antiquity of the Syrian astronomical sciences (obviously meaning what we now call Cuneiform Babylonian Astronomy). In itself, the chapter is a gem because it does not only preserve an early attempt at writing the history of "Syrian" science, and preserves the reference to the Indian decimal system, but because it also preserves the spirit of tension that was already widespread between the Syrians and the Greeks as two cultures in conflict. Putting that enmity between the two cultures in the context of the political events of the time, one is no longer surprised at the widespread belief that the native population of Syria actually welcomed the Arab/Muslim invasion of that Byzantine territory[44] some thirty years earlier in order to rid themselves of the cultural and political hegemony of the Greeks.

Our text, however, falls towards the beginning of the chapter titled "On the Antiquity of the Syrian Knowledge of Astronomical Instruction, and that such Knowledge is General and not Restricted to the Greeks or the Barbarians if they are Diligent, and some Questions, i.e., Doubts, Regarding Certain Issues in this Science." (The title by itself tells the whole story of the context, and tension.)

In the heat of the debate against the Greeks, Sebokht says:

> And I have neglected to tell you now of the science of the Indians, those who are not even Syrians, and of their subtle discoveries regarding this science of astronomy that are much more ingenious than those of the Greeks and even the Babylonians, and the intelligent methods of their calculations, and their calculation that is beyond description, I mean to say that which is [carried out] by the use of nine symbols. Had those who feel that they can think of themselves as they alone having reached the limits of wisdom, only because they speak Greek, been able to know these things, they would visualize, although belatedly, that there are others who know something, and not the Greeks only. But that there are others [who know] of other nations with different tongues. I say these things not to belittle Greek wisdom (and say) that it is not (to be found) in these matters and in things similar to them. Nay! I do not err in all that, rather I wish to demonstrate that science is universal.[45]

This incredibly powerful text, demonstrates beyond any doubt that at least Severus Sebokht knew of the Indian invention of the decimal system. For he speaks of those nine symbols that one uses in computation, and when he thought of the power of that computation he became simply speechless. Nine symbols used in a powerful computation by the Indians could only mean the decimal system.

However, we are accustomed to think of the decimal system as containing a zero as well, that is ten symbols altogether, hence "decimal," and Sebokht speaks of only nine. Before one rushes to think that the Indians did not have such a symbol, or that the zero was added by the Arabs later, as it is so often asserted, remember that the zero, as a concept of a place holder, and as a symbol, was already known in ancient Mesopotamia,[46] and was very well known among the Greeks at least as far back as the early Christian era. It was also known to the Indians.

So, why did Sebokht say that nine symbols were sufficient to constitute that powerful system of the Indians for which he was so full of amazement? Perhaps he did not think of the zero as a number, but rather as a designation of a lack of number, an empty space, and thus did not constitute a number like the other nine. The most sophisticated Greek mathematicians did not think of negative numbers as numbers either. It is in modern times that such numbers, as well as the zero, are now treated as belonging to the same class.

The fact that the Indians employed a zero, and even had a symbol for it, is not subject to doubt.[47] But the Indian decimal system was perfected around the year 600 A.D.,[48] about sixty years before the date of Sebokht's text. Given the context of the time, and the natural human tendency not to acknowledge easily new ways of computation,[49] sixty years is indeed a very short time for the transmission of such ideas.

For those who are accustomed to thinking of the Indian numerals, as the ones used in the eastern part of the Arab/Muslim world, where the zero symbol is usually represented by a dot, rather than a small circle, one more text demonstrates that the circular form of the zero was also known in the Mesopotamian region by at least the early part of the ninth century if not before. About the year 817, another Syriac author has left us a treatise devoted to the discussion of natural philosophical subjects in which there is a mention of such a symbol for zero.

The treatise in question is that of Job of Edessa (fl.817), who was known to Bar Hebraeus as a Nestorian physician, and who wrote in Syriac as well as Arabic. The text under discussion, called *Book of Treasures,* is an encyclopedia of sorts, in which Job moves from a discussion of the fundamental elements that constitute the universe in the first discourse to a discussion of the ranks of angels in the sixth.[50]

In the second chapter of the last discourse, titled "On The Fact that the Hierarchies of the Hosts of Angels are Three, and these are Subdivided into Nine Orders," is found the following description of these orders:

> Indeed numbering does not begin until the number two,[51] which is even, follows the number one (making three); and it continues this until the number three reaches the number nine, where the movement of mounting up stops, according to the angelic division. It is after this that, in the composed beings, on account of suffering an addition begins towards the number ten, as if the number nine wished to make a kind of link, in order to strengthen the numbering on account of its weakness,[52] in accordance with the order required by the composed beings that these beings should be linked in all their compositions; and so that it might be linked, it reverted towards the number one in a circular way. The movement of numbering is thus completed in a kind of cycle. It is for this reason that the ancients invented, as a first sign for this number (ten) the (empty) space between the forefinger and the thumb, formed in a circular way. Indeed when the numbers which we have with us reach a denary ('sīrīyūtā) state they stop, and then turn back and mount up indefinitely. (259-260).

It is obvious that Job is talking about the familiar decimal system, the main feature of which is that numbering goes back to the beginning once we reach ten, just as the numbering in the sexagesimal system (still used very heavily by almost all cultures after thousands of years of its invention in ancient Mesopotamia in the familiar count of hours, minutes, seconds, etc.) begins from the beginning when we reach sixty. By going back to the beginning, we simply mean that we move the base unit one rank to the left, thus reaching the tens, then the hundreds, the thousands and so on.

The importance of Job's text is that it describes this returning to the beginning in such visual terms that it specifically refers to it by the image generated by the empty "space between the forefinger and the thumb, formed in a circular way." The picture is very clear, Job undoubtedly had in mind the rounded zero, which marks the turning over to the beginning.

Job's text was written just about the same time as the famous algebraist Muḥammad b. Mūsā al-Khwārizmī, whose name has given us the common English term *algorithm,* and whose book title gave us the term *algebra.* It is this same Khwārizmī who was also supposed to have written the first text known to the Arabic authors on Indian arithmetic. In retrospect, we can now see that the process of naturalizing the Indian decimal system in the Mesopotamian region had already begun about two centuries earlier, at least by the time of Severus Sebokht if not before.

Conclusion

What lessons can be drawn from these scattered fragments of evidence? First, we note the centrality of the Mesopotamian region in all this traffic. Whether it was doctrines invented in Mesopotamia, or somewhere else, they all passed by Mesopotamia sooner or later.

Second, the early church fathers seem to have considered a variety of subjects while they were carrying out their theological debates. One has to go through the painful process of separating these secular subjects from the surrounding "Byzantine" debates in order to gain some familiarity with their basic scientific information.

Third, the religious, theological schisms may have not been always motivated by theological considerations. The enmity so transparent between the Syrian Sebokht and the Greeks would have been enough to split the community if such a community had to suffer the indignity of the haughty Greeks.

Fourth, these church fathers in their struggles with one another, and in their attempts to refute each other's opinions become very human. They succumb to anger, exaggeration, and at times sheer bias.

Fifth, the little known of Bār Daiṣān's ideas does not justify his excommunication as a heretic, and not all church fathers were of the same opinion regarding his status. His scientific knowledge was obviously far reaching. He knew the philosophical doctrines of the Greeks, the customs and habits of far away nations, and most of all he seems to have had some basic competence in astronomical computations. When that is coupled with his well acknowledged fame in poetic diction one is no longer surprised by the "jealousies?" harbored against him. Even Mar Ephraim, his most vehement critic, had to admit that Bār Daiṣān's poetry was enchanting. It is for that reason that the youth of Edessa followed him.

Sixth, this body of evidence illustrates that the contacts between Mesopotamia and India were much more extensive in the pre-Islamic period than previously thought. Apparently they were not contacts of the commercial type only. They seem to have encompassed a whole variety of subjects, most notably the knowledge of that most powerful system of computation, the decimal system, that we still use.

Seventh, with the current millennium coming to a close, with all the expectations of the end to come, it behooves us to remember that the early church fathers encountered similar ideas in their days, and they refuted them as best they could. The fact that those ideas came from the astrological domain should not surprise us in the least, now that we are accustomed to see the New Age books occupying more and more space on the book shelves of our bookstores. The early church fathers, especially Sebokht, and even Bār Daiṣān, were much more grounded in scientific thought and called the natural phenomena by their names, rather than succumb to the millenarists.

Finally, the part of the Antiochian legacy examined reveals an Antioch that was at the crossroads of all types of cultural trends, and scientific ideas. Its intellectuals absorbed these ideas, passed them on, and most importantly, as Sebokht would say, never felt that science and scientific ideas were the exclusive property of any one nation.

NOTES

[1] Asad Rustum, *Kanīsat Madīnat Allah Anṭākia al-'Uẓmā*, (Beirut:Manshūrāt al-Nūr, 1952-1958).

[2] Acts, 11:26.

[3] For the discussion concerning the origins of Theophilus Indus (Theophile The Indian), see Irfan Shahîd, *Byzantium and the Arabs in the Fourth Century* (Washington D.C.: Dumbarton Oaks, 1984), 96-97 n 84. To complicate things further, even the Syriac references to Indians (*hendwāyā*) does sometimes refer to Ethiopians, Cushites, Nubians as well. See J. Payne Smith (Mrs. Margolioouth), *A Compendious Syriac Dictionary* (Oxford: Clarindon Press, 1903), 104-105.

[4] Albert Abūnā, *Adab al-Lugha al-Ārāmīya* (Beirut: Starco, 1970), 64 ff.

[5] This does not mean that the current Christian community of India, with its long Syriac tradition and historical connections with the Catholicos of Baghdad, was not evangelized by St. Thomas. The problem is whether the evangelization happened when it is supposed to have happened, and whether the missionary activity did take place in modern-day India, or in some other part of the Persian Gulf, and from there later reached modern-day India.

[6] Abūnā, 65. Anton Baumstark, *Geschichte der Syrischen Literatur* (Bonn: Marcus & Webers, 1922), 14. On the history of the Syrian Orthodox Church in India, see, Navakatesh J. Thomas, *Die Syrisch-Orthodoxe Kirche der Südindischen Thomas-Christen* (Würzburg: Augustinus-Verlag, 1967).

[7] Yāqūt al-Ḥamwī, *Muʻjam al-Buldān* (Beirut: Sādir, 1979), 1: 432, column 2. For further evidence supporting this reference to Ubulla, the city which was later incorporated into the encampment of Baṣra (*miṣr al-Baṣra*), as "*arḍ al-Hind*", "land of India," see also Ṣāliḥ Aḥmad ʻAlī, *al-Tanẓīmāt al ijtimāʻīya wa-l-iqtiṣādīya fī al-Baṣra fī al-qarn al-awwal al-hijrī* (Baghdad: Maṭbaʻat al-Maʻārif, 1953), 70 n. 4, where he documents the activities of a group called *al-sayābija* active in early Baṣra life as being from India. At 148 n. 3, ʻAlī refers to an article on Baṣra in *Sumer*, vol. 9 (1952), 72-83 and 281-303, passim, documenting the close commercial activities between Baṣra and India even down to Islamic times. He claims that this trade during the first century of Ḥijra (seventh to eighth century) was only a reflection of the similar trade that went on during the previous centuries. The chapter beginning on page 229 in ʻAlī's work is devoted to the trade with India, and has many references to earlier Roman times. See also pages 231-232 for the specific reference to Ubulla where he says that it was called *arḍ al-hind*, or *farj al-hind*. On page 22, ʻAlī gives all the sources that use this name in reference to early Baṣra in the following sequence: al-Ḥasan al-Baṣrī Schaider, in *Der Islam XIV*

(1925), 3240, Balādhurī, *Futūh*, 341 (sic., see 241), Madā'inī, in Ṭabarī, I, 2016, 2378, and Wāqidī, also in Ṭabarī, I, 2383, Ibn Saʿd, *al Ṭabaqāt al-Kubrā*, vol. 7, part 1, p. 2. The name *arḍ al-Hind* seems to have originated with Madā'inī, Wāqidī, and Ibn Saʿd. See also Pellat, Ch. in *EI*, for early sources on Baṣra, where he adds the names of Ibn al-Athīr, Ibn al-Faqīh, al-Istakhrī, and the remaining geographers as well as locates Aṣmaʿī and Madā'inī in Baṣra. I owe to Professor M. Morony of UCLA a reference to a citation of Ṭabarī referring to the area as *farj al-Hind* (I, 2016, 2023), and to Ibn al-Faqīh (*Buldān*, 188) who also refers to it as *ard al-Hind*.

[8] Yāqūt, 432.

[9] See note 7 above.

[10] See Abūnā, 58, where one finds an extensive bibliography on this author, Baumstark, 12, and Ignatius Aphram I Barsaum, *al-Luʾluʾ al-Manthūr*, 4th. ed. (Holland: Bar Hebraeus Verlag, 1987), 191ff, passim.

[11] For an edition and translation of the Syriac text of Bar Daiṣān, see H.J.W. Drijvers, *The Book of the Laws of Countries* (The Netherlands: Assen Van Gorcum, 1964).

[12] *Ibid.*, 43.

[13] *Ibid.*, 51.

[14] For the origin of Arabic numerals, and the family tree to which they belong, see Karl Menninger, *Number Words and Number Symbols: A Cultural History of Numbers* (Boston: MIT Press, 1969), 418-419.

[15] François Nau, who worked extensively on the works of the Syriac fathers in the first quarter of this century was also puzzled by Bar Daiṣān's accusation of heresy. See, F. Nau, "Notes d'astronomie Syrienne," *Journal Asiatique,* 2e. ser., t. xvi (1910), 209-228, esp. 215-216.

[16] For a brief bio-bibliographical reference to this famous church father, see Abūnā, 76; and Baumstark, 31.

[17] I am referring here to his *Discourse* (Mīmrā) *Against Bār Daiṣān,* now edited and translated by C.W. Mitchell, A.A. Bevan and F.C. Burkitt, *S. Ephraim's Prose Refutations of Mani, Marcion, and Bār Daiṣān,* vol. II (London and Oxford: Williams and Norgate, 1921), lxvi-lxxix; 143-169.

[18] Abūnā, 77; and Barsaum, 196.

[19] Mitchell, *et al., Prose Refutations,* lxxv.

[20] For a discussion of such astrological doctrines, and the series of conjunctions connected with them, see, for example, E.S. Kennedy, "The World Year Concept in Islamic Astrology," (International Congress of the History of Science, 1962), reprinted in *Studies in the Islamic Exact Sciences,* by E.S. Kennedy, Colleagues and Former Students, American University of Beirut (Beirut, 1983), 351-371.

[21] According to astrologers, planets are said to be in conjunction if they fall on the same point of the zodiac, or more loosely if they fall in the same zodiacal sign.

[22] The widespread convention of representing sexagesimal numbers by units separated from fractions by a semicolon simply means in this case 242 + 30/60 degrees, i.e., 242 degrees and a half, or 242 degrees and 30 minutes.

[23] See, for example, E. S. Kennedy, "The Sassanian Astronomical handbook Zīj-i Shāh and The Astrological Doctrine of transit (Mamarr)," *Journal of the American Oriental Society,* 78 (1958), 246-262, esp. 259.

[24] Burgess, Ebenezer, *Sūrya-Sidhanta: A Textbook of Hindu Astronomy* (New Haven, 1860), 17-18.

[25] From Ibn Hibinta (c. 929), quoted in E.S. Kennedy, "Sassanian," 260.

[26] Bryant Tuckerman, *Planetary, Lunar, And Solar Positions A.D. 2 to A.D. 1649* (Philadelphia: American Philosophical Society, 1964), 35.

[27] V. Grumel, *Traité d' études Byzantines, I – Chronologie* (Paris: Presses Universitaires de Frances, 1958), 116.

[28] See Kennedy, "Sassanian," and E.S. Kennedy and D. Pingree, *The Astrological History of Māshā'allāh,* (Cambridge, Mass: Harvard, 1971), 74-75.

[29] E.S. Kennedy and B.L. van der Waerden, "The World Year of the Persians," *Journal of the American Oriental Society,* 83 (1963): 315-327, esp. 316.

[30] Abū al-Raiḥān Bīrūnī, *The Chronology of Ancient Nations,* tr. by E. Sachau, Allen, (London, 1879), 27.

[31] *Ibid.,* p. 28.

[32] This fragment has never been published in its entirety, although it is still preserved in at least one manuscript we know of, namely the famous manuscript Syriac 346, kept at the Bibliotheque Nationale, in Paris, which was summarily described by F. Nau, in "Notes."

[33] *Ibid.*

[34] For a full citation of this conjunction, see Nau, "Notes," and O. Neugebauer, "Regula Philippi Arrhidaei," *Isis,* 50 (1959): 477-478. Neugebauer recomputes the positions for all the seven planets, and finds them to have been indeed in the sign of Taurus as stipulated by the text of Sebokht, with minor mistake in the text.

[35] These periods are obviously astronomically nonsensical, for the first two are crude roundings of 29.49 tropical years for Saturn, and 11.86 for Jupiter, while the others could not be related in any coherent sense to the physical realities of the planets. They appear once more in a later Byzantine Greek text, which obviously derives from such traditions as the ones that were being propagated by Bār Daiṣān. For the Byzantine text, see *Catalogus Codicum Astrologorum Graecorum,* 12 vols. (Brussels, 1898-1953), esp. vol. 4, 116-118, and 183-184. For these periods and others, see also O. Neugebauer, *History of Ancient Mathematical Astronomy* (Berlin and Heidelberg: Springer, 1975), 782-4.

[36] Bibliotheque Nationale, Paris, Syriac Manuscript, 346, fols, 122v-123r.

[37] The text was noted and transcribed by William Cureton, in *Spicilegium Syriacum,* (London: Francis and John Rivington, 1855), 40 (translation), 21 (Syriac text).

[38] This should really be 120 as we have seen in the text quoted by Sebokht. The reason for the error is that the number is written in alphabetical form and the difference between *qn* (=150) and *qk* (=120) in Syriac can be confusing. Cureton's text obviously had a scribal error here, which was noted by Cureton himself but not corrected in the edition or in the translation. See Cureton, 84.

[39] *Ibid.,* 40.

[40] The text begins on folio 61v of that manuscript. It is not clear at this stage whether this text is any way related to the commentary of Olympiadorus on Aristotle's *Meteorologica* which was later known from the Arabic sources. See, F. Sezgin, *Geschichte des Arabischen Schrifttums,* vol. vii (Brill, Leiden, 1979), 229-230.

[41] The first one to draw my attention to the importance of this Indian reference in the work of Sebokht was my friend and colleague, Professor David Pingree of Brown University.

[42] D.M. Bose, et al, *A Concise History of Science in India* (New Delhi: Indian National Science Academy, 1971), 460.

[43] First in Nau, "La Cosmographie au VIIe Siècle," *Revue de l'Orient Chrétien,* 2e ser., t. 5 (xv) (1910), 225-254, esp. 248-252, and then in Nau, "Notes," 225-227.

[44] The echo of that assistance is beautifully preserved in the account of al-Balādhurī of the conquest of Damascus by Khālid Ibn al-Walīd, in the year 635AD. See, *The*

Origins of the Islamic State (Futūḥ al-Buldan), tr. by Philip Hitti (Beirut: Khayyat Oriental Reprints, 1966), 186f.

[45] Syriac Manuscript, fol. 170r-170v.

[46] On the origin of the zero, see O. Neugebauer, *The Exact Sciences in Antiquity* (Providence, RI: Brown University Press, 1957), 14, 26, 27. On the legend that the zero was introduced by the Arabs, I need not give any reference for this legend is repeated *ad nauseam* in too many secondary sources.

[47] See Menninger, 397, 418, passim.

[48] For this date, see Menninger, 396.

[49] Consider how western civilization still holds on tenaciously to the Arabic legacy of writing numbers with their ascending value of units, tens, hundreds, etc., from right to left when everything else in the language moves from left to right. Actually, the earliest representations of the ten, or nine, Indian numerals, which were introduced into the Latin West through Arabic were also written from right to left, i.e., 2 was written to the left of 1, 3 to the left of 2 and so on till 9, this in the midst of Latin texts normally read from left to right.

[50] Edit. and trans., A. Mingana (Cambridge: Heffer and Sons, 1935).

[51] We see here that even the number one was not yet accepted as a number like the other numbers. This philosophical position regarding the number one is well known among the Greeks.

[52] With the "weakness" of the number nine, it is hard not to think of the Pythagorcan perfection attributed to the number 10.

CONTRIBUTIONS OF CHRISTIANS TO ARABIC CIVILIZATION
by George N. Atiyeh

Introduction

Civilizations are advanced states of human society in which a high level of culture, science, art, industry and politics has been reached. In each civilization's development, certain ideals serve as guiding and driving forces. These ideals are the source for the definition of identity and self-knowledge.

In what we now call the classical Arab civilization, these ideals are embodied in the effort to reconcile reason and revelation. The classical Arab person sought to develop into a human being who, while serving God and obeying his will, used reason to understand God's will and his creation. To the classical Arab, man's final goal, besides salvation, was the establishment of a just society.

Arabic civilization did not put God on a shelf, as did other civilizations. To Christian Arabs, the manifestation of his presence served as a lighthouse, keeping them on course. Philosophy and the sciences were rarely distanced from the service of God.

What we call Arabic, and sometimes in a wider sense, Islamic civilization, developed most uniquely. The message brought by Muhammad (d. 632) translated itself into two great phenomena: a wide empire and a synthetic but rich civilization. This civilization developed gradually as the little-sophisticated Arabs absorbed the cultures of the neighboring Fertile Crescent, Egypt and Iran. Many of its roots and branches were not intrinsically Arabic. The three monotheistic religions, Judaism, Christianity, and Islam, sprang up and began their careers in the same region.

Christianity and Islam share some common fundamentals, the most important of which is belief in one Supreme Being. Each espouses similar ethical and spiritual values, belief in life after death, and belief in God's communication with his creatures through prophets. These common fundamentals are the key to understanding how Christians can live together with Muslims and contribute significantly to the particular cultural developments engendered by Islam. It is not far from Jerusalem to Mecca.

Some might wonder whether there were any specific Christian contributions to Arabic or Islamic civilization. This wonder should not last long. Interaction between Arabs and Christianity took place before, during and after the rise of Islam. Most of what is now the Arab world was Christian on the eve of Islam; there were many Christian tribes in the Arabian Peninsula and its peripheries.

After the rise of Islam, these Christian communities steadily became Arabized. More than that, they incorporated their Christian traditions of learning, whether Greek, Coptic, Latin or, most importantly, Syriac, into the fabric of Arabic civilization. Far from being strangers to Arab culture, Christians of all confessions contributed significantly to its formation and development. That is not to say that Arab civilization was created by Christians. The purpose of this short survey is to show that Christians, who were and have been Arabized, were full partners in its development.

Background

To understand the scope and depth of the contributions made by Christians and other Syriac speaking communities, one has to look in perspective at the intellectual and scientific achievements of these communities in the areas where Islam was first established, beginning with the centers of learning in Egypt, the Fertile Crescent and Iran.

During the six centuries predating Islam, Christianity had established itself securely in the heart of the Near East and around the Mediterranean basin. It triumphed over the religions and cults of those areas, but not without experiencing painful damages to its own theological unity. From a cultural perspective, however, the proliferation of Christian sects and the rise of several schools of thought enriched the cultural life that was the precursor to Arabic civilization.

In their struggle to make Christianity triumph over its religious, intellectual, and political opponents, the church fathers and scholars assimilated Greek and Hellenistic philosophical and scientific legacies. Using Greek intellectual modalities as well as biblical citations, Christianity developed into several schools of thought and sects. A new culture, a mix of Greek and Near Eastern, Christian and non-Christian elements, was formed. A great number of Syriac, Egyptian and African philosophers, theologians and scientists, schooled mostly by Greek and Roman scholars, added new and different elements to the core of classical culture, a core characterized by its humanism and rationalism.

All of the schools of thought developed in the first centuries of Christianity carried some elements of Near Eastern spirituality. Hermitism, Stoicism, Gnosticism, Pythagoreanism and Neoplatonism all contained "oriental" or non-rationalist elements, which distinguished them from the highly rationalist standards of Socrates, Plato, and particularly Aristotle. What was particularly significant though, was the transference of the major centers of learning from Athens and Alexandria to different places in the Fertile Crescent. These centers of learning developed a continuous tradition of scholarship that had a strong impact on the early development of Arabic civilization.

The Centers of Learning

The oldest of the centers of scientific and philosophical learning was in Alexandria; its famous library and Museum attracted and produced major Greek and local scholars and doctors. Alexandria was the site where early church fathers and scholars such as Clement (d. 215) and Origen (d. 253) explained and defended a struggling Christianity with arguments derived from philosophical principles. In Alexandria, Plotinus (d. 270), author of the *Enneads*, developed his Neoplatonist school of philosophy, which is characterized by its theory of emanation and the attempt to reconcile the philosophies of Plato and Aristotle. Porphyry of Tyre (d. 305) popularized Plotinus' philosophy. He wrote a biography of Plotinus and edited his *Enneads*, parts of which were translated into Arabic under the wrong title *Theology of Aristotle*. These became a source of inspiration for the Muslim philosophers al-Kindi (d. 873) and al-Farabi (d. 950). Porphyry composed, among other things, the *Isagoge*, a highly-regarded introduction to Aristotle's *Categories*. The *Isagoge* became the foundation for all subsequent formal logic, used and commented upon by philosophers and theologians, Christians and Muslims.

Greek philosophy was accepted by the Muslims as it had previously been accepted by the Christians because it provided a "natural theology," that is, a theory of the divine as revealed in the nature of reality and accessible to human reason. Christian thinkers like John Philoponus — most likely the source of many of al-Kindi's theories on creation out of nothing and on prophetic knowledge — used Greek logic to prove the truth of the Christian doctrines. His thesis on creation was based on the argument that the body of the universe, being finite, cannot be eternal: finitude and eternity are mutually exclusive. He further believed that reason and revelation have the same attainable goals. Philoponus was well known to the Arabs and Muslims and it is possible that his theological and philosophical views were disseminated by his fellow Jacobite writers.

The activities of the school of Alexandria, which lasted until the Arab conquest, were not limited to the philosophical field, they also included the pure sciences. Alexandria produced many distinguished scholars and professionals such as Ptolemy (d. 170) the geographer and Galen (d. ca. 201) the doctor. In the field of theology, it was Athanasius (d. 373), opponent of Arianism, who explored the full implication of the Nicene creed, that God is one in essence.

But it was also in Alexandria that the Christological controversy took place, which flared and led to a division in the Universal Church during the fifth century. Looking positively at this disconcerting phenomenon, one cannot fail to notice the development it engendered in the intellectual and scientific fields. Thousands of books were produced, filling the shelves of many libraries in the areas where Arabic civilization was destined to prosper.

One of the leading figures of the controversy was Eutychus (d. 455), who taught that Jesus Christ had only one nature and that Christ's humanity was completely absorbed and identified with his divinity. This implied that he never became perfect man. The controversy culminated in the Council of Chalcedon (451) and led to the final clarification of the position of the Universal Church: though Jesus Christ is one in essence with the Father, Christ has two real and perfect natures, he is perfect in Godhead and perfect in manhood.

Antioch was the most important Christian city in Syria. Christianity as a church organization started there. From it came the Nestorian movement which was, in a way, a nationalist movement against Byzantium and the Greek language.

Like Alexandria, Antioch was a source of illumination for many intellectual causes, Christian and otherwise. Very early it brought forth Saint Ignatius the Great (d. 107) and Theophilus (d. 180), the bishop whose writings impacted greatly on the dissemination of Christianity in the West and on the early formulation of the dogma of the Trinity. John Chrysostom, the Golden Mouthed (d. 407), was another Antiochian. He was a fluent and eloquent preacher who expounded in popular terms the complicated concepts of Christianity. Another famous Antiochian was Theodore of Mopsuestia (d. 429), teacher of Nestorius (d. 451). Though heterodox in certain areas, he was a great scholar who left a lasting impact on the school of Antioch by using a literal method of interpretation. This simplicity in method and clarity in explanation was the approach for which the school of Antioch became known.

The theological importance of the school of Antioch rests on the distinction made by its scholars between the human and the divine in the person of Christ. Those who moved away from Orthodoxy were mostly from the Antiochian school. Apollinarius (d. 390) maintained that the incarnate Logos resided only in Christ's body and animal soul but not in his rational soul. This, according to Apollinarius, was unchangingly divine. The implication is that the humanity of Christ was incomplete, a thesis contrary to the Universal Church's teaching of perfect God and perfect man in one divine person. Apollinarius prepared the way for Nestorius, who emphasized the separateness of the divine and human natures of Christ. Nestorius also maintained that Mary was the mother of Christ the man; that Christ was born a man and that the Logos entered his body after birth.

Antioch was a Hellenized city. Greek was the language of scholarship and literature, but Syriac was the language of the people. The rise of the Nestorian movement elicited strong opposition from both the Universal Church and the Byzantine government. The Nestorians were consequently forced to move to the interior, to Nisibis (Nasibin) and Edessa (al-Ruha). The cities of the interior, especially Qinnisrin, Membij, Amid and Harran, became important centers of learning and played an impressive role in the transfer of Greek learning into Syriac.

Edessa's great contribution was the transference of the Greek philosophical and scientific legacies into Syriac. Its professors taught Aristotelian and other philosophies together with religion and literature. A glimpse at Edessa's history shows its great importance.

Before the appearance of Islam, the school of Edessa had gone through three stages of development. In the first stage, the name of Saint Ephraim (d. 373), a great Syriac poet and interpreter of the Bible, is the most notable. In the second stage, because of the heated controversy between the Universal Church on one side and the Nestorians and Jacobites on the other, Emperor Zeno closed the school (489), and its eminent professors moved to Nisibis which was under the Persian rule. As a consequence, in the third stage, Nisibis became the center of the Nestorian movement. It kept the Edessan program of using logic and science in the service of religion very much alive. Its professors continued to translate and author books in philosophy, religion and literature.

The most distinguished of those was Sergius Ras Ayni (d. 536), one of the greatest translators from Greek into Syriac. Sergius had studied medicine and chemistry in Alexandria before settling down in his hometown of Ras al-Ayn. He was the first and most important translator of the medical books of Galen (d. ca. 200). For two centuries Serigus' books were considered most authoritative. Of his philosophical works, his versions of Porphyry's *Isagoge* and *Table* have survived together with an original treatise on logic.

The other non-Chalcedonian Christian group that played a great role was the Monophysites, known in Syria and Iraq as the "Jacobites." They upheld the thesis, promulgated earlier by Eutychus, of the one (singular) nature of Christ. According to them the human and the divine aspects of Christ constituted one composite nature, the one nature of the incarnated Word (Logos) of God. The Monophysite church in Syria and Iraq was organized by Jacob of Serugh (d. 578), hence the name "Jacobites."

The Jacobites had no great schools like the Nestorians, but their convent at Qinnisrin was an important center for Greek studies. Several eminent scholars appeared there. Among them was Severus Sebokht (d. 668), author of a commentary on Aristotle's *De Interpretatione*, and a treatise on the terms used in that book. He also wrote a treatise on syllogisms of the *Analytica Priora*. In astronomy, he wrote on the figures of the Zodiac and on the astrolabe. Among the disciples of Sebokht was Athanasius of Balad (d. 686), who edited a new version of a commentary on the *Isagoge*. Athanasius, a contemporary of some of the Rashidun caliphs and early Umayyads, wrote an epistle on how the Christians should behave among Muslims.

Jacob of Edessa (d. 709), another disciple of Sebokht, became fluent in Greek and Hebrew. The scope of his learning included theology, geography and grammar. He authored more than thirty works, the best known of which were the *Encheridion*, a treatise on technical terms used in philosophy, and a Syriac version of Aristotle's *Categories*. George, the bishop of the Arabs (d. 724), disciple of Athanasius and bishop of the Tay, Aqil and Tanukh tribes, translated and commented on the complete *Organon* of Aristotle.

There were other schools in the Fertile Crescent, one of them non-Christian, in Harran, and one, with a Christian faculty, in Jundishapur, under Persian rule. Both played significant roles during the Islamic period.

One can conclude from this short survey that Syriac and other Christian centers of learning were abundant and productive, and that the schools of the Fertile Crescent not only transmitted Greek philosophy and sciences, but also kept scholarly traditions alive throughout the centuries. They added knowledge that was destined to serve as a basis for many aspects of Arabic civilization. Their function did not cease with the coming of Islam; they continued to produce and enrich the Arabic civilization which began to take shape and to which, in time, they became assimilated.

Christian Influence in Early Islamic Development

If we consider — and we should — that Arabic civilization had strong pre-Islamic roots, we should examine the role of the Christians in the areas where Islam began.

Christianity existed in the Arabian Peninsula in Najrān as well as in some Arab towns and villages mentioned by the historian Zosimus (fifth century). Areas bordering southern Syria were inhabited by Christian Arab tribes. In places such as Tabuk and Wadi-al-Qura, Christian monks lived in special hermitages.

We also know that there were Christians in Mecca, including members of the Quraysh family, Abyssinian followers of the Monophysite sect, and passing traders. Certain historians, in particular Ibn Ishaq (d. 768), refer to Warqah ibn Nawfal as a Christian. Khadijah, wife of Muhammad, sought his advice when Muhammad saw his first vision at Mount Hirah. Warqah, it is said, identified the source of the vision as Gabriel, the archangel, and related its manifestation to similar experiences had by other prophets. The figure of a Christian monk who clairvoyantly recognized the hidden greatness of Muhammad appears repeatedly in Muslim biographical traditions about his early years.

The particular aspects of the development of early Islam to which the Christians of the Peninsula and its peripheries have contributed are still in dispute among scholars. Christianity was not as dominant a religion in the Peninsula as it was in Egypt and the Fertile Crescent. Christianity existed, however, among certain important tribes such as Banu Bakr, Ṭay, Rabi'ah, Quda'ah and Tamim. Other tribes, such as the Ghassanids and the Banu Tanūkh, built large kingdoms in southern Syria and Hira, Iraq, respectively. Both kingdoms attained a high degree of culture and built political centers of power that made their influence felt all over the area.

The Ghassanids, a buffer state for Byzantium in southern and eastern Syria, mediated certain vital elements of their flourishing culture to their original kinsmen in Arabia, particularly in Hijaz, the future birth place of Islam. The Ghassanids, who were Jacobites, probably passed on Christian ideas, which, with other ideas, germinated into Islam. According to Muslim tradition, Muhammad and his caravan passed through Busra, there to learn much of what he knew of Christianity.

In the pre-Islamic period and in early Islam many Christians distinguished themselves as great poets. 'Adi ibn Zayd (d. 587) produced poetry in a style different from the bedouin style of other pre-Islamic poets. His beautiful wife Hind bint al-Nu'man was another poet who, after his death, became a nun and built a famous convent. Another poet was Maysun, the wife of the caliph Mu'awiyah I. A famous poem expressing a yearning for the simple life of the desert is attributed to her. Al-Akhtal (d. 710), the bard who championed the cause of the Umayyads, was also a Christian.

Poets at the time were leaders of public opinion, so when the Umayyad caliph Yazid I wished to take revenge on the people of Medina because one of their poets had addressed amatory verses to the caliph's sister, he turned to al-Akhtal to respond. Al-Akhtal's forceful eulogies of other Umayyad caliphs made them prefer him to their own Muslim poets. Al-Akhtal is commended by literary critics for the great number and excellence of his long poems as well as for the purity, polish and correctness of his style.

In his introduction to Luis Cheikho's book *'Ulamā' al-Masiḥiyah fi al-Islam* (Christian Scholars in Islam), Father Camille Hecheime counts 363 scholars who flourished and contributed between 622-1300 A.D. They included 215 medical scholars and doctors, 63 translators, 40 philosophers, and 5 astronomers. What is striking here is not the numbers but the concentration of the scholars in the fields of medicine, translation and philosophy.

Christians shone in these fields because their socio-religious situation and traditions limited their participation to these fields. Having come mostly from the Fertile Crescent, these scholars had the advantage of being bilingual or trilingual. They knew Syriac, Greek and Arabic. In addition to their trustworthiness, this linguistic ability was the main reason the caliphs called upon them for medical treatment and for translation of the riches of the Greek and Syriac cultures into Arabic.

Furthermore, many Christian philosophers and scientists tutored the great Islamic philosophers in the early centuries of Islam. Islamic science and philosophy grew from a ground saturated with the Hellenic and Syriac cultures. It could be said that through Arabization, Islam underwent a counter-process of Syrianization and Hellenization.

More than any other group, the Syriac-speaking Christians contributed to the early scientific and intellectual awakening during the classical or golden age of Arabic civilization. Yet, in a sense, it is difficult to measure these contributions quantitatively, one cannot thus encompass the breadth of Christian influence. Specific examples may help to demonstrate its scope.

Eighty years after the fall of the Umayyads, the burgeoning Arabic civilization had reached one of its major peaks. Thanks to Christian translators, it already possessed Arabic translations of the works of Aristotle, Plato, the leading Neoplatonic commentators such as Alexander of Aphrodisias, Proclus, Porphyry and others, as well as the works of famous geographers, astronomers, mathematicians and doctors of medicine.

The contact and interaction between the Christian and Muslim theologians during and after the Umayyad era had a demonstrable impact on some Muslim theologians, particularly the Qadarites, the Murjites and the Mu'tazilah. The polemic between the two groups did not only center on the creeds of each religion, it went much beyond that.

Scholars are still debating the amount of influence Christian theology had on the Mu'tazilah. The similarity between the teachings of John of Damascus (d. 749) and Theodore Abu Qurrah (d. ca. 825) on the one hand, and some of the early Muslim scholars on the other, is so obvious that it is hard to say that there were no interactions between the two. The Murji'ites (following the Damascene), maintained that God is the source of what is good, and he always does the best for his creatures.

Both religions were faced with a similar problem regarding the relation of the eternal with the temporal. For the Muslims, the Koran is the "very speech of God." The Book in time was on earth, was one with the Book preserved eternally in heaven; as such it must be "uncreated," yet the Koran came in the seventh century, what is really its relationship to God?

This was the same problem which faced the Christians when they tried to solve the problem of Jesus the incarnate as Logos and son of God on earth. There is no doubt that Muslim scholars benefitted from the Christian speculation on this subject. In other words the issue of God's attributes such as wisdom and power, whether they are or not a part of his very nature, troubled both religions. To say they are not would mean that God is composite, and what is composite is not eternal.

In the dispute among the Muslim theologians on the relation of the Koran to God, the Mu'tazilah believed the Koran was the speech (Logos) of God, but they also believed that it was created. They insisted on the perfect unity and simplicity of God. The divine attributes were recognized but according to the Mu'tazilah they had no intrinsic existence apart from God. Although identical with the Divine Being, they were entities appended to him. If the Koran was not created, that is eternal, there would be two eternals, then God is not one and simple; therefore he is composite, an unacceptable conclusion.

Perhaps the most controversial issue, other than the creation of the Koran, centered around free will — man's responsibility for his actions. It is very probable that the Mu'tazilah were influenced by the first creative Christian theologian to write in Arabic at a time when this language was just becoming the medium of the wider Islamic civilization. Having in mind the new environment in which he was writing, Theodore Abu Qurrah debated the Mu'tazilah in the court of the caliph al-Ma'mun (813-833). Many of Abu Qurrah's ideas are similar to those of the Damascene, but he further emphasized man's capability to know God by reason. If man is able to know God by reason he should also be able to know what is good or evil by reason. Proving the principles of religion by reason was the methodology used by the Mu'tazilah.

Christian Influence in Secular Arab Civilization

The role of the Christians was essential in developing those sciences of the ancients which were the backbone of the humanistic non-religious aspects of Arab civilization, although several of the sciences, particularly mathematics and astronomy, were used by Muslims for religious purposes. Let us consider some examples of that role.

Jurjis (George) ibn Bakhtishu' (d. ca. 770) the dean of the school of Jundishapur, was summoned by the caliph al-Mansur (754-775) when the latter fell sick. Impressed by his methods of treatment and knowledge, the caliph retained him in his service. After years of service, Jurjis fell sick and wanted to go back to his hometown. Al-Mansur invited him to adopt Islam, but Jurjis replied that he preferred the company of his brothers, be they in heaven or hell. In fact, Jurjis became the founder of a family of physicians which almost monopolized the entire caliphal courts' medical practices and which produced a great number of medical works, original and translated. Gabriel, son of Jurjis wrote a *Kannash,* a manual of medicine, based on the works of the great doctors of antiquity Dioscurides (fl. ca. 60) and Galen. Like most Christian scholars of the time, Gabriel also wrote on subjects related to religion and philosophy, including a treatise on the agreement between the sayings of the prophets and philosophers.

Yahya ibn al-Batriq (d. ca. 806), another Christian scholar of the times, translated the major works of Galen and Hippocrates (fl. ca. 436 B.C.) as well as the great astronomy work *al-Majisti*. Yuhanna ibn Masawayh (d. 857), a famous doctor, was commissioned by the caliph Harun al-Rashid to translate certain manuscripts, mainly medical, which the caliph had brought back from raids into Asia Minor. Ibn al-Nadim, author of the oldest Arabic bio-bibliographical work *al-Fihrist*, lists forty-four works by Yuhanna on medical and public health.

Yuhanna's pupil, Hunayn ibn Ishaq (d. 873), stands out as one of the greatest translators, creative authors, and most noble characters of the Abassid period. In fact, he was the most important expositor of ancient Greek science to the Arabs. He was appointed by the caliph al-Ma'mun to head *Bayt al-Hikmah* (House of Wisdom), a major learning institution that combined the functions of an academy, library and center for translation and learning. Hunayn's reliable and clearly written translations of Hippocrates, Galen, and others, enabled the Arab physicians of the Middle Ages to produce the authoritative works they contributed to world civilization.

A master of Syriac, Greek, and Arabic, Hunayn travelled in Iraq, Syria, Palestine, and Egypt in search of rare manuscripts. He is credited with an immense number of translations in fields ranging from medicine, philosophy, astronomy, and mathematics to magic and divination through dreams.

Hunayn left an impressive treatise on the translations made of Galen's works, in which he enumerates and discusses one hundred and twenty other treatises. Of these, he translated about one hundred into Syriac or Arabic. He also corrected many of the earliest translations, especially those of Sergius of Ras al-'Ayn. His method of translation did not differ much from our modern methods: he collected as many manuscripts as he could find, collated them and established an authoritative text before translating it.

He was also among the first to translate the Old Testament into Arabic. His disciples, of whom his son Ishaq and his nephew were the most prominent, produced some thirteen Syriac and thirty Arabic translations. He coined new Arabic terminology to convey previously unknown terms.

Hunayn was no mere translator; he wrote several books, mostly concentrating on medicine. His *Ten Treatises on the Eye* was translated into Latin in more than one version. The influence of this work on the development of ophthalmology was profound, not only in Islam, but in the West as well. Occulists quoted and consulted the *Treatises* for many centuries. His *Masa' il fi al-tibb* (Questions on Medicine), a standard work for many years, was translated into Latin and Hebrew. It was the most dependable manual used by the examiners who approved physicians for licensing.

Hunayn's interests, like those of most scholars of the time, were not confined to the pure sciences, but extended to all fields of human knowledge. He translated and commented on Aristotle's logical works and Porphyry's *Isagoge*. His book *Nawadir al-falasifah* (Anecdotes of the Philosophers), a collection of stories, letters and sayings of the ancient Greek philosophers, became the basis and source for many similar works in Arabic, such as Miskawayh's *al-Hikmah al-khalidah* (Eternal Wisdom), Abu Sulayman al-Sijistani's *Siwan al-hikmah* (Repository of Wisdom), and Ibn Fatik's *Mukhtar al-hikam* (Selections of Wise Sayings).

His story about the death of Alexander the Great in *al-Nawadir* prompted the development of the Alexander Romance, a romance very popular in the literature of the Middle Ages. Finally, his book *Fi idrak haqiqat al-adyan* (On Understanding the True Nature of Religion) shows his continuous interest in religion and in defending his Christian beliefs.

Yahia ibn 'Adi (d. 974), a Jacobite scholar, one of the greatest Christian translators, philosophers and logicians, deserves a place of honor in the annals of Christian contributions. Ibn 'Adi studied under another famous Christian scholar, Abu Bishr Matta ibn Yunis (d. 940) the logician, who was the first to translate Aristotle's *Poetics* into Arabic. Ibn 'Adi, who tutored many of the Muslim scholars of the time, became the mentor of the Baghdad philosophers after his contemporary, al-Farabi, (d. 950) left for Syria. His students included

Abu Sulayman al-Sijistani (d. 1001), Abu Hayyan al-Tawhidi (d. 971), Muhammad Miskawayh (1030), and the famous Orthodox doctor, Nazif ibn Yuman (d. 983).

More than one hundred and forty-one books are attributed to Ibn 'Adi, several of which have survived to the present. He wrote on ethics as well as logic. His book *Tahdhib al-akhlaq* (The Refinement of Character) is one of the finest Arabic books that have survived. In it, Ibn 'Adi attributes the fundamental differences in ethical behavior to the disharmony that may result from the stresses and strains that beset the three faculties of the soul: the appetitive, the passionate and the rational. This last faculty sets man apart from the beast. Man's excellence is bound up with the rational faculty's domination over the other two. Therefore, the primary aim of education should be the cultivation of the rational mind. Once the soul is controlled by this faculty, the distinction between good and evil becomes clear.

The theological interests of Ibn 'Adi are as important as his ethical interests. He was one of the few tenth century Christian scholars to have taken an active part in theological debates with his Muslim contemporaries. One of his polemical works was directed against the attacks upon Christianity by Abu 'Isa al-Warraq.

Another was a rebuttal of al-Kindi's (d. 873) philosophical rejection of the Trinity. Al-Kindi used Porphyry's *Isagoge* to show that the Trinity would make of God a composite being. What is composite is caused, and what is caused cannot be the cause of itself, in other words, it cannot be eternal. Using Aristotelian concepts, Ibn 'Adi responded that al-Kindi's argument cannot be accepted without question. He argued that in the efficient cause, one has to distinguish between that which is responsible for the supervention of the form upon the matter and that which caused the form rather than its mere supervention. In regard to its effects, the relationship shared by the Father, the Son and the Holy Spirit is of the latter type.

One of the earliest complete works in Arabic on the unity of God is Ibn 'Adi's book *Fi al-tawhid* in which he tried to show that God is One in one sense and a Trinity in another. God as the subject of qualification (mawsuf), is one, but insofar as he possesses attributes of goodness (Father), wisdom (Son) and power (Holy Spirit), he is three. As a person he is one. What this argument defines is not a trinity of persons, but a trinity of attributes. An attribute (for example, the Sun's rays) is not different in nature from its source (the Sun). Sun rays are the same as the Sun since there can be no suns without rays.

Ibn 'Adi's influence on Muslim as well as Christian philosophers was significant. His school of thought lasted for centuries. Al-Bayhaqi, one of the important historians of Muslim philosophy, said of him, "he was a complete philosopher"; al-Qifti, another important historian, considered him "the chief spokesman of the philosophical circle"; and Ibn al-Nadim, the oldest Arab bibliographer, refers to him as "unique for his times." It was mostly through his many students that his teachings permeated the works of many of the Muslim scholars. Averroes used Ibn 'Adi's arguments in refuting Avicenna's contention that "God does not know the particulars." In general Ibn 'Adi played a very significant role in Aristotelian studies in Islam. As a teacher, critic, translator and commentator, he gave a new impetus to Aristotelian and other philosophical studies.

Many other Christian scholars contributed significantly to Arabic civilization. 'Ali ibn 'Isa al-Kahhal (d. ca. 1038) wrote a much-used work on ophthalmology, and his method of cataract operation was practiced in some parts of Europe until the seventeenth century. Ibn Butlan, author of many books on medicine, philosophy and religion, was another Christian who defended the concept that one need not rely solely on Greek medicine to become a great doctor. Qusta ibn Luqa (d. 912) of Baalbeck in Lebanon was an expert in engineering in addition to being a philosopher and mathematician. Finally Ibn al-Quff (d. 1286), was one of the last in a series of famous Christian physicians and surgeons.

It is impossible to detail in this short space all the Christian contributions to Arabic civilization during the Middle Ages; suffice it to say that Christians continued to contribute throughout the Abbasid, Seljuk, Fatimid, Mamluk and Ottoman periods.

In Modern Times

Beginning in the nineteenth century, and in some cases earlier, Christians played an important role in bringing about *al-Nahdah*, or Arab awakening, particularly in Syria and Lebanon, as well as in Egypt.

After the fall of Baghdad at the hands of Hulagu (1258), the Arab world suffered a prolonged period of decline, culturally and otherwise. There was little inventiveness and a great reliance on traditions. Sufism and salafi thought became dominant. One may correctly consider the period between the fourteenth and nineteenth centuries as the cultural dark ages of the Arab world, although it was not completely devoid of a few bright spots.

The revolutionary changes that were taking place in Europe and the great transformations in thought and power that were bursting all over Europe found no echo in the Arab world. Arabic language and literature, important components and symbols of Arab culture, whithered into desiccated rhetorical and verbal platitudes. Politically, the entire Arab world fell under the heavy hands of the Ottomans early in the sixteenth century.

The first important and effective stirrings of *al-Nahdah* came from the Syrian and Lebanese writers and thinkers, including a great number of Christians. The new interest shown by them in Arabic language and literature had a profound impact on their mental life. This brought them to a new historical consciousness of the Arab past and to a desire for self-definition. "Who are we?" and "where are we?" became critical issues, and remain so even now.

When the nineteenth century opened, the Arab world found itself invaded by Europe and the West. It was politically and culturally challenged in the name of civilization. The response to the challenge came from different corners and in different ways. The Christians, who were in greater contact with the West, were able to effect a switch of emphasis in the Arab world's views on social life, science and literature. This is best shown in the areas of printing, education and journalism.

The Christians were the first to introduce the Arabic printing press. The first movable-type press was introduced in Lebanon as early as the year 1610 in Dayr Qizhayya, North Lebanon. In 1723 'Abdallah al-Zakhir (d. 1748), a skilled artisan and intellectual from Aleppo, established a press at the monastery of Yuhanna al-Sabigh, in the village of Shuwayr, al-Matn. Because of its clear and beautiful type, Zakhir's press became a model for St. George Orthodox press, established in Beirut in 1751.

Both the Shuwayr and the St. George's presses printed mostly religious works, particularly the *Psalms*, because they were used both as a prayerbook and as a textbook to learn Arabic. The fact that the *Psalms* were printed fifteen times between 1610 and 1775 was a sign of the slowly growing interest of the Christian population in the Arabic language. This was the beginning of a love affair with Arabic that had important consequences later on.

Because of early contacts with Europe, because of the establishment of schools as early as the eighteenth century in Lebanon, because of the arrival of missionary schools and presses, and finally because of new liberal laws introduced by the Ottomans in the mid-nineteenth century, there arose a new, educated generation that desired to change the social order and political reality of the Arab world.

The role of the press in making education available to all classes, and consequently enabling them to make the jump into modern times, cannot be overstated. During the second half of the nineteenth century, American, French, British and Russian missionary presses and schools gave a strong boost to higher education. This opened wide the doors for new trends destined to revive the Arab literary heritage. Western intellectual, literary, and scientific trends could now flow freely into the Arab world.

The Christians' admiration of the Arabic language led to a greater admiration of Arabic literature, but it also had other consequences. By assimilating Arabic, the Christians assimilated a culture which was basically non-Christian. In due time, this opened for them new vistas. The religious sects under whose wings they had sought protection looked, to many, like barriers to reaching these new vistas.

They saw a great opportunity to bypass these barriers in secularism and nationalism, which leading Christian writers adopted. Several literary and scientific societies were formed, and the new journalism invigorated the assimilation of the new trends.

Furthermore, the new education produced new literary genres. The dramatic arts were introduced by a Christian, Marun al-Naqqash, and the novel was promoted in its beginnings by Christians. A new style of writing, different from the Koranic, was popularized by the new trends.

Journalism, a Western innovation, flourished during the second half of the century both in its scholarly and popular forms. At its inception in Egypt, journalism was in the hands of the government. Private non-governmental publication was almost completely in the hands of Christians.

The first general Arabic newspaper, *Mir'at al-ahwal*, was published by Rizqallah Hassun of Aleppo, in Istanbul (1855). It was followed by Khalil Khuri's *Hadiqat al-al-akhbar* (1858), in Beirut. Ahmad Faris al-Shidiyaq, who was born Christian, published *al-Jawa'ib* in Istanbul (1860); Salim Taqla *al-Ahram* in Egypt (1875); and Khalil Sarkis *Lisan al-hal* (1877) in Beirut. The role of periodicals such as *al Diya', al-Jinan, al-Muqtataf,* and *al-Hilal,* was immense.

Although many, such as Nasif al-Yaziji and his son Ibrahim, distinguished themselves in bringing about the literary and intellectual renaissance, the one who personified the love of Arabic and the new trends of progress, nationalism and secularism was Butrus al-Bustani (d. 1883). He was the founder of the National School; author of the Arabic dictionary *al-Muhit;* editor of the first modern encyclopedia in Arabic, *Da'irat al-ma'arif;* publisher and editor of the periodical, *al-Jinan;* and a major contributor to the new translation of the Bible into Arabic by American missionaries.

Butrus and his son Salim lifted high the banner of progress, education, freedom and love of country. In his short-lived newspaper *Nafir Suriya,* al-Bustani raised the motto "Love of country is an article of faith." According to him, only by national unity could the people transcend religious differences. His appeals for patriotic consciousness were based on the distinction between fanaticism and mutual respect between the faiths; on the possibility of reconciling science and religion; and on the need for establishing a constitutional government, all these being principles that would assure strong bonds between the individual and his community, his God and his government.

These and similar principles were adopted by many Christian writers. Shibly Shumayyil (d. 1917) introduced Darwinist philosophy, which intensified the polemics around science and religion. Another Christian writer, Farah Antun (d. 1922), stands out as the Arab theoretician of the reconciliation between science and religion. According to him, man has two major faculties: the intellect, which uses observation as a method to learn the truth; and the heart, which accepts the truth of sacred books without examination. Since neither can refute the findings of the other, let them respect each other by not invading each other's territory.

Antun's ideas about the difference between science and religion led him to advocate the political and social principles of separation between state and religion. The state, he maintained, should be based on freedom and equality, goals which can be achieved only when secular power is autonomous. Antun, like many of the other writers of *al-Nahdah,* tackled the issue of backwardness in the East. He attributed it to the lack of good education, ignorance, corruption, disunity and the depreciated role of women. His basic theme was that the Muslim past will only catch up with the present civilization and progress when the union between the civil and the religious is dissolved.

Also important was the role of Christians in demanding and actively seeking independence from the Turks, particularly their contributions to the different ideas and ideologies of nationalism. Najib 'Azuri (d. 1916) was among the first to express the idea of an Arab nation in a coherent and integrated manner. It was he who raised the issue of a definition of the Arab countries' national identity (Arab, Syrian or Lebanese), which developed later into a major aspect of Arab political thought. Beginning with Butrus al-Bustani, and continuing with Bulus Nujaym, Najib 'Azuri, Antun Sa'adeh, Constantine Zurayq, and Michel Aflaq, among others, the association of the Christian thinkers with the rise and growth of the nationalist schools of political thought is easily evident.

It must be noted that although they differed on the question of national identity, all their nationalist ideas contained the seeds for equality and freedom for all citizens.

The contributions of the Christians to the modern renaissance were not limited to Lebanese, Syrian and Palestinian Christians. Space does not allow us to go into the achievements of the Christians of Egypt, or those Syrian and Lebanese living in Egypt. Scholars, writers and poets such as Ya'qub Sarruf, Jurji Zaydan and Khalil Mutran left an indelible impact on modern life and thought. A few words should be written about the literary movement known as *al-Adab al-mahjari* (Immigrant Literature), produced almost completely by Christian immigrants in North and South America.

Finding themselves in a new environment where they could express themselves more freely, a few immigrant free spirits decided to produce a new Arabic literature. Aware of the lack in both form and content in almost all that was written in the Arab world, the leaders of the Mahjari literature, Kahlil Gibran, Mikhail Naimy, Nasib 'Arida, Nadra Haddad and Iliyya Abu Madi, among others, began to express themselves in a new manner appropriate to the literary spirit of their new environment.

In 1920, this group of free spirits in North America formed the Pen Bond (*al-Rabita al-Qalamiyya*), which was set on "emancipating Arabic literature from its state of sterility and traditionalism" and turning it into a state of beautiful originality in both meaning and style. In fact, they proceeded to create a literary school characterized by simplicity of language; nostalgia for the "Old Country" and its natural beauty; and a strong message calling for tolerance among the sects, democracy and freedom. Immigrant literature impacted greatly over all the Arab world, and supplemented the budding and tender reformist trends already underway there.

These contributions covered and extended beyond the field of literature into the advocacy of political and social freedom, and promulgated equality and justice for all citizens, especially women. To a great extent their message was revolutionary in its criticism of literary verbosity as well as its opposition to tyranny in all its forms.

Christians of the Arab world, as full partners, are still playing a great role in all aspects of society, and hand in hand with their liberal minded Muslim brothers and sisters, are forging ahead in building the ideal society where all may live in peace, harmony, freedom and equality.

NOTES

The author's bibliography has been incorporated into the Selected Bibliography at the end of this volume.

PART THREE:

The Antiochian Orthodox Christian Archdiocese of North America

A RETROSPECTIVE: ONE HUNDRED YEARS OF ANTIOCHIAN ORTHODOXY IN NORTH AMERICA
by Antony Gabriel

Decisive historic changes do not come from great wars, terrible cataclysms or ingenious inventions. It is enough that the heart of man incline its sensitive crown to one side or the other of the horizon, toward optimism or pessimism, toward heroism or utility, toward combat or peace. (Ortega Y Gasset)

The history of the Antiochian Orthodox Church in North America is rich and exciting, full of larger-than-life personalities and a struggle for power and influence not unlike that in the political arena. It begins with the faithful who crossed the ocean and planted the seeds of Antiochian Orthodoxy upon this continent. Their noble and at times ignoble deeds flesh out the real story.

This article is not intended to be a definitive or exhaustive work on the history of the Antiochian Orthodox Church but is rather an attempt, on the occasion of its centennial celebration, to recapture elements from the exciting and complex history of the Church in North America.

I. THE EARLY PERIOD

Historical and Political Background

The story unfolds with the election in 1899 of the Arab Patriarch Meletios II (Doumani) as head of the Church of Antioch. Meletios assumed the patriarchal office after a bitter struggle in the Syrian Orient during which the Arabs of the Greek Orthodox Patriarchate of

Antioch, as it was so incorporated in the empire, sought to wrest control of the throne from the Hellenes.

During several centuries of Ottoman rule, the patriarchs of the ancient See of Antioch were Greek ethnics, originally from Constantinople and later selected from the Brotherhood of the Holy Sepulchre in Jerusalem. The Greek monastics, together with some Arabs, were overseers of the properties and holy places of the Greek Orthodox Patriarchate of Jerusalem. Hierarchs for the various sees or archdioceses in the empire were frequently drawn from this ecclesiastical pool.

The sultanate in Istanbul (the "Sublime Porte") maintained a watchful eye over the Christians in the Middle East through the Millet System (Nation).[1] Syria fell under Ottoman rule in 1516, and the patriarchate was transferred from the city of Antioch to Damascus following a series of political, economic, religious and environmental calamities in 1531.

The Sublime Porte later turned a blind eye to the increasing intervention by European powers within the empire, allegedly to protect the Christians. The Melchite schism in 1724 and the Protestant missionary incursion into Arab lands in the eighteenth and nineteenth centuries[2] resulted in a rather uneven spiritual and educational church life that sapped the community's energy and gave impetus to the appointment of Greek monastics to the Antiochian Throne to counteract the western missionaries. The ecumenical patriarch was viewed as "the king," the civil and religious head of the Greek Orthodox people who were also subjects of the Ottoman Empire.

Of all the patriarchates, Antioch suffered the most throughout its long history. This suffering often was at the hands of outsiders who, under the pretext of religion, and for reasons which were political and economic, almost succeeded in destroying the venerable Church of Antioch. It was therefore not surprising that the calls for men of their own to govern the Church of Antioch grew louder. Metropolitan Antony Bashir wrote in *The Word* (Jan. 1957) of the persecuted Church of Antioch: "The Middle East has been a battleground of ideas and armies since the dawn of time.... The troubled history of the Church founded by the Apostles indicates the constant miracle implied by its survival."

In the waning years of the Ottoman Empire, nascent Arab nationalism began to blossom throughout Syria. The Arabs who had been constantly subjected to arbitrary rule began calling for the liberation of their patriarchate from alien domination.[3] The cause of restoring the Patriarchate of Antioch to the Arabs was furthered by the presence of the Russian Consulate and the Russian Imperial Orthodox Palestine Society.

Arab Orthodox Christian Immigration to North America

Waves of Arab Orthodox Christians immigrated to North America (and elsewhere) at the turn of the twentieth century, searching for religious freedom, political liberation and a better way of life. The Christians of Syria — like their forefathers before them — had always been adventurous, seeking new venues for their restlessness. Some left to escape oppression while others left to satisfy their longing to conquer new worlds.

Before World War I, the tide of immigration from Greater Syria (here including modern Lebanon) took place against the backdrop of the geo-political struggles of the times. While North American shores were considered to be a beacon of hope and a new frontier for the peoples of the Levant, their journey to North America was fraught with uncertainty and terrible hardships. There were many cultural and linguistic barriers to overcome as well as poverty, isolation and inexperience once they arrived. Many immigrants thought that after achieving success they would return home, and some eventually did. Most, however, remained in North America and carved out for themselves and for future generations a bright and exemplary life. They contributed hugely to the economic, cultural and literary mosaic on this continent.[4]

The most important contribution to North America made by these pilgrims was, in a word, *Orthodoxy*. They were sustained in crisis and adversity by the simplicity of their faith experienced in life and liturgy. Their world was shaped by the Christian humanism of the

Syrian East, giving these pioneers in North America a holistic vision almost unmatched by any other ethnic group arriving on her shores.

Russian-Arab Cooperation

A history of the Antiochian Patriarchate must also take into account the important role the Russian Church played among the Christians of the Middle East, especially in the nineteenth century. The Church of Russia saw herself as the protector of the Orthodox Arabs through the Russian Imperial Orthodox Palestine Society (1882-1917). This was crucial to the development of the Antiochian Patriarchate and to establishing new religious and educational institutions in Palestine and Syria, and many hierarchs were encouraged to seek advanced theological degrees in Russia. Affinity with Russian spirituality, education and culture was a strong factor in shaping the spirit of the Syrians who came to these shores. Indeed, some credit the final restoration of the Arabs to the Patriarchate of Antioch to the direct and indirect intervention of the Russians in Syria.

Orthodoxy in America began with the Russian mission to Kodiak, Alaska in 1794. When Alaska was sold to the United States in 1867, the see was transferred to Sitka and then to San Francisco. A new chapter opened when Archbishop Tikhon (Bellavin)[5] made New York City the headquarters of the emerging Orthodox Church in North America in 1905.

It was thus virtually inevitable that the Church in the New World would come under the canonical protection of the Russian Church. At the same time, the strong national sentiments among the Syrians in North America led them to organize themselves along ethnic lines.

Raphael Hawaweeny and Syrian Orthodoxy

The Syrian Orthodox Benevolent Society of New York was organized through the efforts of George Bek Qodsy and Dr. Ibrahim Arbeely, its first president. Dr. Arbeely contacted the then Archimandrite Raphael Hawaweeny, professor of Arabic and Islam at the Academy of Kazan in Russia, and petitioned the Holy Synod of Russia, asking that Hawaweeny be sent to serve the spiritual needs of the Orthodox of the city and of all the United States.[6] There had already been two unsuccessful attempts to establish a church for the New York community. Father Constantine Tarazi and Archimandrite Christopher Jabara, who had arrived in 1892, were unable to maintain a viable community structure, lacking full support at home and abroad.

Hawaweeny's arrival inaugurated the first official Antiochian presence and the formation of the Syrian Orthodox Ecclesiastical Mission in North America in 1895. He was appointed head of the Syrian Mission under the Russian Orthodox Archdiocese. By the time he was elected and consecrated bishop of Brooklyn in 1904 as vicar to Archbishop Tikhon, he had already established his missionary, administrative and literary credentials.

Raphael Hawaweeny was born in Beirut on or about November 8, 1860. A "Syro-Arab by birth, a Greek by education and an American by residence, but a Russian at heart and a Slav in soul," as he himself proudly said. He was shaped by both his priestly family connections and the religious and national movements of his time. He spent his formative years in Syria where he was exposed to the leading Greek and Arab hierarchs. He was educated in his own country and later at the theological school of the Ecumenical Patriarchate (1879-86) at Halki and finally in Russia at Kiev (1888-89).

Hawaweeny was a charismatic leader with an authoritative manner and a compassionate and humble heart. When he arrived in America to begin his real mission in life, the establishment of Antiochian Orthodoxy in the New World, he absorbed and integrated all the diverse linguistic, cultural and spiritual elements that had nourished his intellect and soul.

His travels, publications and evangelical pastorship mark him as one of the most outstanding hierarchs of the Antiochian Church of the twentieth century. He travelled the length and breadth of the country, often under difficult conditions, to visit the faithful in scattered communities. The magazine *al-Kalimat* (1905), now *The Word*, is one of his most enduring literary bequests to this archdiocese, as are his many liturgical books. He was receptive to the use of English in the Liturgy, and translated a number of liturgical texts; many are still in use. He was even open to discussion with other religious groups, notably the Episcopalians.[7] His ecumenical relations in general, linked to his Episcopalian connections in particular, are especially noteworthy.

Hawaweeny was a member of the Russian Church and keenly aware of the canonical norm for the ecclesiastical authority in a new mission and land. He was a staunch nationalist and patriot, but championed the cause of the Antiochian Patriarchate. In his life and ministry one can see the Russian line from the nineteenth century in Syria to the beginnings of the Church in the New World.

Raphael Hawaweeny died on February 27, 1915. He succeeded in laying a solid foundation for the Church in North America through its ministry to the Syrians. As the first Orthodox bishop of any nationality to be consecrated on North American soil, Raphael Hawaweeny planted and nurtured the Antiochian presence in this hemisphere.

He was a man of extraordinary gifts. His disciplined mind and creative spirit inaugurated a process in North America that carries the Antiochian Archdiocese securely into the twenty-first century.

The First Priests

The first generation of priests and their families endured great hardship, and the celibate priests knew great loneliness as well. They left a culture far different from the one they encountered in the New World. Some of the newcomers were educated while others were the children or grandchildren of priests or chanters. Some entered the business world and were later ordained to serve their communities; others were elected by their congregations because they were literate or knew the liturgical worship or had fine singing voices. Most loved the Church and sacrificed heartily for her survival in the New World.

Many priests were simple folk, imbued with the Orthodox spirit, who had migrated to these shores without much knowledge of the intricacies of Orthodox theology. The celebration of the Liturgy was what knitted the community together.

The clergy who came to this country at the turn of the century hoped for freedom and a better life. They were, however, often at the mercy of contentious boards and insufficient revenues, and they suffered from the political controversies which divided parishes and often devastated their homes or families. For many of them, their hopes were only achieved by their children. Even as they labored under grave limitations, they created the foundation of a strong archdiocese.

The Americanization of Orthodoxy

In spite of the vicissitudes suffered by the early faithful, there was a unity of purpose and a structure: the Russian Orthodox Archdiocese and its Syrian Mission. The first seedlings of the Americanization of Orthodoxy arose with the reception of convert clergy as well as those of Middle Eastern ancestry who initiated English into the periodicals and the Divine Services.

Loyalty to the Russian hierarchy was not an issue; the relationship within the American synod was an easy one. Russians, Greeks, Arabs and Serbs were mutually administered by the hierarchs present in North America at that time. The authority and primacy of the Russians and their bishops, as well as that of the vision of Archbishop Tikhon, were locally acknowledged. In 1907, the archbishop was transferred to Russia and later elected patriarch just as an American Church was beginning to take root.

Russy-Antacky Cooperation and Division; the Agony Begins

The seeds of dissent and chaos for the Syrian Mission were sown with the arrival of Metropolitan Germanos (Shehadi) of Seleucia in 1914 shortly before the death of Bishop Raphael Hawaweeny. He came to America on a fundraising mission on behalf of his archdiocese, with accreditation for a limited stay as a guest of Bishop Raphael. Before long, however, his presence and the message he carried to the Syrian nationals brought tension.

With World War I (1914) and the October Bolshevik Revolution in Russia (1917), communications with the Russian and the

Antiochian Church became difficult. Funding from the Russian Holy Synod was abruptly cut off. In the United States and Canada political strife developed within the Russian communities, stifling efforts by the Russian Orthodox to preserve Orthodox unity in the New World. The dislocation of authority and fragmentation of the Russian Church as well as the resurgence of desire on the part of national Orthodox Churches to reattach themselves to the Mother Churches also created uncertainty.

The Succession: Aftimios Ofiesh

After Bishop Raphael died in 1915, a period of instability ensued in which no clear successor emerged. Negotiations as to who among his closest confidants would succeed him began — during his funeral services! Documents of the period reveal that Germanos saw himself as the successor to Raphael. In a letter to Archbishop Evdokim, dated June 1/14, 1915, he raised questions about Hawaweeny's citizenship and consecration.[8] In another letter (April 24, 1917), he claimed he was the acting bishop of the Syrian Antiochian Orthodox Church of North America.[9]

Archdeacon Emmanuel Abo Hatab, who had come to America in 1900 to assist Bishop Raphael, now stepped aside. Aftimios Ofiesh of Montreal emerged as leader of the "Russy" faction. With the support of the Russian Diocese of New York, he was named bishop of Brooklyn. Before his consecration, Germanos attempted to persuade him to submit to Antioch with the assurance the patriarch would authorize his consecration by Antiochian hierarchs. He was consecrated on May 13, 1917 by Russian Archbishop Evdokim (Merchevsky).

Aftimios had the support of thirty-four of the forty-one clergy who cast their ballots in the election and the loyal parish supporters of the canonical Russian hierarchical overseers. But some fifty telegrams were sent to Archbishop Evdokim accusing Aftimios of being an active member of the Masonic order, an accusation he vehemently denied.[10] Many editorials attacking him were published in the media of this period as well.

In 1908, the Ecumenical Patriarchate, for reasons of its own, placed the Greek parishes in America under the jurisdiction of the autocephalous Church of Greece. However, the arrival in 1918 of Archbishop Meletios (Metaxakes), of Athens, accompanied by Alexander, bishop of Rodostolou would create a change. When Meletios was elected patriarch of Constantinople in 1922, he placed his compatriots in North America under his jurisdiction. This was in spite of his observation, based on his experience in America, that he had seen the largest and best part of the Orthodox Church in the diaspora. And that he understood how exalted the name of Orthodoxy could be, especially in the United States of America, *if more than two million Orthodox people here were united into one church organization, an American Orthodox Church.*

Meanwhile, the Russian Church in America was in turmoil. In 1921, Patriarch Gregory IV of Antioch corresponded with the Russian Holy Synod in Moscow — and later with the exiled Russian bishops who formed a synod at Karlovsky, Yugoslavia — to regularize the Church of Antioch's relationship with the Church in the New World. The answers he received were unsatisfactory. One stated the situation was not impossible within canonical norms. The other suggested dividing Arab Orthodox Christians into two dioceses, one under Russian authority and the other under Antiochian control. It was even suggested that Bishop Aftimios and Metropolitan Germanos resign and that Archdeacon Thomas Mallouf be elevated in their stead.

Neither the recently restored patriarchate in Moscow nor the newly established Synod of Exile Bishops had the will or the know-how to deal effectively with the deteriorating situation in the New World. Patriarch Tikhon, however, showed sensitivity to Bishop Aftimios' position and wanted a harmonious transition. Also, it is probable that the first Orthodox council to meet in North America, on November 16, 1923, had a pressing issue to deal with: a pending schism in the Russian Church. A resolution was passed to reaffirm the unity of the Russian Orthodox Church in America under Metropolitan Platon.[11]

Metropolitan Germanos, meanwhile, had free rein to pursue his own interests and start churches where he could. He identified himself with those Syrians who rejected any authority but their own, and he unleashed the aspirations of the Antiochenes for the "legitimate" return to their Mother Church. The rise of nationalism paralleled his immense personal appeal[12] and ignited Russy/Antacky antagonism.

In 1923, Metropolitan Germanos was recalled to Antioch by Patriarch Gregory IV. Archbishop Evdokim and Alexander, archbishop of the Greek Diocese, issued decrees against his remaining in North America in a series of letters. Charges and counter-charges between clergy and laity exacerbated the situation. Churches, communities and families were split along party lines.[13]

At a meeting in Detroit on April 4, 1924, the Russians declared themselves independent of Moscow, and proclaimed an independent self-governing Metropolia until conditions in Russia would allow the resumption of normal relations. This action could not be officially sanctioned by Patriarch Tikhon. But it appears his tacit agreement was transmitted through intermediaries, appointing Metropolitan Platon head of the Russian Archdiocese during these turbulent times.

These divisive problems cast a long shadow on the episcopacy of Aftimios Ofiesh, who early-on had revealed brilliance, coupled with enormous energy, integrity and strong individualism. Although he was a visionary leader and far-sighted thinker, he spent much of his life in conflict. In Syria he had organized the Young Syrians, but his efforts were censured by Patriarch Meletios II (Doumani). In the New World, he was pastor of the fractious Montreal community, a microcosm of the Russy/Antacky controversy, which ultimately divided. During his episcopate he and his assistants, Archimandrite Emmanuel Abo Hatab and the Reverend Basil Kherbawy, spent much time travelling from city to city and law court to law court trying to prevent Germanos and his followers from gaining control of the communities in the diocese.

The Election of the Archbishop of New York and All North America: Victor Abou-Assaley

Patriarch Gregory IV sent Metropolitan Gerasimos (Messara) of Beirut to attend the General Convention of the Episcopal Church in Portland, Oregon, at the invitation of the Reverend W. C. Emhart, envoy of the American Episcopalian Church. He was accompanied by his secretary, Deacon Antony Bashir, and Archimandrite Victor Abou-Assaley.

Both the Russian Church in America and the Patriarchate of Antioch were seeking financial assistance from the Episcopal Church since the Church in Russia could no longer sustain its financial commitments abroad. The Episcopalians agreed to make a grant to the Patriarchate of Antioch and to finance the missionary work of Deacon Antony Bashir who was subsequently ordained a priest by Metropolitan Gerasimos.

Today it is believed that Metropolitan Gerasimos had another agenda. Before returning to the Middle East, he had sent a letter dated June 8, 1923 to a leading Arab newspaper, announcing the decision of the Patriarchate of Antioch to assume jurisdiction over the Orthodox of Syria and Lebanon in the New World. The letter also invited the faithful to nominate three candidates for the episcopate of the new Antiochian jurisdiction, and was echoed in an encyclical and an official call for nominations (June 1923):

> ... I have been favoured by his beatitude with the joyful tidings announcing his esteemed determination to include the parish of North America as related to the Orthodox Syrian, within the number of parishes, constituting the holy apostolic See of Antioch, and his fatherly readiness to ordain a regular shepherd who will work for their unity and take full care of their religious and moral needs....Accordingly I call upon the children of the Syrian Orthodox Church scattered all over North America to make the nomination in accordance with aforesaid canonical rules.... [14]

The stage was finally set for the first recognized hierarch affiliated with the Antiochian Patriarchate to be selected and consecrated as "Archbishop of New York and All North America." On November 8, 1924, in Worcester, Massachusetts, Victor Abou-Assaley was consecrated by Metropolitan Zachariah (Ragy), delegated by Gregory IV. Archbishop Panteleimon of Neopolis of the Jerusalem Patriarchate was delegated to be his co-consecrator. Archimandrite Ananias Kassab was appointed vicar-general and remained in this post until Victor's death.

Both Archbishop Aftimios and, ironically, Metropolitan Germanos protested at the alleged interference of Gregory IV [15] in the internal affairs of the North American Church. The Holy Synod of Antioch itself was divided. Dissenting were Metropolitans Alexander (Tahan), Arsenios (Haddad), Basilios (Dibs) of Akkar, and Boulos (Abou-Adal) of Beirut.

It was an amazing time. Everyone took sides and was prepared to fight to the bitter end. During this period, a brief attempt was made in the United States and Canada to negotiate a settlement of the division between the three hierarchs serving in North America: Aftimios of Brooklyn, Germanos of Brooklyn, and Victor of New York.

It was in this context that Archbishop Aftimios sought and received permission from Russian Metropolitan Platon and the Russian Synod to simultaneously remain a member of the American synod and primate of an independent church and elevated to rank of archbishop. He felt an indigenous church was needed to serve those born and raised in North America. He ordained qualified American converts to produce a program of religious educational materials and music to serve the needs of the young people. The work of Archpriest Michael Gelsinger is a testimony to his vision.

The diocese meeting held in 1925 culminated in the formation of a new ecclesiastical phenomenon. After many attempts to negotiate unity with the other Syrian bishops had failed, Archbishop Aftimios's plan for a united Orthodox Church was finally blessed by his superior, Russian Metropolitan Platon, in February, 1927. The Russian Synod approved the establishment of the autocephalous American

Orthodox Church which would incorporate the faithful of the Syro-Arab Mission as well as the Orthodox born in the New World into one jurisdiction. Archbishop Aftimios was named primate; Archimandrite Emmanuel was consecrated as bishop of Montreal and administrative assistant on September 11, 1927, and Archimandrite Sophronios Bishara, as bishop of Los Angeles in 1928. This venture, however, was short-lived.

Archbishop Aftimios later claimed jurisdiction over all the Orthodox in North America, a posture that was rejected by Constantinople, Alexandria, Antioch and even parishes that had remained loyal to him during the Russy/Antacky dispute.

In a revealing exchange of letters on the subject of jurisdiction and unity between Archbishop Aftimios and Archbishop Alexander of the Greek Orthodox Archdiocese, Alexander asserted in a communique dated February 11, 1929 that all Orthodox elements should be united under the Ecumenical Patriarchate. His reasoning was based on the traditional interpretation of the canons (with regard to the diaspora) and on the argument that since Alaska had been sold to America in 1867, Russia no longer had claim over the Church in America.[16]

Archbishop Aftimios finally lost the support of Metropolitan Platon and the Metropolia when he questioned Platon's authority[17] (and that of the other Russian bishops) after becoming engaged in a local controversy. As well, the Metropolia needed the material assistance of the Episcopal Church which viewed the new independent church under Aftimios as a threat to its interests. After his study, *The Orthodox Situation in America*, a practical and lucid survey and program of unity, was published, Aftimos offered to resign so the newly-appointed Greek Orthodox Archbishop (later Patriarch) Athenagoras would assume the leadership, an honor Athenagoras declined, preferring to remain loyal to his superiors in Istanbul.[18] He also lost his position in the Syrian community as bishop of Brooklyn.[19] Emmanuel (Abo Hatab) was appointed in his place.[20]

It has been suggested that in despair, after everything collapsed around him, Aftimios took the step which ultimately ended his episcopacy: his marriage to Mariam Namey in 1933. He resigned and was deposed. He died in seclusion in 1966.

Metropolitan Germanos returned to Beirut in 1933 and died a year later. Bishop Sophronios, who remained *de facto* independent after the demise of the autocephalous church, died in 1934. Archbishop Victor, the canonical hierarch, died on April 19, 1934. Bishop Emmanuel Abo Hatab, who was recalled by Platon, continued to serve the few parishes remaining under the 'Russy' Mission. Towards the end of his life he worked in co-operation with his long-time friend Patriarch Alexander III to secure the canonical release from the Russy Mission for the Antiochian Orthodox Christian Archdiocese under Archbishop Victor (Abou-Assaley). The release was granted after Emmanuel's death on May 29, 1933.[21]

With the departure from the scene of all the major controversial players in the Antiochian drama, it was hoped that peace would reign. However, there were several other mitigating factors, among them the Arab mentality or "memory," the ability to recall to the minute detail an event long past. Second, the Holy Synod now fully restored to the Arabs, continued over the years a uniquely Turkish diplomatic stance: it appeared to take all sides, issuing a decision and then reversing policy in mid-stream. This was frustrating to North American Orthodox Arabs who had become accustomed to debate and decision-making. Third, there was conflict between the village mentality and a more global mind set. Finally, there were past community bipartisan controversies having the church as their focus.

II. THE MIDDLE PERIOD

Antony Bashir and Samuel David: A Time of Hope

A new chapter in this troubling era opened when His Beatitude Alexander III, Patriarch of Antioch and All the East, delegated Metropolitan Theodosios (Abourjaily) of Tyre and Sidon in 1935 to visit North America to conduct the nomination process for a successor to the late Archbishop Victor (Abou-Assaley) and to unite the Antiochian Archdiocese in North America.

Metropolitan Theodosios, accompanied by Archimandrite Antony Bashir, pastor of St. George of Detroit (1932-1935) and patriarchal-vicar (1934) travelled throughout North America. Three candidates for the vacancy emerged after the views of the faithful, their leaders and notables across North America had been polled: Antony Bashir, Samuel David (Toledo), and Ananias Kassab (Ottawa).

The Unity Proposal

A unity agreement amongst the candidates was drawn up in the interest of the archdiocese. It stated that there should be "one head of the Church;" that nominations should come from the people; and that the candidate obtaining the majority of the votes would "guide the ship."

The agreement promised that all candidates would support the chosen nominee. The archdiocese would be defined in two zones, with two bishops to assist in administering it. The agreement was signed by all parties and cabled to His Beatitude on October 15, 1935, from Brooklyn, New York.

This proposal was fraught with difficulties, however, and had repercussions for years on the policies of the church. The election of auxiliaries was not a common practice in the patriarchate; the right of succession abrogates the nomination and election of a new primate according to canonical order.

The Election of Antony Bashir

Final voting took place on November 10, 1935, in Detroit, Michigan, with the patriarchal delegate presiding and the pastor and parish leaders participating in the process to which all parties agreed. The list of candidates finally included Antony Bashir, Samuel David and Agapius Golam, with Ananias Kassab withdrawing his candidacy. When Antony Bashir was declared the winner, there was a brief period of quiet. The possibility of uniting all the factions had been short-lived, and evaporated as soon as the nominating process was completed. Meetings and discussions continued, but the seeds of dissension were once again sown within the Antiochian family.

To further exacerbate the controversy, the supporters of Samuel David intercepted a telegram sent by Metropolitan Theodosios to Patriarch Alexander III, allegedly abrogating an agreement between Theodosios and Samuel David.[22] Metropolitan Theodosios, apparently trying to appease all parties, had assured Samuel David that he would be elevated in due course to assist Antony Bashir in the administration of his vast archdiocese. However, this was a commitment which he should not have given without first consulting with the Holy Synod of Antioch. Samuel David was urged to be patient until the canonical process leading to a successor to Archbishop Victor was accomplished and he was assured of his elevation by all parties. Realistically, it was necessary that Metropolitan Theodosios return to the Middle East to report on the election and discuss ratification of the unique agreement. The intercepted telegram, however, was seen as a betrayal by David's followers, and they insisted on his immediate consecration.

Archimandrite Antony's nomination was confirmed on November 19, 1935, in the United States, and in Damascus, on February 5, 1936. His consecration as Archbishop of New York and All North America took place on April 19, 1936, at St. Nicholas Cathedral in Brooklyn, New York (two years to the day after Victor's death) by Metropolitan Theodosios, assisted by Bishop Vitaly of the Russian Orthodox Church. Patriarch Alexander III, following the agreement drafted earlier, issued a statement on April 6, 1937, confirming "the Most Reverend Archbishop Antony Bashir, Syrian Orthodox Antiochian Archbishop, is the only representative of the Patriarchate of the Greek Orthodox Church of Antioch and all the Orient in the United States of America...."

Samuel David, Archbishop of Toledo

Archimandrite Samuel David was consecrated on April 19, 1936 in Toledo, Ohio, by Archbishop Adam of Philadelphia, Bishop Arseny of Detroit, and Bishop Leonty of Chicago (later metropolitan of the Metropolia).[23] Samuel David was immediately suspended by the patriarch of Antioch, and remained so until he was restored in 1939.[24]

He originally claimed that his consecration was consistent with the norms of the Syrian Mission which was under the canonical jurisdiction of the Metropolia, and that he no longer belonged to the Antiochian Patriarchate.

Thus there emerged two archdioceses on this continent. Toledo was established as Samuel David's headquarters, with parishes in parts of the Mid- and Far West as well as Charleston (West Virginia), Ottawa, Cambridge (Massachusetts), Mexico City, and St. Nicholas of Montreal, plus several areas without churches. The vast majority of the parishes, however, remained under the authority of the Archdiocese of New York and All North America.

In response to the situation, Metropolitan Antony said:

> We have depended a great deal on the old country. We still feel that the mother church in the old world can help us but we must realize that what we cannot do through unity ... we cannot expect any one else to do for us. His Eminence and I have ... agreed never to disagree. We both realize that we will not have many years left for us and those years ... must be used for the glory of our church, for the benefit of our faith, for the future of our youth because if we do not do that, we are going to be the losers.... I assure you that ... maybe even 90% of our differences ... were imposed on us by the selfishness of individuals who wanted to use the clergy for their own spiteful purposes. It is time we realized these things.[25]

The Evolution of the Church and the Role of the Laity

The heightened role of the laity brought new complexities to a hierarchical church in a democratic society. In the Middle East, where the hierarch is the quasi-ecclesiastical/civil leader, he has considerable power while the laity have a much less important role. The first and second generation of Antiochian Orthodox Christians in North America wanted control over the parishes and in some cases actually gained it. They were then able to influence the decisions of bishops as well. Many were uneducated in the faith and their new positions gave them power and a certain prestige within the community. North American Orthodox Arabs had not yet reached the level of sophistication to enter local or national politics; the church, therefore, was their preferred arena. This created enormous tensions in the North American Church, unknown to the parish councils and clergy of today.

The laity in North America also turned their attention to less controversial concerns. Children of Orthodoxy who were nourished by their faith likewise passed on their love of the Orthodox Church to their children. The Orthodox Church became a haven of security and the center that nurtured family values, morality and Christian education for their growth.

The Canonical Situation in North America: Unity and Disunity

The political influences of the day at home and in the Middle East, and the power exerted by some who had a vested interest in the perpetuation of disunity in the archdiocese on this continent caused the patriarchate to pursue an uneven course in dealing with the canonical situation in North America. Confusion reigned, and energy and resources that could have been utilized for the growth of Orthodoxy were dissipated.

In 1953, a proposal for succession, the Detroit Agreement, was put forward. It was not accepted in its entirety by the Holy Synod of Antioch since it might alter the canonical process of nomination and election. What was interesting in the proposal was the agreement that *no successor* would be elected to succeed Samuel David upon his death:

> Immediately upon the decease of Archbishop Samuel David, or in the event of his succession to the office of Metropolitan Archbishop, the existence of the present Archdiocese of Toledo and dependencies shall automatically be terminated, and no successor to Archbishop Samuel shall be elected.[26]

Actions taken at this convention, and succeeding ones in 1954, 1955, and later, confirmed the tradition of the canonical rights of the laity in the nomination process. Metropolitan Antony demanded and received support for a strong constitution as well as by-laws that would enshrine the legitimate legal rights of the North American clergy and laity. This was prophetic in view of the patriarchate's later reaffirmation of the tradition in Syria and Lebanon whereby the Holy Synod assumed the entire process of nomination and election.

In 1954, during Patriarch Alexander III's golden jubilee celebration, and in later years, Metropolitan Antony pursued a vigorous policy of attempting to regularize the canonical situation in North America. His position, consistently held, was that there had been no canonical election for the bishop of Toledo and no canonical delineation of boundaries other than that of the original Praxis of 1924 for North America.

After a visit to Syria in September 1955, Archbishop Samuel had been granted the title of "Metropolitan" along with a vote in the Holy Synod of Antioch by Patriarch Alexander III on October, 29 1953.[27] No archdiocese in the Antiochian Church had ever possessed two votes nor had a Mixed General Council created a new diocese in North America. The patriarch reasoned that this exception was in honor of Archbishop Samuel's long service to the Church.

When the official publication of the New Constitution and Canons of the patriarchate were ratified on November 19-20, 1955, Antony Bashir believed that the North American situation was finally resolved. Patriarch Alexander III had removed the reference to Toledo and listed only one archdiocese in North America.[28]

Preservation of a united archdiocese, protection of the institution of the archdiocese from outside intervention, and development of a process for full participation in the selection of a successor to the metropolitan when such a need would arise were matters of great concern. Metropolitan Antony had tremendous influence on these deliberations, and history has since validated his efforts to spare future generations a struggle over division of the archdiocese, both at home and abroad.

During the archdiocesan convention in Los Angeles in 1958, Metropolitan Antony learned that Archbishop Samuel (David) fell asleep in the Lord on August 12 in Toledo, Ohio, while sitting in a chair with the Bible in his hand. After the business of the convention was concluded, Metropolitan Antony with a delegation of clergy travelled to Toledo, Ohio, and visited the home of Oscar Joseph to express the sympathies of the archdiocese.

Samuel David, from Aitha al-Fakar [29] (August 26, 1893) was a sincere and gentle person who remained through his life a villager at heart. His real strength was his love of the Church, the Divine Liturgy and his magnificent voice. In later years, he recorded the most famous and best loved liturgical hymns which were sold throughout North America. Samuel David utilized the literary skills of Ananias Kassab and the solidity of the members of the David family as well as other powerful laymen. His generosity abides in the lives of today's churchmen whom he sponsored with his family resources to these shores. Memorial testimonies to his gifts can be seen at the Convent of Saidnaya as well as in the patriarchal Grand Salon in Damascus.

The Administration of the Archdiocese under Metropolitan Antony

Antony was a commanding figure in the Orthodox Church, a born leader with an expansive world view. Born in the village of Douma, Lebanon (March 15, 1898), he displayed strong individualism that served him both in adversity and good times. His keen wit and sense of humour helped him bear the burdens of high office and deal effectively with constant conflicts among the people after his election. He was also a writer and intellectual, an extraordinarily articulate man, in contact with the leading thinkers and writers of his day.[30] Metropolitan Antony's presence was a major factor in knitting together his flock and subsequently elevating their vision beyond narrow parochial interests. While he had the heart of a villager, and understood people as they were, at the same time, he towered above many of his contemporaries with his breadth of vision and intellectual depth.

Heroic efforts were made to elevate the organizational standards of the archdiocese. The task of bringing the ancient Church of Antioch in the New World in line with the mainstream churches in North America weighed heavily on the minds of Metropolitan Antony and his co-workers. Their commitment to the future displayed far-reaching vision.

One of the earliest accomplishments was the establishment of the general convention, comprised of clergy/lay delegates with its uniquely North American concerns[31] and the nominations process. This institution, an innovation of the Antiochian Church drawn from the political arena, later became popular in other jurisdictions. The concept of the board of trustees, with fiscal accountability, modelled on structures in Protestant churches, was instituted throughout the archdiocese and was the forerunner of the parish councils of today (now in line with Orthodox ecclesiology).

Antony as a visionary was active in the formation of the Federation of the Primary Jurisdictions in 1942 (transformed into the Standing Conference of Orthodox Bishops in America in 1960).

The archdiocese also had to adjust to the growing demands of its adherents, especially the youth. Metropolitan Antony was active in launching the Syrian Orthodox Youth Organization (SOYO), and he inaugurated Sunday School and Sacred Music programs and innumerable publications, among them *The Word* (revived), *The SOYO Digest* and many religious educational materials.

Church and Politics in the Middle East
On June 17, 1958, Patriarch Alexander III died. In the context of the great achievements of his patriarchate, his action vis-à-vis North America were puzzling. He was a skillful churchman and a consummate politician, but managed to obfuscate the centrality of a principle of canon law by his actions.

The election of a successor to Alexander III was no easy task because of the tradition of conflict in the Middle East and the emerging political forces that left their mark on the Eastern Church. The hiatus between June 1958, when the patriarch died, and the nomination/

election of a successor in November 1958 resulted from the political disturbances in Lebanon at that time which made it impossible for the metropolitans of Lebanon to travel to Syria. President Eisenhower, in fact, was obliged to send in U.S. Marines to quell the storm in September 1958, during the final days of Camille Chamoun's mandate.[32]

In his enthronement speech, the new Patriarch Theodosios VI spoke of his conviction that Orthodoxy was an integral part of the Arab world. It should be noted that at the time of his election to the patriarchal office, he was metropolitan of Tripoli, therefore a bishop from Lebanon and, significantly, on good terms with the then Premier Rachid Karami. Politics, as always, played a central part in the church's survival in the region. The Middle East is an important sphere of influence in which the various foreign powers (particularly Russia and the United States) and their agents and the Eastern Church were engaged in an uneasy struggle. Theodosios' pro-western leanings were part of the reason for Metropolitan Antony's support[33] and, subsequently, his elevation. Metropolitan Antony's prestige and shrewd presence helped defuse the difficult situation.[34]

The co-mingling of church/state relations was a part of the fabric of the Byzantine Empire and later during the period of Ottoman rule and Czarist Russia. Easterners draw a subtle distinction between the two. Theologians have argued about the separation of the twin eagles of power: the emperor and the patriarch, but in fact, both realities had an impact on one another.

North American Unity

During the November 17, 1958 meeting of the Mixed General Council of the Antiochian Patriarchate for the nomination of the new patriarch, it was decided to upgrade the North American delegation from three to five members as was done for Damascus and Beirut. Metropolitan Antony included some members from Toledo in a gesture of good will.

After his election by the Holy Synod, Theodosios VI presided over a meeting of the council. It was affirmed, again, that there was one undivided archdiocese in North America. The council approved a plan to establish a bishopric with geographic boundaries under the jurisdiction of the presiding metropolitan, whose name would be commemorated in all services.

Once again, Metropolitan Antony believed the thorny unity problem in North America was finally resolved. However, letters continued to be exchanged between Theodosios VI and Metropolitan Antony regarding the future of the archdiocese in North America.

Antony called for a "Special General Convention" of the archdiocese on January 12 and 13, 1960 in Toledo, to set geographical boundaries for a new episcopate of Toledo, as ordered by the patriarch and the council, and to nominate by secret ballot three qualified clergymen for the episcopacy from within the archdiocese. Forty-eight thousand parishioners were present in person or by proxy. (The seven Toledo parishes representing twenty-two hundred parishioners were not in attendance.) One hundred and thirty-seven delegates, clergy and laity, were represented.

Metropolitan Antony submitted the list of ten qualified candidates, the names of the three receiving the majority of votes to be submitted to the Holy Synod of Antioch. Four removed their names: Archimandrites Ellis Khouri, George Ghannem, Gabriel Samné and the Reverend Philip Saliba. Remaining as candidates were Archimandrites Ilyas Kurban, Ananias Kassab, Gregory Abboud, Basil Kazan, Athanasius Saliba and Michael Shaheen.

The three clergymen who had received the most votes were officially accepted as candidates with a resolution from the assembly asking that His Beatitude and the Holy Synod elect one, and only one, official candidate. Antony accepted, despite his uneasiness, the creation of an episcopate in Toledo, thinking of the Greek model in North America: one archdiocese with geographical bishoprics. He hoped this would lay the foundation for unity on this continent.

The Election of Archbishop Michael Shaheen

When Metropolitan Antony returned to Damascus for a meeting of the Holy Synod of Antioch, December 8, 1961, the unity of the North American archdiocese was affirmed once again. However, on

Saturday, December 9, the Holy Synod convened and unexpectedly elected Archimandrite Michael Shaheen of Montreal. He was to be consecrated in North America.

Archimandrite Ilyas Kurban was later elected metropolitan of Tripoli, a move that was very popular in Tripoli. Archimandrite Basil Samaha was elected metropolitan of the almost non-existent Archdiocese of Hauran, and Archimandrite Ignatius Hazim of Beirut was elected patriarchal-vicar of Damascus (Palmyras) in February, 1962. Participants asserted that these moves were intended to resolve the crisis between the pro-western and eastern bloc partisans within the patriarchate.[35]

Ignatius Hazim was consecrated patriarchal-vicar to Theodosios VI, and Michael Shaheen as assistant to Metropolitan Antony. It was intended that the new bishop's role would be to assist Metropolitan Antony and minister to the archdiocese; he was not bishop of a geographical zone, nor bishop of one group in the archdiocese. Metropolitan Antony returned to Damascus with Archimandrite Michael Shaheen for his consecration on February 11, 1962, at the Church of the Holy Cross.

At the meeting of the Board of Trustees of the Antiochian Archdiocese of North America held in Montreal, May 18 and 19, 1962, a request by Toledo to omit Metropolitan Antony's name from the liturgical services was granted by Metropolitan Antony as a concession. Bishop Michael pledged to uphold the unity of the archdiocese, and Toledo insisted it would maintain its own treasury. The minutes reflected relief among all the participants with these solutions.

Antony next received an invitation to attend a synod meeting on May 22, 1962. With little time to prepare, he sent his regrets. On July 6, 1962, he learned that a meeting of the Holy Synod of Antioch had been held on May 24, at which the subject of the North American archdiocese had been reopened: Toledo was granted the status of a diocese within a diocese.

Bishop Michael left North America at this time, and later reappeared with a new praxis from the patriarch dated July 22, 1962 naming him metropolitan of Toledo. This appeared paradoxical since after Samuel David's death, no *Locum Tenens* had been appointed; there was no nomination from the "archdiocese" of Toledo since it did not exist;[36] and there was no canonical appointment for him to assume this title. Had it not been for the interventions of certain members of the synod, it would never have occurred.

At the archdiocesan convention in Asbury Park, New Jersey, August 24, 1962, the clergy led by Protosyngelos Ellis Khouri along with trustees, lay delegates and youth leaders unanimously pledged their loyalty to Metropolitan Antony and issued a protest against the decision that jeopardized the relationship between New York and Antioch.

With his last trip to the patriarchate in May of 1964, Metropolitan Antony made another attempt at reconciliation, only to have his efforts thwarted. His final journey was to Rome where he was received by Pope Paul VI; to Istanbul, to reunite with Patriarch Athenagoras, his long-time friend, and to Jerusalem, to visit Patriarch Benedict.

Metropolitan Antony's Place in History

Metropolitan Antony was a central figure in American Orthodoxy. While he had his share of human weaknesses, in balance and contextually, his strengths far outweighed them. He was a gifted, literate and articulate spokesman for Orthodoxy in North America. He had the prophetic insight, grace and awareness to initiate impressive reforms, and yet he knew the limits of his power. He borrowed from ideas circulating at the time, from thinkers and from institutions, and integrated them to construct a viable archdiocese in the twentieth century through his writings and his ministry.

He was for years both archbishop and archdiocese. The archdiocese was built on his leadership as a fundraiser. He lived simply, allowing himself few luxuries. In the early years, he used to visit the homes of the archdiocese wherever he travelled and he used the *nourieh,* or gifts given, to maintain the archdiocese. This was later transformed into the assessment system and major financial contributions of members of the archdiocese and the board of trustees. He also used the revenues accrued from his successful publishing business for the archdiocese.

Paradoxical as it may seem, while he continued to press at home for canonical reform he continued to provide material support for the Mother Church and its institutions. He had a sensitive heart for the Balamand, the patriarchate itself, for his village church and other facilities in Syria and Lebanon. He negotiated with the old country based on both the canons and the traditions that became a part of the fabric of North American church life.

Metropolitan Antony was immersed daily in the political and secular tribulations affecting the Orthodox Church he served. To fully appreciate his life, one must remember the times: the dislocations and the political tensions in the Middle East and Russia, and between the patriarchates of Constantinople and Moscow, as well as the pressures brought to bear on Patriarch Theodosios VI.

The End of an Era; the Death of Antony Bashir

Suddenly and unexpectedly, Metropolitan Antony, after a career that spanned nearly fifty years, died of lymphatic cancer on February 15, 1966. His death took the archdiocese, the patriarchate, and the Orthodox world by surprise. The letter he sent to the parishes of the archdiocese on February 8, 1966 informing all that he was being admitted to the hospital gave no indication of the seriousness of his illness. He was later joined by his family and, after receiving the sacraments, slipped into a deep coma and died peacefully.

Metropolitan Ilyas (Kurban) of Tripoli was appointed *Locum Tenens* by Patriarch Theodosios VI to take charge of the archdiocese and funeral arrangements. Thousands of religious and civic leaders, and people from all walks of life, came from across North America to pay tribute to the man whose ministry had affected so many. The then Reverend Philip Saliba was selected by Protosyngelos Ellis Khouri to deliver the official eulogy on behalf of the archdiocese.

Other eulogies and scores of messages were delivered in recognition of the great contributions of this visionary churchman throughout his life. His most enduring legacy was an archdiocese with his imprint on every facet of its organized life. The late Protopresbyter Alexander Schmemann, dean of St. Vladimir's Seminary, called him the real father of American Orthodoxy, and so he was.

III. A NEW ERA BEGINS

Philip Saliba

If the historical significance of Metropolitan Philip's election and consecration is to be fully comprehended, it is imperative to record the motivations and machinations of men who set the stage for one of the most dramatic episodes in the contemporary period.

The "Special General Assembly" called to consider the election of a successor to Metropolitan Antony was convened on March 16-17, 1966 in New York City. The meeting was presided over by the *Locum Tenens*, Metropolitan Ilyas. At the opening session on March 16, Monsour Laham, vice chairman, and John Khouri, chancellor of the board of trustees, outlined the rationale for the legal procedures to be followed. At the time of the balloting, a full 94.7% of the qualified clergy and lay delegates of the archdiocese were present in person or by proxy.

There were attempts at caucusing, even some outright campaigning, as rumors concerning the candidates circulated during those intense two days in New York. However, when the time arrived to take action, the gap between the Old and New World was bridged: the mechanism in the archdiocesan constitution worked, and the process of selecting a leader went ahead smoothly.

The final list of accredited candidates included Archimandrites Gibran Ramlaoui and Athanasius Saliba, and the Reverends Philip Saliba and Antoun Khouri. Protosyngelos Ellis Khouri and Metropolitan Ilyas declined to be nominated; Archimandrite Gregory Abboud's name was offered from the floor, and Bishop Ignatius Hazim, known to the archdiocese since 1963 when he attended the archdiocese convention in Washington, D.C., was presented.

When Philip Saliba approached the podium, he stirred the assembly as at Metropolitan Antony's funeral with a maturity far beyond his years. The archdiocesan assembly produced a slate of nominees with one prominent candidate, without rancor, quibbling or disturbance. When it came time to vote, the chairman of the Department of Credentials and his committee conducted the roll call, and balloting took place in an orderly fashion.

When Metropolitan Ilyas Kurban announced that a consensus had been reached, the assembly was overjoyed. Philip Saliba received almost twice the aggregate of other votes. The consensus was an eloquent testimony by the clergy and lay delegates to their confidence in Philip Saliba to lead the archdiocese.

It is now known that Philip Saliba was caught completely off guard by the massive mandate he was given. In all the deliberations he had deferred to others, not believing he would receive the majority of the votes. Overwhelmed yet inspired, he humbly accepted at the tender age of thirty-five the challenge before him.

It was little wonder that the mantle of leadership fell to Philip. His inner fortitude, intellectual capacity, leadership skills and spiritual development had been in evidence from the earliest days. Born in Abou-Mizan, Lebanon on June 10, 1931, he entered the Balamand Monastery at age fourteen. Later in the schools of the patriarchate in Syria, Kelham Theological School and the University of London in England, Holy Cross Theological Seminary in Brookline, Massachusetts, Wayne State University in Detroit and St. Vladimir's Seminary in New York, he continuously sought to satisfy his intellectual curiosity. As a young deacon, he held positions as secretary to Patriarch Alexander III, and dean of students and lecturer of Arabic language and literature at Balamand Seminary. After his ordination to the priesthood, he served as pastor of St. George, Cleveland, Ohio (1959-1966).

In retrospect, the meeting in New York in 1966 was a dazzling occurrence in the life of the archdiocese. The participants at this unusual conclave clearly believed they were free agents in the process for change and renewal; they set a pattern for generations to come. The archdiocese was sorely tested and, in the distinctively North

American but Orthodox fashion, responded appropriately. This provided a fitting epitaph to the legacy of Metropolitan Antony. But it was only one act in a protracted drama still to be played in the Middle East.

The Worsening Situation in the Middle East

Metropolitan Ilyas (Kurban) played a key role in this unfolding situation. In transmitting the results of the nomination convention to the patriarch and members of the Holy Synod of Antioch, he was unwavering in his support for the legality of the Special General Convention — unknown in the Middle East — and was able courageously to frustrate delaying tactics by the synod to send a delegation from Damascus to North America.

He communicated regularly with the archdiocese. On May 19, 1966, he issued a communique reporting on the meeting of the board of trustees held on May 7, 1966, and again on May 24, 1966, informing all that he was leaving to attend a meeting of the executive committee of the Mixed General Council and the Holy Synod of Antioch, accompanied by Monsour Laham and Rudy George, archdiocesan trustees, at the patriarchate in Damascus.

He also noted that the nominating committee for the vacant Archdiocese of Latakia had selected three candidates: Bishop Ignatius Hazim, the Reverend George Khodre and Archimandrite Constantine Papastephanou.

On May 31, 1966, Monsour Laham reported that at the final meeting on May 21, between the North American delegation and the patriarch and members from the Mixed General Council of the Antiochian Patriarchate, the nominations of March 17, 1966 had been accepted. A promise was made to convene the Holy Synod of Antioch before the end of June, and Metropolitan Ilyas was requested to remain in North America until the synod meeting. There seemed to be hope for a speedy resolution.

Rump Synod: Election of Metropolitan of Latakia

However, when Metropolitan Ilyas returned to the United States on June 21, 1966, he brought news of an uncanonical meeting of several metropolitans on May 25, at which Antonio Chedraoui had been elected and consecrated as metropolitan of Latakia. The Arab and North American press was full of news at this time of the government of Syria, the Antiochian Patriarchate and the people of Latakia locked in a bitter struggle. These revelations only increased the anxiety of the North American archdiocese. Members feared a repetition of the same tactics. In fact, the rump synod did elect Ignatius for North America; to which he replied, "Thank you for your election to China."[37]

On July 9, a special meeting of the Board of Trustees of the Antiochian Archdiocese in North America was called. All the deans were present. It was decided that a delegation headed by Protosyngelos Ellis Khouri, including several members of the clergy[38] should represent the archdiocese at the patriarchate, both preceding and during the next meeting of the Holy Synod. During the 1960 archdiocese convention in Houston, Archimandrite Ellis Khouri had been elevated to the rank of Protosyngelos in recognition of his unique role in the history of the archdiocese. The ninth generation of priests in his family, Father Ellis was the ultimate example of humility and service combined with a brilliant and poetic mind. His stature was unmatched in the entire history of the Antiochian Orthodox Christian Archdiocese in North America.

Holy Synod Preparations

In Beirut, where there was intense interest in the upcoming synod and election of the North American prelate, the Protosyngelos Ellis Khouri headed off all attempts to undermine the delegation's mission. Dayton Mak, first secretary to the American ambassador, met with the American delegation at the American embassy. He stated there had been no problem of such complexity in the history of his diplomatic career and in the history of the American relationship with

Lebanon. The results of the upcoming synod would determine the destiny of the Patriarchate of Antioch for centuries to come.[39]

The North American delegation was subjected to scurrilous attacks in the press. With the support of the Latakia community leaders there, the role of Ellis Khouri widened, and he proved to be an able statesman for the resolution of the emerging crisis. As chief spokesman, he explained eloquently the position of the Archdiocese of North America: that a special convention had been held; a legal consensus had been taken; one candidate had received an overwhelming majority of the votes; and the clergy and laity stood firm with absolutely no compromise on any of the issues.

The delegation, he noted, had travelled thousands of miles to appeal to the patriarch and the Holy Synod of Antioch to expedite the nomination and immediately elect Philip Saliba as successor to the late Antony Bashir. The message was conveyed to His Beatitude Theodosios VI and Metropolitans Elia (Beirut), Elias (Mt. Lebanon), Elias (Aleppo), Paul (Tyre and Sidon, Marjayoun), Ignatius (Hama), Ignatius (Sao Paulo), Meletios (Argentina), Ilyas (Tripoli), and Ignatius Hazim, dean of Balamand Seminary.

In a highly unusual step, Orthodox parliamentarians, with Orthodox senators, deputies, ministers from both the Syrian and Lebanese parliaments and members of the patriarchal Mixed General Council concerned over the beleaguered patriarchate, met with Theodosios VI. They confirmed "that the faithful in Syria and Lebanon urge this synod to act decisively, with legality, without compromise, since the decisions of this synod meeting would have far-reaching consequences in the history of the patriarchate."

Protosyngelos Ellis Khouri met with His Beatitude at the patriarchal headquarters in Damascus. The patriarch spoke with his friend in English in deference to the American clergy. Perhaps sensing he was at the apex of his ecclesiastical career, he called for the synod meeting to convene at the Monastery of the Prophet Elias (Dhor El Shweir), to assert his authority to convene the synod anywhere within the boundaries of the patriarchate, and most importantly to diffuse the climate of crisis.

As the synod was preparing to assemble on July 25, 1966, five dissenting bishops issued a mocking statement published in Lebanon in the *Lisan al-Hal*. Patriarch Theodosios VI, with the support of the clergy and laity of the patriarchate and the archdioceses involved, did not budge from his decision to hold the meeting at the monastery.

In the end, the five opposing bishops did attend the synod meeting but only to disrupt the procedures. They ultimately walked out.

When the patriarch reconvened the meeting, Metropolitans Salibi, Karam, Hureiki, Forzley, Moawad, Swaity and Kurban were present, making a quorum. They accepted the nominations, and the following day elected Philip Saliba as Metropolitan of New York and All North America, and Ignatius Hazim as Metropolitan of Latakia. This election ended a painful chapter in the Church's history, and the victory for North America became a victory for the patriarchate.

The Consecration of Metropolitan Philip

Philip Saliba was consecrated on Sunday, August 14, 1966, at St. Elias Monastery where he began his ministry, before a wildly enthusiastic congregation of thousands. The event was widely covered by the media throughout the Arab world. He then lay the cornerstone for the new St. John of Damascus Academy at the Balamand Seminary, fulfilling the long-standing commitment by the late Metropolitan Antony Bashir.

Metropolitan Philip was enthroned at St. Nicholas Cathedral, Brooklyn, New York, on October 13, 1966 in the presence of a multitude of Orthodox hierarchs, clergy and laity of the archdiocese and a large contingent of ecumenical representatives and diplomats. Archbishop Iakovos, primate of the Greek Orthodox Archdiocese of North and South America and chairman of the Standing Conference of Canonical Orthodox Bishops in America (SCOBA), delivered the main address to the new metropolitan.

The Early Ministry

Soon after presiding over the archdiocesan convention in San Francisco, Metropolitan Philip returned to the Middle East for the continuation of the meetings of the Holy Synod of Antioch which had elected him on August 5 and was still in session. There his election became a symbol of the future as well as an essential precursor in the recovery of the dignity and prestige of the patriarchate.[40]

During the archpastoral charge to the 1969 General Assembly of the 24th Annual Convention of the Antiochian Archdiocese in Miami, Florida, merely three years after assuming office, Metropolitan Philip implemented decisions that would have far reaching consequences in the future of Antiochian Orthodoxy in North America. He began tackling the reforms of the constitution and by-laws of the archdiocese, the clergy-laity relations and the ethnic self-designation of the archdiocese. The highlights included here, signify a drastic change with bold and inclusive initiatives that would eventually define the course of the archdiocese:

1. To drop the word "Syrian" from the official title of the archdiocese;
2. To support the early formation of an autocephalous Orthodox Church in America;
3. To overhaul and revise the archdiocesan constitution, following two years of work by a special commission;
4. To admit elected representatives of teen-agers to full voting status in archdiocesan conventions;
5. To authorize a comprehensive survey to determine the future possibilities of the Syrian Orthodox Youth Organizations SOYO, the archdiocesan youth society;
6. To erect a new archdiocesan headquarters.

The Death of Patriarch Theodosius VI and Election of Patriarch Elias IV

The octogenarian Patriarch Theodosios VI died on September 19, 1970 in the hospital in Beirut while members of the Holy Synod were in session at the Monastery of the Prophet Elias in Dhor El Shweir. In an ironical twist, the patriarch ushered in a new era as the non-political metropolitans he consecrated in his twilight years opened a fresh chapter in the Antiochian Church.

Following the funeral rites, the Holy Synod of Antioch was convened on September 25, 1970. Metropolitan Elias of Aleppo was elected patriarch. Metropolitan Philip later observed, "Never in the history of Antioch was the Holy Spirit so manifest in the election of a Patriarch." The Holy Synod, foreseeing the political situation unfolding in the Middle East, acted decisively with the election of Elias IV, called, "the sturdy man of Antioch" and "Patriarch of the Arabs."

The Unity Agreement: New York and Toledo

A unity agreement was finally reached between the Archdiocese of New York and the Archdiocese of Toledo, through the efforts of Metropolitans Philip and Michael to end the divisions in the North American Church. It was signed on June 24, 1975 and ratified on August 19 at the patriarchal Monastery of the Prophet Elias, by the Holy Synod of Antioch. This agreement united the Archdiocese of New York and All North America with the Archdiocese of Toledo and Dependencies into one archdiocese, called the Antiochian Orthodox Christian Archdiocese of North America. Metropolitan Philip Saliba was named primate and Archbishop Michael Shaheen his auxiliary.

Thus ended a most divisive period of church history. The long march the two men had begun in 1973 to end the sad chapter of division in North America was over. The discussions were at times difficult and tortuous, but in the end Metropolitan Philip and Archbishop Michael rose to their task and brought their negotiations to a timely conclusion. The unification would have an enduring impact in North America and serve as an example for the See of Antioch. It was a propitious moment, with peace in the patriarchate and North America, to extend an invitation for a first patriarchal visit.

Antiochian Holy Year, 1977: The Visit of Patriarch Elias IV

In 1977, the Antiochian Holy Year was proclaimed by Metropolitan Philip throughout the archdiocese. The presence of Patriarch Elias IV brought the Antiochian experience to North American Christians. Elias repeated throughout his archdiocesan tour, "Antioch is you! You are Antioch!" The patriarchal visit was timely since it came during a period of great theological and moral uncertainty throughout the world, and reaffirmed the spiritual heritage of the Antiochian Orthodox Church. To commemorate the event, the Patriarch Elias IV Endowment Fund was established in support of the Balamand Theological School of St. John of Damascus, considered vital to the interests of the patriarchate.

On June 21, 1979, Metropolitan Philip received the shocking news that Patriarch Elias IV had died suddenly after a massive heart attack. The North American delegation accompanying Metropolitan Philip arrived in Damascus on June 28, two days after the funeral. Of paramount importance to Philip was the expeditious election of the successor to Elias IV. According to the patriarchal constitution, the Holy Synod of Antioch must elect a successor within ten days after the patriarchal seat becomes vacant. During the interim, Philip himself was pressed to be a candidate. He refused stating that there was much left undone in North America and that he could best serve the patriarchate by his episcopacy in North America.

Metropolitan Ilyas (Kurban), as the *Locum Tenens*, convened the Holy Synod for the nominations and election. The candidates were Metropolitans Ignatius Hazim, George Khodre and Elias Youssef. After the nominations were closed, the Holy Synod proceeded to the Cathedral of the Virgin Mary for the election. Ignatius was named the one hundred and sixty-fifth successor to the Apostles Peter and Paul. Metropolitan Philip stated, "We Antiochians have had many great patriarchs... and again we probably have one of the best patriarchs in the entire Orthodox world; a learned man, freely elected to serve the Church." This was of great importance to a church which included state-dominated churches in Istanbul, Russia, Rumania and Yugoslavia.

Patriarch Ignatius is seen as a bridge between two worlds: traditional Orthodoxy and the twentieth century. He is Syrian, has lived mostly in Lebanon and has held several posts there, including dean of the Balamand Seminary. He received his advanced theological degree from St. Sergius Orthodox Institute in Paris, has travelled widely, and is well known in ecumenical circles around the world.

Constitutional Issues

After the thirty-fifth archdiocesan convention, held in Los Angeles in 1981, there occurred a deadlock on nominations for the election of an auxiliary to assist Metropolitan Philip in meeting the expanding needs of the enlarging archdiocese. A confrontation loomed between the archdiocese and the patriarch who was resisting inclusion of this item on the agenda of the Holy Synod. What was at issue was not simply the right of the laity to nominate candidates for the episcopacy or the matter of an auxiliary bishop; there was also deep concern regarding the inter-Orthodox dialogues and their implications for the future.

Metropolitan Philip began a discussion with the Holy Synod regarding the disparities between the 1955 and 1972 patriarchal constitutions and that of the archdiocese. He indicated that in 1966, the Archdiocese of North America had followed the canonical tradition of the 1936 nomination, election and official praxis issued in 1924, and the constitution drawn up under the primacy of Alexander III. The later accretions of 1972 by Elias IV were added to protect the patriarchate from the factionalism that had afflicted the Church.

Metropolitan Philip assured the Holy Synod that the Archdiocese of North America had no intention of going its own way, and that the laity would never relinquish their sacred responsibility in the nominations process. He further added that the archdiocese would not be subjected to division to satisfy some intricate casuistry for auxiliaries. Finally a proposal was hammered out under the joint sponsorship of Metropolitans Philip and George Khodre to nominate three members of its clergy: Archimandrites Antoun Khouri and George

M. Corry, and the Reverend Basil Essey, and to study the election of an auxiliary bishop for North America.

Election of Antoun Khouri

Antoun Khouri was subsequently elected auxiliary to Metropolitan Philip at the meeting of the Holy Synod held on November 4, 1982 and was consecrated titular bishop of Seleucia[41] on January 9, 1983 at St. Nicholas Cathedral in Brooklyn. His consecrators were Metropolitan Philip, Archbishop Michael, Metropolitan Elias (Saliba), Metropolitan Paul (Bendely) (representing the patriarch), and Bishop Antonio (Chedraoui) of Mexico.

The newly consecrated Antoun Khouri had travelled a long journey from Damascus. After serving under the metropolitan of San Paulo, Brazil, he entered St. Vladimir's Seminary, then served several parishes of the archdiocese until he assumed the post of administrative assistant to the metropolitan. He later became dean of St. Nicholas Cathedral in Brooklyn and served until his elevation to the episcopacy.

Antiochian Holy Year 1985: The Patriarchal Visit of Ignatius IV

An invitation was extended to Patriarch Ignatius IV, who has dedicated much of his administration to building and renewing the patriarchate and constructing new facilities such as the St. John of Damascus Theological Academy at the Balamand (underwritten and supported by the Archdiocese of North America and a trust bequeathed by Elias IV) and the new Balamand University, to visit North America on May 16, 1985. He was invited to preside, together with Metropolitan Philip and the auxiliaries and archbishops who accompanied him, in the dedication of the Heritage and Learning Center at the Antiochian Village on July 14, 1985.

During his trip, he met with and approved the ongoing dialogue with the "Evangelical Orthodox Church" (EOC) which was searching for an authoritative spiritual home. This proved to be a bold move as the other autocephalous churches either were unable or unwilling to engage in a meaningful dialogue with them. The evangelicals were received by chrismation in various churches across North America, and the clergy were ordained into the Antiochian Church by Metropolitan Philip, and commissioned to missionize North America.

Traversing the continent during the four-month sojourn convinced the patriarch of the need for another auxiliary to assist the primate in administering the affairs of the archdiocese.

The Holy Synod and the Election of Basil Essey

The agenda of the meeting of the Holy Synod of Antioch convened at the Balamand Theological Academy/Abbey on November 12-14, 1991 included the following issues: the on-going dialogue with the Syrian Orthodox Patriarchate of Antioch; the benefits of comparative study of administration and canon law between Antioch and North America; the canonical guidelines for church discipline and the formation of a spiritual court of the patriarchate. It also addressed the issue of *economia* (oikonomia) and reaffirmed that each metropolitan must dispense economia in his own archdiocese, using his own wise counsel in each situation.

Also at this final session, a new auxiliary for North America was elected. The names of six candidates were submitted from which three were nominated. Archimandrite Basil Essey was elected without any procedural wrangling or politicking. The transition within Antioch, and the acceptance of North American practices, had come to fruition. The Church had come of age.

The American-born priest Basil Essey was consecrated in his parish, St. George Cathedral of Wichita, Kansas, on Sunday, May 31, 1992 by Metropolitans Philip and Elias (Audi) of Beruit and the auxiliaries of the archdiocese. Father Basil had endeared himself to many over the years in his various roles under the direction of the primate, especially those relating to the youth of the archdiocese. His nomination and election symbolized the maturation process on both continents. An American-born cleric, educated in seminaries in the United States and at Balamand in Lebanon, he assumed the episcopacy in the last decade of the twentieth century.

Recent Events

On October 24, 1992, Archbishop Michael died of a massive heart attack in Toledo, Ohio. Funeral services on October 29 were attended by all the hierarchs, scores of clergy and the faithful from the archdiocese. Metropolitan Philip eulogized him as the bishop who confirmed unity in 1975, ending the disunity in North America.

At a special meeting of the enlarged Holy Synod on October 4-12, 1993, at the Balamand Monastery and Theological School in Lebanon, Metropolitan Philip submitted a study of Bishop Raphael Hawaweeny's life for consideration for his canonization.

On January 24, 1995, the Holy Synod of Antioch elected Archimandrite Demetri Khoury and assigned the Right Reverend Bishop Joseph Zehlaoui, auxiliary to His Beatitude, to serve as auxiliary bishops for the Antiochian Orthodox Christian Archdiocese of North America. This action came in response to the request of the board of trustees of the archdiocese. Archimandrite Demetri was consecrated titular bishop of Jāblat on March 12, 1995 in Damascus, Syria.

Mission in North America

Since 1966, when Metropolitan Philip assumed the primacy of the archdiocese, the Department/Commission of Parish Development (Missions) has been a priority in his ministry. The archdiocese has gone through a period of unprecedented growth, tripling in size through both internal and external forces. Emphasis has been placed on reaching out to the unchurched and the creation of new missions in viable areas. In addition, the "uncivil" war in Lebanon has brought thousands of refugees from Lebanon, especially to the Canadian parishes. This immigration has strengthened the Orthodox Church from within.

The reception of Western rite parishes has brought renewed vigour and increased membership. What was a seminal current in the 1950s is today a full-fledged movement. Entire disaffected Anglican and Episcopalian parishes have united with the ecclesiastical authority of Antioch, in large measure because of discontent with the ordination of women, liturgical tinkering and dogmatic relativism in the

Anglican Church. These Western rite churches follow their own liturgy with some modifications to bring it in line with the Orthodox Divine Liturgy. The movement was originally blessed by Patriarch Alexander III in 1958 just prior to his death, and implemented in North America by Metropolitan Antony with the ordination of Alexander Turner, a pioneer in this movement, and the reception of his followers. The current primate, sensitive to the attachment of North American Christians to their own liturgical traditions, has encouraged this process which is taking place in many parts of North America and even in England.

The growth in the Antiochian Church is also attributable to the entry into canonical Orthodoxy of the Evangelical Orthodox Church, now the Antiochian Evangelical Orthodox Mission (A.E.O.M.), whose origins stem from various Protestant denominations, bringing with them a fresh zest and missionary spirit. These new church members follow the Liturgy of St. John Chrysostom in English. The integration of these diverse elements within the archdiocese is a tribute to the openness implicit in the Antiochian tradition and the expansive view of Metropolitan Philip.

Philip Saliba's Ministry

Metropolitan Philip's awareness of the world at large has allowed him to rise above ethnic particularism to search for ways to relieve hunger, racism, totalitarianism, economic exploitation and social injustice. Under his leadership, many episcopal missions have brought humanitarian relief to the people of the Near East — the orphans, the needy, Palestinian, Lebanese, and Syrian refugees. Scholarships have been made available for students; and the governments of Syria, Lebanon and Jordan and many institutions and archdioceses have received financial support for the reconstruction efforts in their war-torn countries.

In his own archdiocese, Metropolitan Philip has looked beyond parochialism and certain fundamentalist tendencies for the larger good of the archdiocese. In the course he has charted, he has attempted to bring church structures into line with the Orthodox theological premises necessary for a balance between the hierarchy, the parish clergy and the archdiocesan board of trustees and local parish councils. He has maintained a constant and vigilant watch over the transformation of the many institutions of the archdiocese into an organic unity of purpose and vision as the Orthodox Church turns towards a new century.

The organizational level has been elevated by the many innovations Metropolitan Philip has initiated: The Order of St. Ignatius of Antioch, the Antiochian Orthodox Christian Women of North America, the Clergy and Parish Council Symposia, Teen SOYO, the Fellowship of St. John the Divine (SOYO), the Antiochian Village and the Heritage and Learning Center, the archdiocesan headquarters and West Coast Chancery, and the Task Force for the Twenty-first Century.

As a "practical theologian," he has tried to move from juridical issues to those of faith in action in his pastoral work. His thesis for his master's degree dealt with the Eucharist in the early church, and this has been a consistent theme throughout his ministry, articulating the Church as a worshipping community. He is known at home and abroad as a charismatic, creative leader, embodying the spirit of Antioch in the breadth of his encounter with the world and its endless need for redemption and transfiguration.

Another hallmark of the ministry of Metropolitan Philip has been his relentless search for ways the Orthodox hierarchs of the Americas can coordinate efforts to meet the vital needs of today's Christians. As vice-chairman of SCOBA he never ceases to urge his co-workers to rise above narrow jurisdictional lines to confront the larger issues. There is an awareness that he has encouraged and nurtured organic Orthodox unity among all the canonical jurisdictions as a realizable goal, as well as addressing the everyday issues that affect the Church daily by implementing a common witness/action.

Orthodox Unity

Metropolitan Philip hosted SCOBA in an unprecedented meeting at the Antiochian Village, Ligonier, Pennsylvania on November 30

– December 2, 1994. Twenty-nine bishops representing the entire spectrum of Orthodox churches and ethnic groups were in attendance. This historic first assembly was presided over by Archbishop Iakovos (Greek Orthodox Archdiocese), chairman of SCOBA, and the agenda covered important topics for the future of the Orthodox Church on this continent: the ongoing struggle for administrative unity; the various programs under the auspices of SCOBA such as International Orthodox Christian Charities (IOCC), the Orthodox Christian Mission Center (OCMC), the Orthodox Theological Society in America (OTSA), the Orthodox Christian Education Commission (OCEC), etc.; and an important statement on mission and evangelism. This gathering affirmed that the Orthodox Church is no longer a foreign implant but at home in the North American cultural setting; ready to engage in coming to terms with the realities of modern life as the twenty-first century looms ahead.[42]

Conclusion

The Antiochian Patriarchate is immeasurably richer for Metropolitan Philip's ministry; not merely because of the vast amounts expended for its varied causes but because he has singlehandedly raised the consciousness of Antiochian ideals throughout this archdiocese. Antioch is no longer simply an ancient reference or a spot in history but a dynamic evangelical challenge for every generation. It is a living "school" that renews and incarnates the apostolic message of hope on this continent as well as in the Middle East.

We may know the human only where we are confronted with the divine;

We may know the temporal only when we ponder the eternal;

And we may know the depth of the Valley only when we look at it from the peak of the Mountain. [43]

NOTES

Some references from the author's extensive bibliography have been incorporated into the Selected Bibliography at the end of this volume.

Author's note: This article is drawn from a forthcoming book. The references listed here are only a part of the extensive bibliography the book will include. The author has arranged to have many of the letters and periodical articles cited translated from the Arabic press. The author used the archives of the Moscow Patriarchate, the Greek Orthodox Archdiocese of North and South America, the Orthodox Church in America, as well as the Antiochian Orthodox Archdiocese of North America. The author has also relied on personal conversations, interviews, tapes of speeches and his own diaries.

[1] The Millet system of the Ottoman Empire kept religion ideologically compacted and under the control of the Sublime Porte. Christians and the Jews had, for example, their own Millet/Nation within the Ottoman Empire. They did not form part of the community of state and had no share in its military or religious organization.

[2] The missions stemmed from the growth of British, French, Italian and American commercial interests as well as the time when the French intervened after the 1860 massacres. On the Protestant sides since the mid-nineteenth century, there arrived in the Middle East missionaries from the Church of England, the Presbyterian Protestant Society, the Scottish United Free Church and American Board for Foreign Mission; in addition to the Danish, Swedish, Irish and German contingents. The Latins, after the formation of the Propagation of the Faith, in 1622, sent Capuchins, Jesuits, Carmelites and Franciscans, to the Middle East. The Christians were easier prey than "those stubborn Mohamedans" in the words of one Protestant missionary. Their interventions posed a direct threat to the indigenous Christians.

[3] Professor Derek Hopwood notes that Meletios II's election as the first Syrian since 1724 was a real victory for Arab nationalism.

[4] Bishop Emmanuel Abo Hatab wrote in *A Brief History of the Syrian Community of Greater New York*, that "New York City ... [had] become the Capital of the Syrian Immigration. It [was] the most important center for the churches, organizations, publishing houses, and business establishments. In New York, you [could] experience their love of tradition and witness their progress and high moral standing."

5 Archbishop Tikhon was glorified on October 19, 1989 in Moscow.

6 The petition, dated August 8, 1895, and freely translated, stated the faithful had for some time felt they needed a priest to care for their spiritual needs:

> The Orthodox community has been less fortunate than other communities and has for a long time prayed to God to grant them what he granted to Catholics and Maronites. Those denominations have indeed found in their superiors and chiefs leaders who have done everything to make them progress spiritually and morally: building churches for them and providing them with priests. Our community was lifeless and scared to ask for help from the Antiochian See fearing no response from them, no help at all....
>
> Our society ... [has] agreed to ask as pastor the Rev. Father Archimandrite Raphael Hawaweeny ... because they found in him a fully religious man, very pious, who loves what is good for the community and especially the attachment to the Russian Holy Synod....
>
> It is with pleasure and pity for our souls that the Archimandrite accepted our wishes... We have... hope in the Holy Synod ...who has the charge to take care of Orthodox[y] everywhere ... that he will support our demand....

7 The article by Metropolitan Antony. "Pastoral Direction and Instruction on Orthodox and Protestant Episcopal Relations and Ministrations in America," July 31, 1944 describes Bishop Rafael's attempts to foster Orthodox aspirations for Christian unity, and includes a pastoral letter written by Hawaweeny in which he outlines the Orthodox Church's position regarding inter-faith practices.

8 The letter purported to raise these questions on behalf of Patriarch Gregory.

9 Metropolitan wrote to Archbishop Evdokim:

> Existing conditions in the Syrian Church and the demands of many churches have forced me to accept the position of acting Bishop of Syrian Antiochian Orthodox Church in North America.
>
> Therefore I ask you in the name of Christ to delay consecration of Archimandrite Ofiesh until we can communicate with our Patriarch in Syria.
>
> For the sake of the peace of the Church, I repeat my request to your Grace to put a stop to all these acts which are creating dissension among my fellow countrymen.

10 Ofiesh read from a statement on August 3, 1914, the day he was made an archimandrite (from the original in the archives of the Diocese of Brooklyn, in Bishop Raphael's handwriting):

> "I, Efim Ofiesh, the poorest of monk-priests, swear before this Holy Gospel, the honorable cross, the holy icon of our Lord Jesus Christ and His most Holy mother, the Virgin Mary and also before you, Bishop Rafael, and all the faithful who are here present, that first I renounce [illegible] and shall avoid participation in any Society or Sect the learning of which is contrary to the teachings, the beliefs and the rites of the orthodox holy and apostolic Church of Christ. Second, in my speech in my [illegible] and in my conduct I shall avoid everything that could cause doubt and temptation. Third I shall consecrate all the days of my earthly life with all my intellectual and corporal strength to the sincere and true service to my Orthodox Church and to my spiritual flock and I shall always obey without any hypocrisy or pretence the local legal spiritual authority."

11 At the meeting, at which were attending Metropolitan Platon; Aftimios, the vicar-archbishop of Brooklyn; Stephan, vicar-bishop of Pittsburgh; Theophilius, vicar-bishop of Chicago; Archimandrite Benjamin, administrator of Canadian Churches and representatives of Eastern Orthodox Churches; Archbishop Alexander and Archbishop Panteleimon, one of the resolutions passed was "…to recognize that the only lawful head of the Russian Orthodox Church in America is Metropolitan Platon."

12 Germanos was a man of enormous stature and presence and great personal magnetism. He had a powerful baritone voice, and was probably the first person to record the liturgy. His recordings of Arabic-Byzantine hymns were widely sold, and stirred the hearts and minds of his countrymen with nostalgia for the homeland. In fact, he was a pioneer in the use of the media.

13 The controversy was widely covered in the Arab press (*al-Hoda, Mir'āt al-Gharb, al-Sā'ih, al-Nasir,* and *al-Samir*). With the exception of Kahlil Gibran, all members of the al-Rabita al-Qalamiyya (the Pen Bond antedates its formal constitution in 1920) 'Abd al-Masih Haddad, Nasib 'Arida, Mikhail Naimy, William Catzeflis, Rashid Ayyub, Nadra Haddad, Wadi' Bahut, Ilyas 'Ata Allah (and later) Ilyya Abu-Madi were members of the Orthodox Church. Najib Badran's *al-Nasir* took an independent route in unconditional support of Germanos' aspirations.

14 Article 22 (Quoted from His Beatitude's letters of May 9 and 22, 1923, No. 688): "Whenever a vacancy takes place in a Bishopric office in one of the parishes, the Patriarch appoints whomever he deems fit to act as his representative and announces the fact to the local authorities to recognize said appointee as such. Thereafter the Patriarch shall announce to that parish through his representative to

nominate three qualified cleric for the office of Bishop within forty days of the announcement, and they shall present those names to his beatitude in an official petition. The Patriarch then shall communicate that to all the bishops of his See within a week." The complete voting procedure is then laid out, with a proviso that since Syria is so far away, the period for submitting nominations has been extended.

15 Patriarch Gregory IV, while pro-Russian, was first and foremost a pro-Arab nationalist. Though he was considered a crafty churchman by some English observers, he was revered by his co-religionists in the Islamic World and regarded as "The Patriarch of the Arabs" for his generosity during the famine in Syria during World War I. Many accounts of Gregory IV are quite sympathetic to him as a fine humble priest of God, one who, as the second Arab patriarch, brought a measure of stability to the Church during his lifetime. The city of Damascus was reported to have come to a halt during his funeral procession as the populace, Christian and Muslim alike, wept openly, lamenting the loss of their saintly Gregory, calling him the "Patriarch of all virtuous humanity."

16 Alexander replied to Aftimios in a letter dated Feb. 11, 1929 that "The jurisdiction over all Orthodox in the Diaspora, including the whole Western Hemisphere, which includes Alaska as well, being no more a Russian territory, belongs indisputably to the Oecumenical Patriarchate of Constantinople," and suggested that to avoid making the situation worse, [Aftimios] should stop interfering in the affairs of the other national churches.

17 The objection to Platon raised by Aftimios, based on the canonical break between Moscow and North America, became the *raison d'être* for Antioch to finally justify canonical links with the Syrian Mission.

18 A letter, dated Dec. 1, 1928, from Patriarch Basilios of Constantinople, repudiated the establishment of this new apparently Russian Church and urged Athenagoras not to come into any communion with it.

19 The legal proceedings, Jan. 9, 1931, were between St. Nicholas Orthodox Church Committee of Brooklyn, Bishop Emmanuel Abo Hatab, and the laity against Aftimios Ofeish and the Syrian Holy Orthodox Greek Catholic Mission in North America.

20 A letter from the Russian Orthodox Greek Church of America dated May 6, 1930 recognized Abo Hatab.

21 A letter from the Reverend Leonid J. Turkevich, dated March 10, 1933 to Bishop Emmanuel Abo Hatab, quotes part of a letter which Metropolitan Platon received from Patriarch Alexander:

> ...Since every Orthodox National Community which is in emigration including this part of the Syrian one, is naturally attracted by the general

and irresistible wave to its own Mother, this bishop (Emmanuel) and his flock themselves begin to dream and yearn... for more close reunion with their own Mother – Holy Church of Antioch... meanwhile saving in their hearts the feeling of unlimited gratitude towards Second Mother – the Holy Russian Church....

Upon receipt of this letter, His Grace Metropolitan Platon put the following resolution: "The wish of His Holyness [sic] Patriarch Alexander can be gratified after Bishop Emmanuel, his clergy and laity have pronounced their opinion upon the question brought up by the Patriarch."

22 The telegram read:

PLEASE CANCEL LETTERS FEBRUARY EIGHTEEN. DETAILS BY MAIL. [signed] THEODOSIOS

23 When the consecrator-bishops were brought before the Council of Bishops in Pittsburgh, May 14-17, 1936, they stated that they had "performed the consecration to avoid the loss of the Syrians to other denominations such as the Maronites if their candidate had not been confirmed."

24 In 1939, the Holy Synod accepted his repentance and recognized his consecration with the understanding that he would assist and refer to Metropolitan Antony in all ecclesiastical matters.

25 From an address to the fourth archdiocesan convention of September 21-25, 1949, in Worcester, Massachusetts.

26 The Detroit Agreement was signed at the August, 1953, archdiocese convention at Detroit.

27 A letter from Alexander III, Nov. 7, 1956, outlined the Holy Synod's position regarding recognition of Archbishop Samuel's long standing in the church, his "full-fledged membership in the Holy Synod", and his title of "Metropolitan," with "all the rights and privileges of each primate of the Holy Synod."

28 As reported in *The Word* (Sept. 1962). The Holy Synod meeting held on Nov. 18, 1955, at the insistence of Patriarch Alexander, removed the name of Toledo "because he feared that by including the name of Toledo... confusion would be caused."

29 One may speculate about whether Samuel David and his followers saw David in the same hierarchical lineage as Victor Abou-Assaley, since both men shared the same village patrimony.

30 Antony Bashir was founder and publisher of the Arab monthly *al-Khalidat*, Detroit, 1926-27, and New York 1927-31. He was also a contributor to Arabic publications throughout the world. He wrote, translated and published (in English)

studies in the Greek Church, Catechism of the Greek Church. (In Arabic), Kahlil Gibran's *The Madman, The Forerunner, The Prophet, Sand and Foam, Jesus the Son of Man, The Earth's Gods*; Dr. Frank Crane's *Why I am a Christian?*; Wagner's *Simple Life*; Pappini's *Life of Christ* and *Prayers to Christ*; Tolstoy's *Confessions*; Brisbanes's *Today and the Future Day*; Barton's *The Man Nobody Knows*, and many others.

31 The first general convention of the archdiocese was held in Cleveland in 1936. It was an early attempt by the newly-consecrated Metropolitan Antony to organize the American Orthodox Church. The second convention was held in Brooklyn in 1947 and was the first annual meeting. A band of younger laymen with Metropolitan Antony felt that the expanding diocese needed a structured central administration and new stability. Many exciting ideas came out of this convention: the constitution, the central archdiocese treasury and the Metropolitan Antony Foundation. Subsequent conventions have dealt with several recurring issues: the constitution, finance, unity, liturgy, education and the Balamand.

32 It was widely reported in the press that the agitation during the election arose from the so-called "Russian," pro-communist faction against the reported American imperialist 'plot' to take over the patriarchate. Metropolitan Antony was successful in his efforts to foil the alleged "left wing" attempts at international intervention in the internal life of the Antiochian Church. His prestige and shrewd presence helped defuse the situation. The North American delegation made no claims in Damascus to represent the government of the United States but only the best interests of the Patriarchate of Antioch.

33 On the occasion of the election of Theodosios VI, Metropolitan Antony offered him a two-volume recording of the liturgy in four-part harmony, arranged by Professor Michael Hilko and the Reverend Michael Simon and directed by Christine Lynch, the first live audio recording of the liturgy in English.

34 A feature in *Time* (Dec. 1, 1958) entitled "New Patriarch" covered this period.

35 Samaha was considered suspect for his Russian connections, while Ilyas Kurban, western-educated, non-controversial and generally considered to be pro-western, could be elected to Tripoli where leftist connections would have been suspect.

36 There is no evidence of the establishment of Toledo, *de jure*, since it had been deleted in the final draft at the 1955 Constitutional Conference which dealt with the establishment of new archdioceses. However, it was argued by a faction within the Holy Synod that since it existed *de facto*, the name of Toledo should be re-recorded in the patriarchal constitution, according to the summary of the Holy Synod's decision of 19 Nov., 1955, reported in the Archdiocesan Office of *The Word* (Sept. 1962).

[37] Metropolitan Ilyas continued to assure the patriarch and members of the Holy Synod that the North American archdiocese would not be side-tracked by efforts of a minority of bishops in the synod to undermine the legal procedures to elect its archbishop. He pointed out succinctly that the meeting which took place outside the patriarchate and without the patriarch in attendance lacked a quorum and had no official mandate from the people of Latakia. It was held in the Damascus home of Metropolitan Basil Samaha and the consecration took place in the Cathedral of Metropolitan Alexander Geha in Homs, Syria, not in Latakia.

[38] Thomas Ruffin, Theodore Ziton, Joseph Shaheen, George Rados, George S. Corey, Antony Gabriel and Mr. Michel Kafoure were part of the delegation, each paying his own way. George Ghannem and Zachariah Nasr later joined the delegation.

[39] For a more complete account, see Antony Gabriel's "Report from Lebanon, Diary of an Election 1966," *The Word* (Nov. 1966).

[40] Writing about that period later in *From Heart Attack to Heart Surgery*, Philip said, "The meetings lacked order, discipline, seriousness and a creative vision of the future to a degree that on one occasion I left the meeting utterly disappointed, and went to my room and wept bitterly."

[41] Auxiliary bishops are given honorary titles to dioceses that are currently existent in name only.

[42] For a more complete account see: "The Episcopal Assembly of the Orthodox Church in North America, Antiochian Village, Ligonier, Pennsylvania November 30 to December 2, 1994," *The Word* (January 1995).

[43] Philip Saliba (1970) Chicago.

TOWARD A MIDDLE EAST PEACE: A CHRONICLE OF EFFORTS FOR PEACE AND JUSTICE IN THE MIDDLE EAST
by John W. Morris

On July 26, 1994, Metropolitan Philip Saliba, the primate of the Antiochian Orthodox Christian Archdiocese of North America, was invited by President and Mrs. Bill Clinton to a briefing in the White House on "the progress of peace in the Middle East," and to a dinner reception at the State Department in honor of His Majesty, King Hussein of Jordan and Prime Minister Yitzhak Rabin of Israel — an event considered impossible just a few years ago. The presence of Metropolitan Philip bore strong testimony to the fact that he, together with the faithful of the Antiochian Archdiocese, have worked long and hard for a just and lasting peace in the Middle East. These efforts in the quest for peace between Jews and Arabs have helped to persuade the leaders of the United States to adopt a more balanced policy in that troubled part of the world.

Ever since the founding of Israel in 1948, America has provided billions of dollars worth of arms and aid to the Jewish state. However, the United States failed to consider the plight of the Palestinian people and their legitimate desire for national self-determination until just recently. Only when the American government began to reconsider its policy of unquestioning support for Israel was it able to stimulate serious discussions for peace between Jews and Arabs. It may be that the Antiochian Archdiocese has played a major role in the shift in American foreign policy that has made this progress possible. Although many problems remain to be resolved, it would appear that

Arabs and Jews have begun the process of learning to live together in peace.*

As one of the largest and best organized branches of the Orthodox Church in North America, the Antiochian Archdiocese is in a unique position to continue to help the American people and their government reach a new understanding of the complex problems of the Middle East. It is part of the ancient Church of Antioch under the spiritual jurisdiction of the patriarch of Antioch who resides in Damascus. Thus it has strong ties to the Middle East, the ancestral home of most of the faithful of the Antiochian Archdiocese.

Metropolitan Philip has been able to use his position as the leader of a major North American religious communion to meet with presidents and other American leaders to help them understand the Arab point of view. The metropolitan's many visits to the Middle East to meet with the religious and governmental leaders have given him opportunities to open communication between the American government and Arab governments, especially the governments of Syria and Lebanon.

The Antiochian Archdiocese has also distributed hundreds of thousands of dollars in humanitarian aid to the victims of the Arab-Israeli conflict, thereby winning goodwill for Americans in the Arab world. The effort has brought together the leaders of the Arab American community to provide humanitarian aid to the people of the Middle East and to inform the American people and their government of the Arab point of view of the complex problems of the Middle East.

Finally, the Antiochian Archdiocese has worked through the inter-faith movement to help the leaders of other American religious groups and their people understand the legitimate concerns of the Palestinian and other Arab peoples.

A Brief History of the Conflict

Although most Americans believe that Jews and Arabs have fought since the struggle between Isaac and Ishmael, the sons of Abraham, the two peoples have actually lived together in comparative peace for many centuries. However, at the end of the nineteenth century, and the birth of Zionism — the movement to establish a Jewish state in the Holy Land — created a series of conflicts that have yet to be resolved.

At the end of the last century, the Arab majority in Palestine began to long for national self-determination, after centuries under Ottoman rule. At the same time, European Jews began their drive to establish a Jewish state in the Holy Land. Naturally, the Palestinian people rejected this attempt to replace Ottoman rule with domination by Jewish settlers fleeing persecution in Europe. Although a few Jewish settlers came to the Holy Land before World War I, the Zionists began their greatest efforts following the war.

The British had promised to help the Arabs in their drive for national self-determination in return for support against the Ottoman Turks, who were allied with Germany. The English also sought Jewish sympathy in their war with Germany and its allies. On November 2, 1917, Arthur Balfour, the British foreign secretary sent a letter to Lord Rothschild, a leading British Zionist, promising support for "the establishment in Palestine of a National Home for the Jewish people."

Following the war, the victors supported the nationalistic aspirations of the European peoples of the former Austro-Hungarian and Ottoman Empires. However, they failed to grant the same rights to the Arab peoples in the Middle East. Instead, the English and French, who considered the Arab peoples incapable of self-rule, divided the Middle East among themselves. This led to the British mandate in Palestine and French domination of Syria and Lebanon. Thus, European Jews immigrated to Palestine where they continued their drive for the establishment of a Jewish state.

Naturally, the Arab majority — feeling betrayed by the British — objected to the formation of a state by foreign colonists on land they had occupied for millennia. This led to a series of clashes that only intensified as more Jews moved to the Holy Land, fleeing Nazi atrocities during World War II.

Finally, deciding that they could no longer control the conflict, the British turned the matter over to the newly formed United Nations. On November 29, 1947, the United Nations voted to partition Palestine into two states, a Jewish state and a Palestinian state. Since this solution would force many Palestinians to live under Jewish domination in the proposed Jewish state, the Arabs rejected the plan. After Zionist terrorists attacked Arab villages to drive the Palestinian people from the future Jewish state, Arab nations provided support for the Palestinians.

On May 14, 1948, the Zionists established the Jewish state of Israel. Significantly, Harry Truman, the president of the United States, who needed Jewish support to win re-election, immediately recognized Israel, thereby lending legitimacy to the new Jewish state. After the outbreak of war between the Arabs and Israelis, the United Nations negotiated a series of armistices between Israel and her Arab neighbors, leading to an uneasy truce. However, the end of the war did not lead to peace. The establishment of Israel sowed the seeds of future conflict by forcing many Palestinians to flee the homeland of their ancestors.

Even before the foundation of Israel, the Antiochian Archdiocese began to work for peace and justice in the Middle East. In 1947, Metropolitan Antony Bashir, then primate of the Antiochian Archdiocese, presided over a meeting at St. Nicholas Cathedral in Brooklyn, New York, the mother church of the archdiocese. This assembly sent telegrams to the archbishops of Canterbury and York, the leaders of the Church of England, asking them to use their influence to persuade the British government to respect the rights of the Palestinian people of the Holy Land. Significantly, the dispatch ended with the prophetic warning, "unless this is done, peace will never be restored in the Holy Land." The refusal of the Zionists to consider the legitimate rights of the Palestinian people has since led to war and suffering for millions of people.

The uneasy truce ending the 1948 war failed to resolve the Arab-Israeli conflict. In 1956, Israel invaded Egypt, leading to a crisis that ended with the sending of an international force under the United Nations to preserve peace between Israel and Egypt. In 1967, General Gamal Abdel Nasser, the leader of Egypt, persuaded the United

Nations to withdraw its troops from the border between Egypt and Israel. After Nasser closed the Gulf of Aqaba to Israeli shipping, Israel launched a surprise attack on her Arab neighbors. The 1967 War ended with the Israeli conquest of East Jerusalem, the Gaza Strip and the West Bank, and the Zionist domination of over one million Palestinian Arabs.

The Oversight of Metropolitan PHILIP

The 1967 war led to new action by the Antiochian Archdiocese, guided since 1966 by the young and energetic Metropolitan Philip Saliba. When the war broke out, the metropolitan met with Syrian Orthodox, Armenian Orthodox, Maronite Catholic and Melkite Catholic leaders to establish the Emergency Relief Committees of the Near East Bishops in the USA. This was the first of his many successful efforts to organize the Arab American religious community. The committee issued an appeal for funds for humanitarian aid. They also called for special prayers on July 9, 1967 "for the souls of the victims and for a just and honorable peace."

On July 15, 1967, Patriarch Theodosius VI of Antioch sent a telegram to Metropolitan Philip asking him to raise funds to provide relief for the victims of the Israeli attack. On August 11, the metropolitan sent letters to his parishes directing them to begin immediate efforts to raise money for humanitarian aid in the Middle East. By the end of 1967, the Antiochian Archdiocese raised over ninety thousand dollars to help those suffering from the war. Metropolitan Philip and his advisors invested the money in an apartment building in Beirut to provide a continuing source of funds for relief projects. By 1970, the income from the apartment building had provided sixty-one scholarships for Palestinian students in Orthodox schools in Damascus and aid for seven university students.

Metropolitan Philip did not confine his efforts to fund-raising, but sought to influence the American government to adopt a more balanced policy in the Middle East. Ever since the establishment of Israel, American political leaders had supported the Zionist cause. When asked why he had recognized Israel without fulfilling promises made to consult with Arab leaders before taking such a step, President Truman replied that he needed Jewish votes to win the 1948 election.

Since the United States provides military and economic aid to the Jewish state, the American government is in a powerful position to influence the leaders of Israel to adopt a more conciliatory policy toward the Palestinian people and her Arab neighbors. The untiring efforts of Metropolitan Philip and the Antiochian Archdiocese to persuade the American government to change its policy from unconditional support for Israel to a more balanced approach in the Middle East have played a major role in the efforts to resolve the Arab-Israeli conflict. The metropolitan and the members of the Antiochian Archdiocese have also acted as patriotic American citizens by working to persuade the American government to promote its own national self-interest by seeking better relations with the Arab world.

Contact with the Presidents

On August 9, 1967, Metropolitan Philip sent a letter to President Lyndon Johnson informing him that he would discuss the situation in the Middle East at the convention of the archdiocese in Detroit on August 27. The prelate asked for a meeting with the president informing him that, "The present situation in the city of Jerusalem and the injustice inflicted upon the suffering victims of the recent Arab-Israeli conflict have reached the point where I feel that I can no longer remain silent."

On August 18, the metropolitan, accompanied by three of his priests, Thomas Ruffin of Detroit, Paul Schneirla of Brooklyn, and Louis Mahshie of Washington, met with the American president. Johnson strongly supported the Zionist cause, arguing that the Arabs had started the 1967 war.

When the metropolitan pointed out that the Egyptian air force had been completely destroyed in five minutes due to the surprise attack by Israel, the president said, "OK, why didn't Mr. Nasser attack? Why did he put this big army in Sinai and holler at the Jews?

Down there in my country, when someone calls you an s-o-b you hit him right away."

However, he did commit himself to "justice for the refugees, and political independence and territorial integrity for all countries in the Middle East." The American leader also stated that he would favor sending additional food to Egypt, but could not because of strong anti-Arab feeling in Congress.

When Metropolitan Philip gave Johnson an icon as a parting gift, the president, betraying his ignorance, looked at him and said, "What is this?" Metropolitan Philip responded, "It is a Byzantine icon." Johnson looked puzzled, saying, "Byzantine? Icon?" Unfortunately, the American leader focused the full attention of his administration on Vietnam and the domestic problems caused by this unpopular war. Thus he was unable to fulfill his modest promises to the metropolitan.

Despite Johnson's unpromising response, Metropolitan Philip did not give up his quest for a just solution to the Arab-Israeli conflict. He planned a trip for January, 1968, to discuss peace in the Middle East with King Hussein of Jordan. Unfortunately, his heart attack, suffered on January 5, prevented the metropolitan from fulfilling his plans. Even as he lay in the hospital recuperating from his affliction, Metropolitan Philip did not forget peace in the Middle East. Instead, he developed a new suggestion to end the conflict in that troubled part of the world. On May 9, 1968, he held a press conference at the Sheraton Chicago to announce his solution to the Arab-Israeli conflict, the formation of a new state named the Holy Land where Jew and Arab could live together as equals.

A month later, Metropolitan Philip began his efforts to win support for his proposal. On April 10, while recuperating in Palm Springs, California, he met with former President Dwight D. Eisenhower. The prelate congratulated the former leader of the United States for his strong stand against Israeli aggression during the 1956 Suez crisis. He also thanked him for supporting "Need," an organization to raise funds to help homeless Arab children.

Eisenhower stated that he had tried to persuade the Arabs and Israelis to resolve their dispute peacefully. He also said he had been prepared to ask Congress for billions of dollars to assist development in the Middle East. He had hoped to develop a plan to use atomic power to remove salt from Mediterranean water to irrigate the Sinai and Negev deserts. This would have helped both Arab and Jew by fostering agricultural development in the area. Upon hearing the Holy Land plan, the former president stated, "The plan proposed by Metropolitan Philip could be the best solution to the bitter conflict between the Arabs and Israel."

Encouraged by Eishenhower's response, the metropolitan began to seek support for his Holy Land plan. As he traveled throughout the nation visiting his parishes, he spoke of his ideas during press conferences and interviews with many reporters. In Fort Lauderdale, Florida, he suggested that if Jews were a majority in the new state, a Jew should be the president with a Muslim prime minister and Christian speaker of Parliament. He discussed his proposals with Pope Paul VI during an audience in Rome on May 30, 1968.

After Richard Nixon won the 1968 election, Metropolitan Philip lost no time seeking to influence the new president to adopt a more balanced policy in the Middle East. He sent Nixon a telegram urging him to work for a just and lasting peace in the Middle East. The metropolitan also sent a letter to the president-elect offering to advise him on Middle Eastern affairs. Comically, Harry S. Flemming, one of Nixon's special assistants, in a letter addressed to "Philip Saliba," replied that his request for a job would "receive careful consideration." Metropolitan Philip replied, "I did not apply for a job in the new administration because I am an archbishop and have a lifetime job in the vineyard of Christ."

Despite this misunderstanding, the leader of the Antiochian Archdiocese sent a telegram to Nixon's first secretary of state, William Rogers, who had shown a willingness to consider the legitimate rights of the Palestinians, congratulating Rogers for his "first step to a more even-handed policy." However, the conclusion of the Vietnam War and the Watergate scandal so preoccupied Nixon and his staff that little progress could be made to influence the Israelis to reach a settlement with the Palestinian people and their supporters in the Arab world.

Instead, the simmering conflict erupted into yet another war when Syria and Egypt attacked Israel on October 6, 1973, Yom Kippur, a high Jewish holy day. At first the advantage of surprise enabled the Syrian and Egyptian armies to win victories against their enemy. But, the United States sent weapons to the Zionist forces, enabling them to turn back the Arab armies.

The United States and the Soviet Union sponsored a cease-fire resolution in the United Nations to take effect on October 22. However, the fighting continued. At this point, the Soviet Union suggested sending Soviet and American troops to enforce a United Nations mandated cease fire. When the United States refused, Moscow threatened to send its own armies to end the fighting. The American government then put its troops on full alert, opening the possibility of war between the world's two super powers over the Middle East.

Finally, the United Nations adopted new resolutions calling for a halt to the fighting and sent an international force to supervise a cease fire, ending the war on October 27.

Metropolitan Philip responded immediately to the new crisis in the Middle East. He sent telegrams to President Nixon, Secretary of State Henry Kissinger, and Senator William Fulbright, chairman of the Foreign Relations Committee of the United States Senate, protesting the shipment of American arms to Israel. The prelate also called on the American leaders to persuade "both sides to accept the United Nations Resolution 242 of November 22, 1967, which is the only guarantee of a just and lasting peace in the entire area." UN Resolution 242 called for Israeli evacuation of all territories occupied during the 1967 war, a "just settlement of the refugee problem," and "acknowledgment of the sovereignty, territorial integrity and political independence of every state in the area."

The Antiochian Archdiocese also raised funds for humanitarian relief for the victims of the fighting. In April, 1974, Metropolitan Philip travelled to the Middle East and presented a check for $175,000 to President Hafez al-Assad of Syria to help those suffering from the war. The Antiochian Archdiocese also provided funds to assist refugees from the village of Kuneitra, a Syrian town in the Golan Heights destroyed by the Israelis. Metropolitan Philip later told a reporter from the *Palm Beach Post Times* that the Syrian leader did not want war. However, President al-Assad did want Israel to return the Golan Heights, which he considered a legitimate part of his country. Before returning to the United States, the metropolitan also discussed the situation in the Middle East with President Suleiman Franjieh of Lebanon.

Aware that the Yom Kippur War had made his plan for the establishment of the state of the Holy Land impossible, Metropolitan Philip adopted a new approach to the Arab-Israeli conflict. He suggested peace based on Israeli withdrawal from the Occupied Territories as mandated by the UN Resolution 242, thereby allowing the Palestinians to establish their state on the West Bank, the Gaza Strip and East Jerusalem. Realistic enough to recognize the Palestinians would never regain the land lost to Israel in 1948, the Metropolitan also suggested the United States influence the leaders of the Jewish state to recognize the rights of the Palestinians in the Occupied Territories by promising to guarantee the borders of Israel against any attack.

However, a new conflict in Lebanon, the homeland of Metropolitan Philip, and ancestral home of many of the faithful of the Antiochian Archdiocese, began to occupy the attention of all concerned with peace in the Middle East. Lebanon had lived for years in uneasy peace between the Maronite Catholics, given dominance over the Lebanese government by the French who had occupied Lebanon following World War I, and the Muslims. When the Palestinian Liberation Organization moved to Lebanon after King Hussein of Jordan expelled them in 1970, the number of Muslims grew. As the Muslims began to demand more political power, civil war erupted in 1975. In 1976, President Suleiman Franjieh of Lebanon asked President Hafez al-Assad to send troops to help halt the fighting, thereby bringing Syria into the conflict.

A New Alliance

Metropolitan Philip lost no time in responding to this new crisis. He invited the leaders of American religious groups with ties to Lebanon to meet at his headquarters in Englewood, New Jersey on October 14, 1975. During the meeting, representatives of the Antiochian Orthodox, Syrian Orthodox, Maronite, Melkite, Armenian Orthodox, and Arab Protestant churches joined representatives of the Druze and Islamic communities to form the Standing Conference of American Middle Eastern Christian and Muslim Leaders. Metropolitan Philip was elected chairman.

"An Appeal to the Lebanese People," supporting an immediate end to the fighting, and Lebanese independence was adopted. They called for dialogue among the leaders of the various factions to insure that they make any change in the constitution of that troubled nation through peaceful negotiations rather than violence. The document also appealed for "peaceful coexistence among different religious confessions and political ideologies." The resolution concluded with a statement in support of the Palestinian cause. Finally, the members of the Standing Conference decided to seek a meeting with President Gerald Ford, Nixon's successor.

On January 2, 1976, Metropolitan Philip sent President Ford a letter containing the resolution of the Standing Conference and asking him to meet with its executive committee to discuss the crisis in Lebanon. On April 15, Metropolitan Philip, Melkite Archbishop Joseph Tawil, Maronite Bishop Francis Zayek, and Imams Mohamad Jawad Chirri and Muhammad Abdul-Rauf of the American Islamic community met with the American leader. The President assured them of his concern for peace in Lebanon.

Metropolitan Philip replied that the fact that Christians and Muslim leaders are working together to achieve peace in Lebanon should dispel the false notion that the Lebanese civil war is a conflict between Christians and Muslims. The metropolitan also noted that the Syrian forces were invited to Lebanon to help bring peace to that troubled land. The president responded that only a political rather than a military solution could end the fighting in Lebanon. The other members of the delegation reminded the American leader that lasting peace in the Middle East depended on a resolution of the Palestinian problem.

Aware that peace would never come to the Middle East until the Palestinians received the right of national self-determination, Metropolitan Philip sought every means possible to seek a solution to this difficult problem. In January 1976, during a trip to Lebanon, he took the bold step of meeting with Yasir Arafat, the chairman of the Palestine Liberation Organization (the PLO). For over an hour the metropolitan and the leader of the Palestinians discussed the many problems of the Middle East, including negotiations between Egypt and Israel, the crisis in Lebanon, and the condition of the Palestinian people. As he departed, Metropolitan Philip gave Arafat funds to help orphaned Palestinian children. The Palestinian leader in return presented the metropolitan with two sets of mother of pearl worry-beads.

Meanwhile the leaders of the Standing Conference continued to work for peace in the Middle East. In June 1976, they sent a letter to President Ford protesting the arrest of Melkite Archbishop Hilarion Capucci by Israeli authorities. The correspondence also called Israeli settlement in the Occupied Territories a violation of the Geneva Convention. On March 14, 1977, the Standing Conference met again in Englewood to discuss the continuing crisis in Lebanon. Again they passed a resolution supporting a united and independent Lebanon. They also called upon the American government to provide humanitarian aid to rebuild the war-torn country. They reiterated that peace in the Middle East would not be achieved until the Palestinian people received the right of national self-determination.

Meanwhile, a new ultra-nationalist government took power in Israel on May 17, 1977. Led by Menachem Begin, a former Zionist terrorist and leader of the militant Likud Party, the new leaders of the Jewish state adopted a more aggressive foreign policy. They established new Jewish settlements in the Occupied Territories to insure continued Jewish domination of the West Bank, the Gaza Strip and East Jerusalem.

Significantly, the new Israeli government also sought to achieve peace with Egypt. In November, 1977, Begin invited President Anwar el-Sadat of Egypt to address the Israeli Parliament, the Knesset. This led to further negotiations, climaxing in a series of meetings hosted by President Jimmy Carter at Camp David in September, 1978.

On March 26, 1979, Begin and Sadat signed a treaty providing for Israeli withdrawal from the Sinai. However, as Metropolitan Philip rightly observed at the time, the Camp David Accord failed to insure a permanent peace in the Middle East by failing to resolve the central issue: the Palestinian problem. Indeed, the Camp David Accord may have actually led to more problems. With its southern border with Egypt secured, Israel was able to intensify its conflict with the Palestinians by intervening in the Lebanese civil war. In 1978 the Israeli army invaded southern Lebanon.

Despite the more aggressive Israeli foreign policy, Metropolitan Philip continued his work for peace in the Middle East. On July 15, 1977, he accompanied Patriarch Elias IV of Antioch to the White House to meet with President Jimmy Carter. During their discussions, the patriarch emphasized that only a solution to the Palestinian problem would bring peace to the Middle East. On March 22, 1978, Metropolitan Philip and the leaders of the Standing Conference sent telegrams to President Carter and Secretary of State Cyrus Vance protesting the Israeli invasion of Lebanon.

On August 29, 1979, the metropolitan sent a letter strongly protesting the forced resignation of Andrew Young, the American ambassador to the United Nations, after Young had unofficial discussions with Zehdi Labib Terzi, the PLO representative to the world body in the home of Abdalla Yaccoub Bishara, the Kuwaiti ambassador to the United Nations. Significantly, the American government learned of the meeting through illegal listening devices placed in Bishara's apartment by the Mossad, Israeli Intelligence, a violation of American sovereignty by an agency of a foreign government.

At this time, Metropolitan Philip began to play a new major role in American foreign relations with the Arab world. While in Damascus for the election of Patriarch Ignatius IV, following the death of

Patriarch Elias IV, the metropolitan met with President Hafez al-Assad of Syria. On August 3, 1979, Metropolitan Philip sent a report to President Carter on his discussions with the Syrian leader. He stated that the Syrian leader had a "genuine desire for peace." He also suggested that the PLO is "anxious for talks with our American government." The metropolitan called upon President Carter to take advantage of the possibility for peace in the Middle East by opening a dialogue with both Syria and the PLO.

Finally, the metropolitan offered his services to assist in the quest for peace in that troubled part of the world. He thus began to play a role in international diplomacy by helping open communications between Damascus and Washington that would be crucial in any effort to resolve the problems of the Middle East. Metropolitan Philip also continued to work with the leaders of the Standing Conference of Middle Eastern Christian and Muslim Religious Leaders, which met at his headquarters on May 6, 1981 to issue another plea for an end to the Lebanese civil war.

The Reagan Years

Unfortunately, the situation in Lebanon continued to deteriorate. On June 4, 1982, the Israelis used the assassination of Shlomo Argov, the Israeli ambassador to England, as an excuse to launch a full-scale invasion of Lebanon. Supported by savage bombing of Tyre and West Beirut, the Zionist armies advanced swiftly into the heart of the country, reaching the Lebanese capital by June 13. On August 21, protected by an international force of American, French and Italian troops, Yasir Arafat and the PLO fighters left Beirut. On September 1, President Ronald Reagan, aware that no peace could come to Lebanon or the rest of the Middle East without a resolution of the Palestinian problem, proposed Palestinian rule in the West Bank and Gaza Strip under Jordanian sovereignty. The President also called for the formation of a Jordanian-Palestinian delegation to begin peace negotiations with Israel.

Two weeks later, Bashir Gemayel, the leader of the Maronite Falangists and president-elect of Lebanon, was assassinated. The Israeli army then invaded West Beirut and looked on while Falangist troops massacred hundreds of civilians in the Palestinian refugee camps of Sabra and Chatila in revenge for the murder of their leader. A few days later, President Reagan sent fifteen hundred marines to Beirut to join French and Italian troops to bring a measure of peace to the troubled city. Unfortunately, the American forces allowed themselves to be drawn into the fighting on the side of the Falangists with tragic results.

Meanwhile, Metropolitan Philip worked feverishly to help bring peace to his homeland. He wrote President Reagan on June 21, 1982 strongly protesting the Israeli invasion of Lebanon. On March 10, 1983, he wrote to the American president to express his support for Reagan's proposals for Palestinian self-rule in the West Bank and the Gaza Strip. The prelate also informed the American chief executive that he was about to leave for a visit to the Middle East during which he planned to meet with King Hussein of Jordan, President Hafez al-Assad of Syria, and President Amin Gemayel of Lebanon. The metropolitan suggested that he meet with Reagan to discuss his trip and offered "to act unofficially in whatever way we can be of service during this visit."

As a result, Metropolitan Philip met with President Reagan on April 7, 1983. The prelate asked the American leader to persuade Israel to withdraw its troops from Lebanon as a sign to the Arab world of the good intentions of the United States. Reagan assured the metropolitan of his unwavering commitment to a free and independent Lebanon and concern for the welfare of the victims of the tragic civil war. Reagan also assured the prelate of his continued efforts to persuade Israel to withdraw its troops from Lebanon. Metropolitan Philip then asked Reagan, "Mr. President, may I carry this as a message to the people of Lebanon from the president of my country." Reagan agreed. He also asked Metropolitan Philip to tell King Hussein that he hoped that talks between Jordan and the PLO would lead to the formation of a joint delegation for negotiations with Israel based on his peace plan of September 1, 1982.

A few days later, Metropolitan Philip began his visit to the Middle East. Although time did not permit a meeting with King Hussein, the prelate did relay greetings from Reagan to the monarch through Jordanian officials. The metropolitan then traveled to Damascus where he met with President Hafez al-Assad. Metropolitan Philip delivered Reagan's plea for Syrian withdrawal from Lebanon and the request for support for his peace plan.

The Syrian leader then expressed his dissatisfaction with the failure of the American government to keep promises made, following the Israeli invasion of Lebanon, by Philip Habib, Reagan's representative in the Middle East. However, the Syrian president expressed a willingness to remove his army from Lebanon once Israel, which occupied a position only twenty five kilometers from Damascus, withdrew its forces. Al-Assad also stated that he would be willing to begin negotiations with Israel once the Jewish state showed an interest in peace by removing its troops from Lebanon, ceasing to establish Jewish settlements in the Occupied Territories and showing a willingness to discuss withdrawal from the Golan Heights.

In his report to President Reagan, Metropolitan Philip appealed to the American leader to open serious talks with Damascus because, "If we can win the Syrians over, the PLO will not be a problem and consequently your excellent and reasonable initiative of September 1, 1982, will have a tremendous chance for success."

Metropolitan Philip next went to Lebanon where he distributed three hundred thousand dollars in aid to the victims of the Israeli invasion. While there, he met with President Amin Gemayel. Once again, the prelate relayed President Reagan's commitment to a free and independent Lebanon and Reagan's promise to work to persuade Israel to withdraw its forces from the war-torn country.

Unfortunately, peace did not return to Lebanon. Despite Metropolitan Philip's warning in a letter to the State Department, the American forces became involved in the fighting on the side of the Falangists. The result was disaster and humiliation for the United States. On October 23, 1983, 241 American marines died at their bunker at the Beirut Airport, the result of a suicide bombing, while another suicide bomber killed 58 French paratroopers at the French headquarters. A few months later, President Reagan ordered the American forces to leave Lebanon.

On December 4, 1983, Syrian gunners shot down Lieutenant Robert Goodman, an American airman attacking Syrian batteries in the Bekaa Valley. Meanwhile, Muslim militants began to capture and hold American journalists and others living in Beirut as hostages.

Once again, Metropolitan Philip sprang into action. He met with Syrian officials in Washington, D.C. to pave the way for the successful efforts of the Reverend Jesse Jackson to win the release of Goodman. Metropolitan Philip also worked to liberate the Americans held captive in Lebanon. He and his clergy gathered over forty thousand signatures from Arab Americans and their friends on petitions appealing to the Muslim militants to release their hostages.

With approval from the United States Department of State, the metropolitan traveled to Damascus in September, 1986. Again, he met with the Syrian president, who agreed to help his efforts to win the release of the American hostages. Finally, the Shiite leaders, who had close ties to the holders of the captives, agreed to meet with the metropolitan. However, before the meeting could take place, Israeli forces bombed the headquarters of Hezbollah, a Shiite group, in eastern Lebanon. As a result the Shiite leaders could not meet with the metropolitan and the mission ended in failure. However, American diplomacy eventually prevailed and the Muslim radicals released the hostages.

The Bush Era

Meanwhile, Metropolitan Philip continued to work for peace in Lebanon. On April 20, 1989, the Standing Conference of American Middle Eastern Christian and Muslim Religious Leaders met at the chancery of the Antiochian Archdiocese. After hearing a report from Clovis Maksoud, the ambassador of the Arab League to the United Nations, they adopted another statement appealing for peace in Lebanon. They asked United States President George Bush to help end the fighting and to provide humanitarian aid to the victims of the tragic civil war. They requested Chedli Klibi, the secretary general of the Arab League, to "intensify his efforts to mediate a permanent cease-fire and bring a lasting peace to Lebanon."

The leaders of the Standing Conference met again on September 5. Calling for a cease-fire on all fronts, they passed a resolution supporting the efforts of the Arab League to find a negotiated settlement of the civil war. They also supported constitutional reforms that would remove all religious qualifications for offices in the Lebanese government. They also asked the president of the United States to support resolutions of the United Nations Security Council calling for Israeli withdrawal from Lebanon. Finally, they called for all foreign military forces to leave Lebanon and asked the American government to provide humanitarian aid to help rebuild that war torn country.

Although the Lebanese civil war eventually ended, peace did not come to the Middle East. Instead the Iraqi invasion of Kuwait on August 2, 1990, led to a new crisis. After months of failed diplomacy, an international force led by the United States attacked Iraq on January 16, 1990. Six weeks later, the multinational army drove the Iraqis from Kuwait. Since Syrian forces had fought alongside American troops during the Gulf War, the conflict began a new phase in Syrian-American relations.

At the same time, the fall of Communism and the demise of the Soviet Union opened up new opportunities for a more even-handed American foreign policy. The United States no longer felt required to support Israel as a counter to Soviet influence in the Middle East.

When the war ended, the American president called for compromise between Israel and the Palestinians. President George Bush launched a new peace initiative that resulted in direct negotiations between Israel and her Arab neighbors, including delegates of the Palestinians. Elections in Israel ended militant Zionist domination of the Israeli government. Eventually, representatives of the Jewish state began direct negotiations with representatives of the PLO, leading to a major breakthrough and the beginning of Palestinian self-rule in parts of the Occupied Territories.

Although Metropolitan Philip had expressed strong reservations about the use of force to resolve the dispute with Iraq, he wrote President Bush a letter of support on March 7, 1990. He expressed his fear that war in the Persian Gulf would "be long and cost us many precious American lives." However, the metropolitan wrote, "Your brilliant conduct of the war proved otherwise. You were right in your assessment of the situation and this is precisely why you are the president." He concluded his letter with an invitation to the president to address the convention of the Antiochian Archdiocese in July, 1991.

In an historic speech before clergy and lay delegates of the parishes of the Antiochian Archdiocese, President Bush pledged his support for the legitimate rights of the Palestinian people. Thus Metropolitan Philip saw the fruits of his long effort to persuade the American government to adopt a more balanced policy in the Middle East. If peace is eventually secured in the Middle East, it will be partially due to his untiring work to open channels of communication between the American government and Arab leaders.

Additional Diplomacy

Meanwhile, Metropolitan Philip was not the only member of the Antiochian Orthodox Church working for peace in the Middle East. Throughout the country, clergy and laity wrote letters to the editor, spoke in public forums and presented programs designed to help educate the American people on the true situation in the Middle East. Naturally, the well-organized and financed pro-Zionist lobby used every possible effort to stifle the voice of anyone who did not advocate unconditional support for Israel. However, even the most fanatical opposition has not prevented the clergy and laity of the Antiochian Archdiocese from introducing the American people to the suffering of the Palestinian people.

Dr. Frank Maria, appointed by Metropolitan Philip to lead the Committee on the Near East and Arab Refugee Affairs, has been one of the most valiant Antiochian Orthodox Christians to work for a just peace in the Middle East. He has spoken on dozens of college campuses and before other public forums. He has appeared on national television programs and has written many letters to protest pro-Zionist bias in the media.

His greatest achievements have been in the National Council of Churches (the "NCC"), the largest and most influential inter-church agency in the United States. Largely through his efforts, the NCC has adopted a series of resolutions recognizing the rights of the Palestinian people. In 1969, the governing board of the NCC adopted a policy statement affirming the right of the Palestinians "to a home acceptable to them." The governing board responded to the Yom Kippur War of 1973 with a resolution calling for an end to the fighting. They also supported negotiations to resolve the Arab-Israeli conflict based on UN Resolution 242. In 1974, the NCC called on the American government to open a dialogue with the PLO as the representative of the Palestinian people.

Dr. Maria's greatest victory came in 1980, when the National Council of Churches adopted a comprehensive policy statement on the Middle East. On October 7, 1976, the executive committee of the NCC ordered its Middle Eastern Committee, headed by the Reverend Tracey K. Jones, general secretary of the Board of Global Ministries of the United Methodist Church, to begin a study of human rights in the Middle East.

Various pro-Israeli groups used the charge of anti-Semitism to try to prevent the NCC from adopting positions critical of Zionism. On February 18, 1977, the Anti-Defamation League of B'nai Brith accused the NCC of "pronounced anti-Israel prejudice." In March, 1977, Rabbi Marc Tannenbaum, national interreligious director of the American Jewish Committee, issued a statement charging the presence of representatives of the Antiochian Archdiocese, which he characterized as "Arab propagandists ... subsidized by Arab governments," on the governing board of the NCC "means there is built into the NCC a constant anti-Jewish lobby."

These charges did not intimidate Dr. Maria who introduced a resolution in the NCC executive board in September, 1979, calling upon the United States to recognize the PLO officially and to condemn Israel for violating the human rights of the Palestinians. After a fiery debate, the board referred the matter to the Middle Eastern Committee. On December 5, 1979 the Anti-Defamation League of B'nai Brith sent an appeal to the leaders of the members of the NCC to reject Dr. Maria's resolution. Although invited to participate, thirteen Jewish organizations refused to appear at public hearings by the Middle Eastern Committee, charging that its deliberations "were slanted against Israel."

After concluding its hearings in the United States and the Middle East, the committee prepared a resolution, which the National Council of Churches adopted on November 7, 1980. This important document recognized the right of Israel to exist, but also recognized the right of the Palestinians to national self-determination. The NCC also accepted the right of the Palestinians to select their own representatives in any negotiations, including the PLO.

Through his work in the NCC, Dr. Maria has been able to gain credibility for the call for a recognition of the rights of the Palestinians. He has also been able to influence the leaders of millions of American Protestants. As a result, several Protestant groups such as the Presbyterian and the United Methodist Churches have adopted resolutions recognizing the rights of the Palestinian people to national self-determination.

Humanitarian Efforts

In addition to the efforts to inform the American people of the plight of the Palestinian people, members of the Antiochian Archdiocese have provided much needed humanitarian aid to the victims of the conflict. The Antiochian Archdiocese has raised funds during every crisis in the Middle East to assist the innocent victims of violence. Following the Gulf War, the Antiochian Archdiocese sent money to the Antiochian Orthodox Archdiocese of Baghdad to provide food and shelter for the children orphaned by the war.

In 1973, Metropolitan Philip made Project Loving Care an official agency of the Antiochian Archdiocese. Originally called Project Ryiat in 1973, by its founder Professor Rajae Busailah of Kokomo, Indiana, this worthy organization provides continuing support for needy Arab children. Now headed by the Very Reverend George Rados, Project Loving Care, now called the Children's Relief Fund, has helped thousands of Arab children, adopted by the parishes and local organizations of the Antiochian Archdiocese, as well as by many individuals.

Throughout all the wars and crises that have plagued the Middle East since World War II, the clergy and laity of the Antiochian Orthodox Christian Archdiocese of North America have been a positive force in the quest for peace in their ancestral homelands. Through the able leadership of Metropolitan Philip, the Antiochian Archdiocese has provided hundreds of thousands of dollars in humanitarian aid to help the victims of the conflict. Metropolitan Philip, the clergy and laity have worked to educate the North American people on the plight of the Palestinians. Metropolitan Philip has also helped to open communication between the American government and Arab leaders, by carrying messages between American presidents and various Arab leaders. Thus if there is hope for peace in the Middle East today, it is partially due to the work of the Antiochian Orthodox Christian Archdiocese of North America.

NOTES

The author's bibliography has been incorporated into the Selected Bibliography at the end of this volume.

* Most of the material used for this article came from the files and archives of the Antiochian Orthodox Christian Archdiocese in North America in Englewood, New Jersey. In addition to these letters, documents, and press clippings, the author consulted *The Word, The New York Times, Time, Newsweek,* and *Christian Century,* among other sources.

CONTRIBUTORS

George N. Atiyeh
Head of the Near East Section, African & Middle Eastern Division
The Library of Congress, Washington, D.C.

John Lawrence Boojamra
Professor of Religious Education and Church History
St. Vladimir Orthodox Theological Seminary, Crestwood, New York

Issa J. Boullata
Professor of Arabic Literature, Institute of Islamic Studies
McGill University, Montreal, Canada

Antony Gabriel
Pastor — Saint George Church
Montreal, Canada

Paul D. Garrett
Archivist and Librarian, Heritage and Learning Center
The Antiochian Village, Ligonier, Pennsylvania

Susan Ashbrook Harvey
Associate Professor of Religious Studies
Brown University, Providence, Rhode Island

John W. Morris
Pastor — Saint George Church, Cedar Rapids, Iowa
Adjunct Instructor of History
Kirkwood Community College, Cedar Rapids, Iowa

Alixa Naff
Research Collaborator and Donor of The Naff Collection
Arab-American Collection, National Museum of American History,
Smithsonian Institution, Washington, D.C.

Michel Najim
Associate Pastor — Saint Nicholas Cathedral, Los Angeles, California
Former Dean and Professor of Patristics
Saint John of Damascus Institute of Orthodox Theology
Balamand, Lebanon

George Saliba
Chairman and Professor of Arabic and Islamic Science
Department of Middle Eastern Languages and Culture
Columbia University, New York, New York

Najib E. Saliba
Professor of History
Worcester State College, Worcester, Massachusetts

Irfan Shahîd
Sultanate of Oman Professor of Arabic and Islamic Literature
Georgetown University, Washington, D.C.

SELECTED BIBLIOGRAPHY

Abdul Razak, Fawzi. *Mundus Arabicus.*, vol. 1, *Arab Writers in America: Critical Essays and Annotated Bibliography.* Cambridge, Mass.: Dar Mahjar, 1981.

Addai. *The Doctrine of Addai the Apostle,* translated by G. Phillips. London, 1876.

Anawati, George. *al-Masihiyah wa-al-hadarah al-'Arabiyah* (Christianity and Arab Civilization). Cairo, 1993.

Arberry, A.J. *Modern Arabic Poetry: An Anthology with English Verse Translations.* Cambridge: Cambridge University Press, 1967.

Assemani, Giuseppe Simone. *Series Chronologica Patriarchum Antiochae.* Farnborough: Gregg International Publishers, 1969.

Atiya, Aziz S. *A History of Eastern Christianity.* Notre Dame, Ind.: University of Notre Dame Press, 1968.

Bar-Hebraeus, Gregory (Abu'l-Faraj). *Chronicon Syriacum.* Edited by P. Bedjan. Paris: Maisonneuve, 1890.

_____. *Chronicon Ecclesiasticum.* Edited and translated by J.B. Abbeloos and Th. J. Lamy. Lourain, 1872-77.

Baumstark, Anton. *Geschicte der Syrischen literatur.* Bonn: A. Marcus und E. Weber, 1922.

_____. *Die christlichen literaturen des Orients.* Leipzig: G.J. Goschen, 1911.

_____. *Das Problem eines vorislamischen Christlischen – Kirschlischen Scrifttums in Arabischer Sprache.* Vol. IV, *Islamica.* (1924-1935).

_____. *Eine Frühislamische unde eine vorislamische Arabische Evangelium übersetzung aus dem Syrischen.* Rome: Atti del XIX Congresso international degli Orientalisti, 1935.

Behr-Sigel, Elisabeth. *The Ministry of Women in the Church.* Translated by Steven Bigham. Redondo Beach, Ca.: Oakwood Publications, 1991.

Bell, Richard. *The Origin of Islam in its Christian Environment.* London: Macmillan, 1926.

Boojamra, John L. *Church Reform in the Late Byzantine Empire.* Thessalonica: Patriarchal Institute for Patristic Studies, 1983.

Boullata, Issa. *Trends and Issues in Contemporary Arab Thought.* Albany, NY: State University of New York Press, 1990.

Chabot, Jean Baptiste, ed. *Chronique de Michel le Syrien, partiarche jacobite d'Antioche, 1166-1199.* Brussels: Culture et Civilization, 1963.

_____, ed. "Documenta ad origines Monophysitarum." In *Corpus Scriptorum Christianorum Orientalium,* Ser. 2, vol. 37, No. 103. Louvain: L. Durbecq, 1952.

_____, ed. *Synodicon Orientale.* Paris: Impr. Nationale, 1902.

Charles, H. *Le Christianisme des Arabes nomades sur le Limes et dans le disert syro-mésopotanien.* Paris, 1936.

_____. *Processus de la sédentarisation des nomades en steppe syrienne.* Actes du 16 Congrès Internationale de Sociologie, 1954.

Cheikho, Louis. *Le Christianisme et la littérature chrétienne en Arabie avant l'Islam.* 2 vols. Beirut: al-Mashriq, 1912-1913.

Clark, Elizabeth A. *Ascetic Piety and Women's Faith: Essays on Late Ancient Christianity.* Lewiston, NY: Edwin Mellen Press, 1986.

_____. *Women in the Early Church.* Wilmington, Del.: Michael Glazier, Inc., 1983.

Cohen, Michael J. *The Origins and Evolution of the Arab-Zionist Conflict.* Berkeley: The University of California Press, 1987.

Comnena, Anna. *The Alexiad of the Princess Anna Comnena.* Translated by Elizabeth Dawes. New York: Barnes & Noble, Inc. 1967.

Cragg, Kenneth. *The Arab Christian: A History in the Middle East.* Louisville, Ky.: Westminster/ John Knox Press, 1991.

Devreesse, R. *Le Patriarcat d'Antioche depuis la paix de L'eglise jusqu'a' la conquête arabe.* Paris: J. Gabalda et cie, 1945.

Drijvers, H.J.W. *The Book of the Laws of Countries.* The Netherlands: Assen, Van Gorcum, 1964.

Fakhry, Majid. *A History of Islamic Philosophy.* New York: Columbia University Press, 1970.

Findley, Paul. *They Dare to Speak Out: People and Institutions Confront Israel's Lobby.* Westport, Conn.: Lawrence Hill Books, 1989.

Fischer, Robert H., ed. *A Tribute to Arthur Vööbus.* Chicago: Lutheran School of Theology at Chicago, 1977.

_____. *East of Antioch: Studies in Early Syriac Christianity.* London: Variorum Reprints, 1984.

Fisher, Sydney Nettleton and William Ochenwald. *The Middle East: A History.* New York: McGraw-Hill, 1990.

Fisk, Robert. *Pity the Nation: The Abduction of Lebanon.* New York: Atheneum, 1990.

Frend, W.H.C. *Martrydom and Persecution in the Early Church: A Study of a Conflict from Maccabees to Donatus.* Oxford: Basil Blackwell, 1965.

Friedman, Thomas L. *From Beirut to Jerusalem.* New York: Farrar Straus Giroux, 1989.

Garrett, Paul. *St. Innocent, Apostle to America.* Crestwood, NY: St. Vladimir's Seminary Press, 1979.

Gillquist, Peter E. *Becoming Orthodox: A Journey to the Ancient Christian Faith.* Brentwood, Tenn.: Wolgemuth & Hyatt, 1989.

_____. *Metropolitan PHILIP: His Life and His Dreams.* Nashville: T. Nelson Publishers, 1991.

Graf, Georg. *Geschicte der christlichen arabischen literatur.* (History of the Christian Arabic Literature). Rome: Bilioteca apostolica vaticana, 1943-1953.

Grousset, Rene. *The Epic of the Crusades.* Translated by Noel Lindsay. New York: Orion Press, 1970.

Haddad, Robert M. *Syrian Christians in Muslim Society, an Interpretation.* Princeton, NJ: Princeton University Press, 1970.

Hagopian, Elaine and Ann Paden, *The Arab-Americans.* Cypress, Calif.: Medina University Press, 1969.

al-Hakim, Yusuf. *Beirut wa-Lubnan fi Ahd al Uthman.* Beirut, 1964.

_____. *Suriyyah wa-al- Ahd al- Uthmani.* Beirut, 1966.

Hamilton, Bernard. *The Latin Church in the Crusader States.* London: Variorum Publications, 1980.

Harvey, Susan Ashbrook. *Asceticism and Society in Crisis: John of Ephesus and the Lives of the Eastern Saints.* Berkeley: University of California Press, 1990.

_____. and S. P. Brock. *Holy Women of the Syrian Orient.* Berkeley: University of California Press, 1987.

Himadeh, Sa'id B. *Economic Organization of Syria.* Beirut, 1936.

Hitti, Philip K. *History of Syria including Lebanon and Palestine.* New York, Macmillan,1951.

_____. *Makers of Arab History.* New York: St. Martin's Press, 1968.

_____. *A Short History of Lebanon.* London: Macmillan, 1965.

Hopwood, Derek. *The Russian Presence in Syria and Palestine, 1843 – 1914; Church and Politics in the Near East.* Oxford: Clarendon Press, 1969.

Hourani, Albert. *A History of the Arab Peoples*. Cambridge, Mass.: Belknap Press of Harvard University Press, 1991.

Issawi, Charles Philip, ed. *The Economic History of the Middle East, 1800 – 1914*. Chicago: University of Chicago Press, 1966.

Jayyusi, Salma Khadra. *Modern Arabic Poetry: An Anthology*. New York: Columbia University Press, 1987.

Jessup, Henry H. *Fifty-three Years in Syria*. New York: Fleming H. Revell Company, 1910.

John of Ephesus (or of Asia). "Ecclesiastical History Part III," edited and translated by E.W. Brooks. In *Corpus Scriptorum Christianorum Orientalium*, Ser. 3. vols. 54-55. Louvain: L. Durbecq, 1952.

Kayal, Philip and Joseph M. *The Syrian-Lebanese in America*. Boston: Twayne Publishers, 1975.

Khalil, Samir. "Ancient Christian Arabic Culture and Its Interaction with Arabo-Muslim Thought." In *Islamochristiana, Islamiyat Masihiyat*. Vol. 8. Roma: Pontificio Istituto di Studi Arabi, 1982.

Khouri, Mounah A. and Hamid Algar. *An Anthology of Modern Arabic Poetry*. Berkeley: University of California Press, 1974.

Khoury, Adel Theodore. *Polémique byzantine contre l'Islam*. Leiden: E.J. Brill, 1972.

Kraemer, Ross Shepard. *Maenads, Martyrs, Matrons, Monastics: A Sourcebook on Women's Religions in the Greco-Roman World*. Philadelphia: Fortress Press, 1988.

Laqueur, Walter, ed. *The Israel – Arab Reader: A Documentary History of the Middle East Conflict*. New York: Bantam Books, 1976.

Leckie, Robert. *The Wars of America*. New York: Harper Perennial, 1992.

Maalouf, Amin. *The Crusades Through Arab Eyes*. New York: Schocken Books, 1985.

Mansfield, Peter. *A History of the Middle East.* New York: Viking, 1991.

Metzger, Bruce. "Early Arabic Versions of the New Testament." In *On Language, Culture and Religion in Honor of Eugene A. Nida,* edited by Matthew Black and William A. Smalley. The Hague: Mouton, 1974.

Michael the Syrian. "Chronica Minora," edited by E.W. Brooks and translated into French by Jean Baptiste Chabot. In *Corpus Scriptorum Christianorum Orientalium,* Ser. 3, vol. 4. Paris: E typographeo reipublicae, 1919-21.

Moubarac, Youakim. *Les chretiens et le monde arabe.* Beirut: Editions du Cenacle libanais, 1972-73.

Naff, Alixa. *The Arab Americans, From 1880 to the Present.* New York: Chelsea House Publishers, 1988.

_____. *Becoming American: The Early Arab Immigrant Experience.* Carbondale, Ill: Southern Illinois University Press, 1985.

Neugebauer, O. *The Exact Sciences in Antiquity.* Providence, RI: Brown University Press, 1957.

_____. *History of Ancient Mathematical Astronomy.* Berlin and Heidelberg: Springer, 1975.

Nida, Eugene A. *On Language, Culture, and Religion in Honor of Eugene A. Nida.* Edited by Matthew Black and William A. Smalley. The Hague: Mouton, 1974.

Orfalea, Gregory and Sharif Elmusa, editors. *Grape Leaves: A Century of Arab American Poetry.* Salt Lake City: University of Utah Press, 1988.

Ostrogorsky, George. *History of the Byzantine State.* Translated by Joan Hussey. New Brunswick, NJ: Rutgers University Press, 1969.

Ostrovsky, Victor and Claire Hoy. *By Way of Deception.* New York: St. Martin's Press, 1990.

Papadopoulos, Chrysostomos (Archbishop of Athens). *Historia tēs Ekklēsias Antiocheias*. Alexandria, 1951. Translated into Arabic by Bishop Istafanus Haddad under the title *Tarikh Kanisat Antakīyah*. Beirut: Manshurat al-Nur, 1984.

Patai, Raphael. *The Arab Mind*. New York: Charles Schribner's Sons, 1973.

Ribhany, Abraham M. *A Far Journey*. Boston: Houghton Mifflin, 1914.

Runciman, Steven. *The Eastern Schism: A Study of the Papacy and the Eastern Churches During the XIth and XIIth Centuries*. Oxford: Clarendon Press, 1935.

_____. *The Historic Role of the Christian Arabs of Palestine*. London: Longmans for the University of Essex, 1970.

_____. *A History of the Crusades*. Cambridge: Cambridge University Press, 1951-1954.

Rustum, Asad. *Kanīsat Madīnat Allāh Antākia al-'Uzmā (The Church of God's City, the Great Antioch)*. Beirut: Manshurat al-Nur, 1952-1958.

Saliba, Najib. *Emigration from Syria and the Syrian-Lebanese Community of Worcester, Massachusetts*. Ligonier, PA: Antakya Press, 1992.

Saliba, Philip. *Feed My Sheep*. Edited by J. Allen. Crestwood, NY: St. Vladimir's Seminary Press, 1987.

Salibi, Kamal S. *The Modern History of Lebanon*. London: Weidenfeld and Nicolson, 1965.

Schussler Fiorenza, Elisabeth. *In Memory of Her: A Feminist Theological Reconstruction of Christian Origins*. New York: Crossroad, 1983.

Shahîd, Irfan. *Byzantium and the Arabs in the Fifth Century*. Washington, D.C.: Dumbarton Oaks Research Library Collection, 1989.

_____. *Byzantium and the Arabs in the Fourth Century*. Washington, D.C.: Dumbarton Oaks Research Library Collection, 1984.

_____. *Byzantium and the Semitic Orient before the Rise of Islam.* London: Variorum Reprints, 1988.

_____. *The Martyrs of Najrān.* Brussels: Société des Bollandistes, 1971.

_____. *Rome and the Arabs: A Prolegomenon to the Study of Byzantium and the Arabs.* Washington, D.C.: Dumbarton Oaks Press, 1984.

Socrates. *The Ecclesiastical History of Socrates Scholasticus.* Translated by A.C. Zenos. New York: Christian Literature Company, 1890.

Sozomen. *The Ecclesiastical History of Sozomen: Comprising a History of the Church from A.D.324 to A.D. 440.* Translated by E. Walford. London: H.G. Bohn, 1855.

Theodoret, bishop of Cyrrhus. "Ecclesiastical History," edited by Léon Parmentier. In *Die Griechischen Christlichen Schriftsteller,* vol. 19. Leipzig: J.C. Hinrich's che Buchhandlung, 1911.

_____. *A History of the Church.* London: S. Bagster, 1843.

Trimingham, John Spencer. *Christianity among the Arabs in Pre-Islamic Times.* London: Longman Group Ltd., 1979.

Vööbus, Arthur. "A History of Asceticism in the Syrian Orient." In *Corpus Scriptorum Christianorum Orientalum,* vols. 14, 17. Louvain: L. Durbecq, 1958, 1960.

Wallace-Hadrill, D.S. *Christian Antioch: A Study of Early Christian Thought in the East.* Cambridge: Cambridge University Press, 1982.

Wilken, Robert L. *The Land Called Holy: Palestine in Christian History and Thought.* New Haven, Conn.: Yale University Press, 1992.

Zacharias, bishop of Mytilene. "Historia Ecclesiastica, Zacharie Rhetori vulgo adscripta," edited by E.W. Brooks. In *Corpus Scriptorum Christianorum Orientalium.* Ser. 3, vols. 5-6. Louvain, L. Durbecq, 1953.

al-Zerekly, al-A'lam. *Biographical Dictionary.* Beirut: Dar El-ilm Lilmalayin, 1980.

GENERAL THEOLOGICAL SEMINARY
NEW YORK